MW01291630

READ and PRAY
Through
the Bible

*To Vonnecia
Go forward!*

Dr. [signature]

2/19/17

READ and PRAY
Through
the Bible

A DAILY Devotional Journey of READING and PRAYING
Through the Scriptures

Start Anytime
Read it over and over

Dr. Minnie Claiborne

Copyright © 2010 by Dr. Minnie Claiborne.

ISBN: Softcover   978-1-4535-4582-9
               Ebook   978-1-4535-4583-6

All rights reserved. No parts of this publication may be reproduced, stored in a retrieval system, or transmitted in any form or by any means, electronic, mechanical, photocopying or otherwise, without the prior written consent of the publisher. Short extracts may be used for review purposes.

The scripture quotations in this book are taken from the New American Standard Bible (NASB). Copyright © 1960, 1962, 1963, 1968, 1971, 1972, 1973, 1975, 1977, 1995 by the Lockman Foundation. Used by permission.

This book was printed in the United States of America.

To order additional copies of this book, contact:
Xlibris Corporation
1-888-795-4274
www.Xlibris.com
Orders@Xlibris.com
84242

Dedication

To my favorite oldest daughter, Shannon, my first prayer partner. Thanks Tid. (You were and are the prettiest baby in the world. I love you.)

To my favorite youngest daughter, Keturah, (Ruth Jr.), who really remembers how to pray when the "going gets tough" (smile). "I love you, Kitty!"

To my favorite son, Emmanuel, who taught all of us to pray more than we planned, (smile). You're the wonderful son that I prayed for, I love you so-o-o much.

To my son-in-loves, Keith and Andre and my grandsons Justin, Keith Jr, Kieron, Uriah, Isaiah and my ONE favorite grand-daughter, Kennedi. You are wonderful gifts to me. I love you.

To my late husband, Dr. H.L. Claiborne, whose vision for me expanded my vision for myself.

Foreword

Dr. Minnie's book is simply fantastic!

I read it from cover to cover and found it to be thoroughly enlightening.

It will provoke and inspire you.

It should be required reading for every believer.

Matthew Barnett, Pastor
The Los Angeles Dream Center and
Angeles Temple Four Square Church

Acknowledgements

In order to write this prayer book, a lot of prayer was required. If anyone prayed for this project almost more than I, it was my friend and prayer-partner, Evy E.E. Armando Valdez-Lara, you are a mighty prayer warrior. Thank you so much for your prayers and encouragement. Special thanks to the Monday night prayer groups, Rev. Juanda Green, thank you for being in my life. Keep praying; keep soaring! Dr. LaVerne Tolbert, thank you for being a friend and prayer-partner over the years. Mrs. Elean Newsome, my long-term prayer-partner-you are a tower of faith and strength. Shannon Battiste-Pender, thank you for editing and helping me to avoid too many E.H. mistakes. Lynne Stinson—let's take the word to the world! I love you and pray for you, my brothers and sisters: Walter, Anthony, Ts. Chanavia, Michael and Cynthia and all who are dear to you.

Gary Curtis, The Church on the Way—thank you for your encouragement. Frances and David Comacho, thank you for your love and support. To all the people who I have had the privilege of praying with over the years, you're special to me. To my special friend and 'school of the spirit' sister, Leslie Arroyo-thank you.

To the wonderful sister, Joanne Montgomery, THANK YOU, for your diligence, your prayers and dedication. You came as an amazing answer to prayer and became: "the wind beneath my wings" for the final editing of this book. Thank you with all of my heart.

God bless You.

Introduction

USE THIS BOOK ALONG WITH YOUR BIBLE

"Thy kingdom come, Thy will be done," is implied in every chapter and verse in the Scriptures. The Holy Bible is replete with truths, revelations and wisdom that often hover in the heavenlies, waiting for the force of prayer to grasp and pull them into earth's atmosphere where their reality can impact and transform lives and situations.

READ and PRAY *Through the Bible* is divided into daily Bible verses, but it also contains a synopsis of the verses and a prayer that embraces the principles and truths inherent in the verses of Scripture.

What an opportunity to actively agree with the Word of God daily for our lives, our families, our circumstances and our world. In one year, the Bible can be read and its truths appropriated through prayer. READ AND PRAY *Through the Bible* encourages much more than a mental or intellectual collection of good information. It calls for an agreement with, and appropriation of, life-changing spiritual truths that will definitely enrich and strengthen our lives perpetually.

Your life will be transformed as you submit to the Word of God through praying out loud the prayers that are written, as well as through praying according to what the Holy Spirit inspires in you personally.

If you READ and PRAY through the Bible, your life will change dramatically and delightfully for the better.

I promise.

Minnie Claiborne PhD

DAY ONE: READ Genesis 1-2

In Genesis chapters one and two, we see the Almighty God as Creator of the Heavens, the earth, and all living things, including the human race. God establishes order and purpose out of chaos. He also establishes the fact that males and females are created in His image; and are given provision as well as dominion or responsibility.

PRAYER

Dear Heavenly Father, Creator of the Heavens and the earth,
I honor You also as the One who made me in Your image and likeness. Dear God in places or at points in my life where there is confusion and darkness, I pray, let there be the light of Your wisdom and counsel. Where there is chaos in my spirit, soul, body or relationships, please bring Your divine order.

Where I have lacked purpose, remind me that I was created by You with a divine destiny and a specific purpose. I pray that You will provide me with whatever I need in order to take my responsibility and fulfill Your great purpose in my life.

I pray for forgiveness for the times that I have tried to be in control of my own life. I now submit to You, and Your plans Heavenly Father, in the name of Jesus Christ. Amen.

TODAY'S CHALLENGE: To realize that God has the wisdom and the ability to direct every aspect of my life perfectly.

What else is God saying to me today?

What is my response?

DAY TWO: READ Genesis 3-5

In these verses the tempter, the serpent, enters the scene with the sole purpose of usurping God's word and tempting man, God's highest creation, to sin against God and nullify His purposes and blessings in their lives. The cunning serpent challenges the word of God. The woman and man eat of the forbidden tree, disobeying God, and bringing judgment upon themselves and the entire human race. Intimate fellowship with God is replaced with fear, shame and curses. The evidence of Adam and Eve's sin culminates in deception, jealousy and murder through their firstborn son, Cain. However, because of God's great love, we also see redemption on the horizon through their son Seth and grandson Enosh.

PRAYER
Most Holy, Awesome God,
Please help me to never doubt or compromise Your word, or be a victim of satanic deception or manipulation which will lead me to disobey You. Please forgive my sins and those of Your erring children. Help me to never evoke curses upon myself or my family through willful sin and disobedience.

Please remove any curses of sin that I have inherited or initiated. May all such curses be removed from me and my family through every generation; past, present and future. Let the restoration that comes by calling upon Your name be evident and active in my life and in the lives of my family members. In the name of Jesus Christ, I pray. Amen

TODAY'S CHALLENGE: To know that the truth of God's word planted in my heart and spoken through my mouth is able to pierce through generational sins and produce a harvest of blessings.

What else is God saying to me today?

What is my response?

DAY THREE: READ Genesis 6-9

As mankind continues to multiply upon the earth, sin's legacy continues to the point that God decides to destroy His own creation. How this must have grieved the heart of God. In His mercy, God spares Noah and his family, thus preserving mankind, with the purpose of continuing His redemptive plan. He makes a covenant with Noah and his sons and reiterates the original command "Be fruitful and multiply."

PRAYER
My Dear God,
Please forgive me and all of Your people for choosing to sin and for grieving Your heart. What wickedness we have brought upon the beautiful earth that You created for us to enjoy.

Help me to find grace in Your eyes. Help me to walk with You and follow all that You command. In the midst of a sin-infested society, help me to be salt and light and obey Your word.

After Your miraculous deliverances and provisions for me, please help me to not be drunk with the wine of complacency; but alert and sober, so that I can fulfill my responsibilities admirably. In the name of Jesus Christ, I pray. Amen.

TODAY'S CHALLENGE: To what extent can I listen to the voices of my world and still hear and obey the voice of my God? Is there an area of compromise that God is challenging me to abandon today?

What else is God saying to me today?

What is my response?

DAY FOUR: READ Genesis 10-11

The families of the sons of Noah indeed multiply and inhabit the earth; they all speak one language. What an opportunity to unite and worship God the Creator, united with one language, in one accord. What glory that would have brought to God, and what blessings to the people.

Instead, we see another of sin's off springs, rebellion. The people begin to unite together to challenge God, and attempt to make a city and a name for themselves. God intervenes so that the people do not destroy themselves through idolatry. He confuses their language and scatters them abroad so that their wicked plans do not succeed.

PRAYER

Dear Heavenly Father,

Please reveal to me any areas in my life where I tend to rely upon my genealogy, intellect, ethnicity, money or anything earthly, instead of You. I know that reliance upon any of these things is idolatry and rebellion: which is sin. Help me to not make unholy alliances; simply because of what I might have in common with a person or groups of people. You alone are God, and I choose to honor You above all things and seek Your Wisdom and Counsel each day.

Help me not to attempt to build or make any plans of which You have not approved. Thank You for constantly guiding me back onto the right path so that I will see Your precious promises fulfilled in my life. In the name of Jesus Christ, I pray. Amen.

TODAY'S CHALLENGE: To answer this question. Can I, with my own understanding really accomplish what I think I can and get *God's* results?

What else is God saying to me today?

What is my response?

DAY FIVE: READ Genesis 12-15

Abram is a key figure in the history of mankind. God chooses to reveal Himself to and through Abraham with a promise to bless him personally, to bless his descendants, and indeed through him to bless all the families of the earth.

Abram is challenged to leave all that is familiar and dear to him and to simply follow God with only the reward of a promise. "And he believed in the Lord, and He accounted it to him for righteousness."

There is a sense of awe as we see evidence of God's commitment by covenant to Abraham, and His faithfulness to His promises in spite of Abram's flaws.

PRAYER

Dear God, Most High, Possessor of Heaven and earth,

May my fellowship with You be so special, so honest and so trusting, that I will have faith to leave the familiar if necessary, in order to follow Your wonderful plan.

Help me to be submitted to You in a posture of perpetual worship, so that my life will be an extension of Your plan and so that I may be blessed, my descendants may be blessed, and that I may be a blessing to the families of the earth that You may send me to.

May I honor You in worship, in tithes and in faith. Thank You for revealing aspects of Your nature to us by allowing the record of Your relationship with Abram to be preserved. Please feel free to speak to me, and help me to have a heart that will obey. In the name of Jesus Christ I pray. Amen.

TODAY'S CHALLENGE: To know what does God's voice sound like. To listen to him often enough to recognize His voice?

What else is God saying to me today?

What is my response?

DAY SIX: READ Genesis 16-19

Our carnal plans sorely contrast with God's promises. In these chapters we see Sarai and Abram trying to help God's plan along. God had promised them a son. They are both past childbearing age, and the promise has not been fulfilled. Their impatience is understandable. God continues to reiterate His promises to them because He knows that in spite of their detour into carnality, Abraham will perpetuate his faith through his descendants, and the promises of God will be fulfilled. God continues to encourage Abraham and Sarah, even affirming them by changing their names.

In direct contrast to the righteousness of God, the men of Sodom are so depraved, that they practically tear Lot's house down in order to sleep with two men who are actually angels. God destroys the cities of Sodom and Gomorrah with fire and brimstone. The angels usher Lot and his family out, commanding them to not look back. His wife disobeys and turns into a pillar of salt.

PRAYER

Dear God Almighty,
How faithful You are to Your word despite our doubts, anxieties and fears. As You were faithful to Abraham and Sarah in their weakness, please be so to me.

Take the mistakes that I have made and use them for Your purpose. Help me never to doubt You or Your promises. There is nothing too hard for You. I receive from You the faith, patience, perseverance and wisdom to wait for the fulfillment of Your promises in my life. Help me to also recognize Your presence in my present situations and receive Your comfort and counsel. When You want to destroy the things in my past, help me to not set my affections on them and look back as Lot's wife did. I ask these things in the name of Jesus Christ. Amen.

TODAY'S CHALLENGE: To *rest* while I wait on the Lord to fulfill His promises in my life, and in the lives of those who I love and pray for.

What else is God saying to me today?

What is my response?

DAY SEVEN: READ Genesis 20-22

Evidence of God's incredible grace is constantly revealed in Abraham and Sarah's lives. Out of fear, Abraham is not completely honest with Abimelech; again God intervenes. In the following chapter, Isaac, the long awaited promise is about to be conceived. It's unthinkable to imagine what would have happened if Abimelech's plans for Sarah had been carried out.

God is perfectly arranging every thing in order to fulfill His promises to Abraham and Sarah at just the right time, and in just the right place, for just the right purpose. Meanwhile, He is working many miracles while they wait. What incredible trust and friendship Abraham had with God. His obedience and faith are at their zenith when he proceeds to offer his son of promise as a burnt sacrifice on the altar to God.

PRAYER
Most Holy God,
I'm sure I've failed many tests, but I pray to have a pure heart. Please intervene when I am afraid or unsure. As You did with Abraham and Sarah, keep me from hindering the fulfillment of Your promises in my life. Help me to remember that You are with me, even when I feel alone.

May Your grace, favor and peace preserve me from fear and doubt. May I continually read Your word so that I may be reassured of Your presence. And Lord, the things that I hold most dear, I offer up to You by faith. Please overshadow my fears with the faith to know that in the hour of my greatest tests, Your miraculous provisions will always manifest. In the name of Jesus Christ, I pray. Amen

TODAY'S CHALLENGE: To know that one of the smallest words in my language, FAITH, is the biggest key to receiving Your greatest promises.

What else is God saying to me today?

What is my response?

DAY EIGHT: READ Genesis 23-26

Abraham loses his beloved Sarah to death. As is normal, he mourns the wife that he loves. He secures a burial place for her. God had expressed confidence that Abraham would command his descendents in the way of the Lord. Abraham realizing that he is advanced in age, makes provisions for his son Isaac. He sends his servant out to be divinely led to Rebekah: the woman who will become Isaacs's wife.

Abraham later marries Keturah and has six more sons. As God promised, Abraham blesses all of his sons and sends them to various parts of the earth. Because of Abraham's obedience to God, the promises of God are passed on to Isaac and his descendants.

PRAYER
Dear Faithful, Loving God,
Some of life's experiences are very painful. We see Abraham mourning the death of the love of his life, yet not forgetting to honor You. Please help me to not close You out because of bitter and painful events that have occurred in my life. Abraham's life was not without many trials and tests, but he remained committed to God, and committed to passing the legacy on to his descendants. In my weaknesses and disappointments help me to see and let others know that You are still a good God. In the name of Jesus Christ. Amen.

TODAY'S CHALLENGE: To experience the reality that my faith's anchor will hold during stormy weather?

What else is God saying to me today?

What is my response?

DAY NINE: READ Genesis Chapters 27-29

In these and the preceding chapters, we see the promises of God continuing in spite of imperfect vessels. The promises that God made to Abraham remain in Isaac, and his sons Esau and Jacob. The interesting thing is that both the promises of God and the weaknesses of their humanity are passed from one generation to the next. Isaac fails in the same ways that Abraham did. Both Esau and Jacob fail also. Only God's word remains true.

Although God's word remains true, the descendants of Abraham suffer greatly due to their human weaknesses

PRAYER
Dear God,
How we fail in our efforts to find our way in life just like the patriarchs in the Bible. However, we have the help of the Holy Spirit and the written word which gives us the ability to analyze their mistakes. I pray that I will learn from the lessons of the past and not enter into the same temptations.

O Lord, may I have the faith of Abraham without the failures, the blessings as Isaac without the blindness, the inheritance of Your promises as Esau and Jacob, without the deception and greed. In the name of Jesus Christ. Amen.

TODAY'S CHALLENGE: To allow my human weaknesses and that of others to cause me to draw closer to God who is the only truly reliable refuge.

What else is God saying to me today?

What is my response?

DAY TEN: READ Genesis 30-32

Jacob, whose name means supplanter, is reaping what he has sown. His uncle Laban treats him the same way he and his mother treated his father Isaac and his brother Esau. Jacob works hard and is treated poorly by Laban, yet in the midst of his affliction God speaks to him and directs him to go back to the land of his fathers. During his period of suffering, God does not forsake Jacob, but blesses him greatly in spite of his adverse circumstances.

Finally, Jacob has a monumental life-changing encounter with angels. He "wrestles" all night until he receives a blessing from the Lord. At this time, God changes his name from Jacob to Israel: from supplanter to prince.

PRAYER
Dear Lord,
These scriptures show the very human side of Jacob. Yet he called out to You for deliverance and You blessed and changed him. I have areas of my life that need to be blessed and changed. I ask You to be gracious to me in areas where I must reap what I have sown.

May I also encounter Your very presence in the midst of my struggles. Please forgive me and change me, wherever change is needed, so that I may go wherever You send me without the burden of guilt and fear. In the name of Jesus Christ, I pray. Amen.

TODAY'S CHALLENGE: To not allow shame and pride to serve as padlocks and chains to keep me bound, but to sincerely and earnestly cry out to God for deliverance right now.

What else is God saying to me today?

What is my response?

DAY ELEVEN: READ Genesis 33-36

God moves on the heart of Esau who had issued a death threat against Jacob twenty years earlier, and the brothers are reconciled.

After much growth, struggle and finally transformation, Jacob enters into his place of promise. As a way of life, we see that upon entering each place of rest, Jacob erects an altar to God first. As Israel, formerly Jacob, makes a habit of honoring God first, God reaffirms His name and reaffirms His promises.

PRAYER
Most Holy God in Heaven,
Please let my past sins be forgiven, let there be reconciliation wherever needed, and let me see Your vision of who I am and who I am becoming with Your help.

May I not struggle to hold on to behaviors that belie who I am; but to enter into a place of rest in Your presence, Lord; so that You can show me who You have created me to be. In the name of Jesus Christ, I pray, Amen.

TODAY'S CHALLENGE: To trust that the struggles which God permits me to experience, are part of an incredible process of positive transformation.

What else is God saying to me today?

What is my response?

DAY TWELVE: READ Genesis 37-39

Joseph's brothers sin against him because he is favored by his father. They are further infuriated when Joseph shares a dream and vision of being elevated to a position of leadership over them. Moved with jealousy and envy, they stage his death and sell him into slavery.

Despite being a victim of such cruelty, the Bible tells us that the hand of the Lord is upon Joseph so that he finds favor, and is blessed and he prospers wherever he goes. Just when things are going well for Joseph in Egypt, he is wrongly accused and sent to prison; but the Lord's hand is still with him and he finds mercy and favor.

Meanwhile his brother Judah, who is free, acts outside of the will of God and sins with the Canaanites, which begins a chain-reaction of unholy consequences.

PRAYER
Dear Heavenly Father,
Help me to remember that *where* I am is not as important as *who* I am and who is with me. Seemingly plagued with misfortune, Joseph still prospered where he was placed and did not compromise his integrity even when no one was watching.

Help me to see that in the most unfortunate situations, as I remain connected to You, and faithful to whom You have ordained me to be; You will find a way to bless me. In the name of Jesus Christ, I pray. Amen.

TODAY'S CHALLENGE: To search for the presence of the Lord's hand upon me during the times of adversity.

What else is God saying to me today?

What is my response?

DAY THIRTEEN: READ Genesis 40-42

In these chapters, we see Joseph's gifts emerge. Just as we think that we will see him released because of the promise of his fellow prison mate, the chief butler is restored, but, forgets about speaking to the Pharaoh on Joseph's behalf.

Amazingly, the Bible does not suggest in any way that Joseph becomes bitter. He accepts his lot, and waits upon the Lord.

It's two years later before the opportunity comes for Joseph to witness to Pharaoh through the gift that God has given him. Finally God, through Pharaoh, elevates Joseph to the place of destiny where he can do the most good, and God can get the most glory.

Joseph's dream, which was really God's dream, has come to pass. Circumstances cause Joseph's brothers to come to Egypt for provisions because of a famine in their country. They bow down to Joseph. He recognizes them, but he is so blessed of God that the family that sinned against him does not recognize him.

PRAYER
O Lord,
Only with Your grace and mercy and Your hand upon me will I be able to bear such mistreatments as Joseph did without sinning. Perhaps a clearer vision of Your dream and destiny for me will help me to be totally focused on Your purpose for my life. May that vision so consume me, that I will not be moved by adversities that I encounter.

May God's presence, in me, be so comforting and healing, that if someone sins against me and expects to see me full of anger, bitterness and unforgiveness: I will be so full of the love, healing, and forgiveness of God that they won't recognize me. In the name of Jesus Christ, I pray, Amen.

TODAY'S CHALLENGE: To allow God's vision within me to be bigger and more influential in my life than the adversities that I encounter while I wait for it to come to pass.

What else is God saying to me today?

What is my response?

DAY FOURTEEN: READ Genesis 43-46

Although Joseph gives his brothers provisions, the famine is so great that they have to return to Egypt and ask Joseph for help. Joseph continues to investigate and interrogate them. As Judah intercedes and humbles himself before Joseph, Joseph can no longer constrain his compassion and his longing to see his father.

He reveals himself to his brothers who become speechless with dismay. Joseph comforts and assures them that what they did worked into God's plan to send him to Egypt to be a Savior and Deliverer for them.

Because God blessed Joseph, he is able to bless his entire family and be the instrument that God used to secure them in the best land in Egypt with abundant provisions despite the famine throughout their country.

Before Israel departs for Egypt he offers sacrifices to God. God reassures him and promises to make him a great nation in Egypt.

PRAYER
Lord God of Abraham, Isaac and Jacob, and my God,
I bow before You in awe. You are the God who makes promises and keeps them, who gives dreams and fulfills them, in spite of adversities, delays and human weaknesses.

My faith is refreshed by Your word today. I pray again with expectation that in my life too; You will fulfill every God-given dream and promise that work for my good and the good of others, and for Your glory. In the Jesus of Jesus Christ, I pray. Amen.

TODAY'S CHALLENGE: To offer the sacrifices of praise and worship to my God who is faithful to fulfill His promises to me and make His dreams for me come true.

What else is God saying to me today?

What is my response?

DAY FIFTEEN: READ Genesis 47-50

When Joseph tells Pharaoh about his family and introduces him to his father, Jacob, Jacob blesses Pharaoh and because of Joseph's faithfulness and subsequent promotion; Jacob and his entire family, which by now has grown tremendously, is blessed.

Interestingly, before he dies, Jacob bestows the blessings of the first born of Joseph's sons on the younger. Jacob does not follow tradition, but, is led by the Holy Spirit. He prophesies over, and blesses each of his sons; specifying and foretelling that the kingly lineage of the Messiah, Jesus Christ, will come through the lineage of Judah.

After the death of Jacob, Joseph reassures his brothers that he will not retaliate against them. It is here that we find the immortal phrase: "you meant it for evil, but God meant it for good." Joseph continues to prosper in Egypt until his death.

PRAYER
Dear God,
Joseph is such a clear typification of the Savior, Jesus Christ. His attitude, his life, his ultimate ascension to the right hand of Pharaoh, all point to Christ the Messiah. Thank You for Your great and manifold provisions. Please help me to live my life in such a manner that You will bless me and cause me to be a blessing to others In the name of Jesus Christ, I pray. Amen.

TODAY'S CHALLENGE: Who do people say I remind them of?

What else is God saying to me today?

What is my response?

DAY SIXTEEN: READ Job 1-4

In this book, we are introduced to a man named Job, who is upright, blameless, fears God and shuns evil. He also has great material possessions.

Suddenly, overwhelming calamity befalls Job. He loses his children and all of his possessions in one day. Apparent to us as readers, but, not to Job immediately, this is a vicious attack from Satan, with God's permission. A second attack of Satan leaves Job with painful boils on his body from the soles of his feet to the crown of his head. Instead of luxuriating in splendor and grandeur with maid and menservants, which his previous wealth could afford him, he now sits in a pile of ashes, scraping himself with a potsherd. At this point, his fate looks so eminent that his wife tells him to curse God and die. The Bible says. "In all of this, Job does not sin with his lips." He looks so bad that his friends do not recognize him. When they do, they weep out loud and sprinkled dust on their heads toward Heaven. Job's grief is so heavy that for seven days and seven nights his friends sit and mourn with him in silence. No one says a word.

Job's wife and friends are completely baffled because, according to their understanding of God, good things happen to good people, and bad things happen to bad people. In the words of Job's friend, Eliphaz, "No one perishes if he is not guilty." Job feels such grief that he wishes he had never been born.

PRAYER
Dear Lord,
Job's calamities seem more than I would ever be able to bear. I know that in my world the attitude of Job's friends and wife are pervasive. "If you're suffering calamity, or having a hard time, there must be sin in your life, there must be something that you're doing wrong." Job's experience illustrates the fact that bad things actually do happen to good people. If ever I am the victim of calamity, help me to not curse You. If ever I am in a position of comforting someone, on whom calamity has fallen, please help me not to be smug, suspicious or judgmental; but to show mercy and kindness and to offer prayer to God on their behalf. In Jesus name I pray. Amen.

TODAY'S CHALLENGE: To not offer human explanation for things that only God can answer, but to pray instead.

What else is God saying to me today?

What is my response?

DAY SEVENTEEN: READ Job 5-7

Eliphaz, one of Job's friends, conjectures that God is disciplining Job, correcting him because he is guilty of something. In his mind, it is unfathomable that someone could be upright and suffer such affliction. Eliphaz presents an entire treatise on how God operates, to prove to Job that it is his sin that God is judging.

In anguish, Job prays for God to kill him. He does not understand what is happening to him, and feels as if he is a target for God's wrath.

He appeals to his friend for kindness, but, his friend only adds to his affliction by undermining and judging him. Job questions God.

PRAYER

Oh Lord, in times of great affliction, when I may feel like a target of Your wrath; help me to know that I am more likely a target of Satan's wrath, and that You have not forsaken me. Help me to remember that Satan does not have the permission or the freedom to destroy my life. Help me to remain steadfast in the times of trouble. In the name of Jesus Christ, I pray. Amen.

TODAY'S CHALLENGE: To hold on to my faith in God beyond what my mind can comprehend.

What else is God saying to me today?

What is my response?

DAY EIGHTEEN: READ Job 8-10

Another of Job's friends, Bildad, also questions Job's integrity, and suggests that he is really a hypocrite, stating: that if Job were really upright, God would help him. Job's answers reflect his utter frustration. He knows that he is crying out to God, that he did not sin, but, feels that he has no recourse to defend himself before his friends or before God.

He questions the seemingly senselessness of his affliction. He asks God questions, such as "Why did You so intricately fashion me only to destroy me?"

PRAYER
Heavenly Father,
I don't always understand the things that happen to me or to other people. I can only learn day by day to trust in Your goodness and integrity. In the midst of my questions, because of various situations, help me to maintain a sense of Your presence by faith if not by sight. Just as I walk into a darkened room and feel my way along the wall until I find the light switch; help me to reach out for Your light in the middle of my darkest midnights until I feel Your strong hand sustaining me. In the name of Jesus Christ, I pray, Amen.

TODAY'S CHALLENGE: To base my hope for deliverance on God's integrity, not on my own, or my friend's.

What else is God saying to me today?

What is my response?

DAY NINETEEN: READ Job 11-13

Zophar, another of Job's friends, affirms the verdict of the other two. His summation of the situation is: if Job were righteous, this evil would not have befallen him, and that he should repent. In Job's distress, he begs God for answers. He continually acknowledges the Sovereignty of God and is certain that it is God who is afflicting him. His famous words, "Though He slay me, yet will I trust Him," reflects Job's love for God that defies comprehension; especially given the fact that he thought that the God that he had given his life to honoring: has betrayed him, afflicted him, and sentenced him to shame and defeat.

PRAYER
Dear God,
At times when I feel like You, who are sovereign, have let me down, either because You did not prevent trouble or because I think You actually sent the trouble; help my faith to say sincerely, "though He slay me, yet will I trust Him." You are a good God despite what my circumstances look like. In the mighty name of Jesus Christ, I pray. Amen.

TODAY'S CHALLENGE: To offer up praise and worship to God instead of engaging in human discussions and discourse?

What else is God saying to me today?

What is my response?

DAY TWENTY: READ Job 14-17

Job feels sure of his demise and compares himself to a dry plant that will not be watered and revived. His hope is so crushed that he envies the life of plants; they have hope of recovery.

He continues to examine his life and cannot understand the futility of being born and living righteously, only to die a miserable death, while his friends mock him. He calls his friends miserable comforters; while he contends that he is innocent. He concedes that his days are over and prepares to die.

PRAYER
Oh God,
You alone are our hope in hopeless situations. At such times, help me to shut out the counsel of unwise people and trust in Your unfailing love. In the name of Jesus Christ, I pray. Amen.

TODAY'S CHALLENGE: To avoid anger and disillusionment toward God when I don't understand what is happening in my life?

What else is God saying to me today?

What is my response?

DAY TWENTY-ONE: READ Job 18-20

Job's friends continue to torment him. He describes Bildad's words as "breaking him into pieces." He describes the utter humility of his situation and begs his friends to have pity on him. Zophar, too, consents to Job's doom. He tells Job that his blessings did not endure because he is wicked, and that heaven, earth and God has appointed him to wrath.

Job sees no hope for his natural life, but, it seems that somewhere from within his spirit, Job makes a prophetic declaration. "I know my Redeemer lives, and after my skin is destroyed, this I know, in my flesh I shall see God!"

PRAYER
Oh Lord God Almighty,
When I feel deeply discouraged, in my mind and soul, may Your spirit, like an eagle, rise up within me and give me a view of my situation from a loftier perspective. In the name of Jesus Christ. Amen.

TODAY'S CHALLENGE: To thank God that when my mind and my body resign itself to the grave; whether in anguish or in reality, my spirit is still in communion with God.

What else is God saying to me today?

What is my response?

DAY TWENTY-TWO: READ Job 21-24

Job's friends only offer him prejudiced advice. Job refuses their condemnation and continues to bring his case before God. Job contends that he is righteous and declares that after God has tried him, he will come forth as "pure gold."

He contrasts his future with that of the wicked. He realizes that although it may seem that God is indifferent, in the end, the wicked will dry up like heads of grain.

PRAYER
Dear God,
By faith, I too declare that when I am tested, "I will come forth as pure gold." Help me to know that tests will not destroy me, but they will purify and strengthen me. In the name of Jesus Christ. Amen.

TODAY'S CHALLENGE: May I not faint during the time of testing, but, look forward to the revelation of the glory of God in my life which the testing will produce.

What else is God saying to me today?

What is my response?

DAY TWENTY-THREE: READ *Job 25-27*

Job refuses to condemn himself, despite his friend's condemnation of him. He holds fast to his integrity. Amazingly, Job is certain of his righteousness before God, which makes his situation most perplexing. His friends can only judge by appearance, Job knows his own heart. He has esteemed God's word "above his necessary food." His is sure that his walk before God is upright.

Job tells the cynical Bildad, "My righteousness I hold fast, and will not let go; my heart shall not reproach me as long as I live."

PRAYER
Dear Lord,
Help my relationship with You to be so intimate, that it is unshakable; regardless of the duration of the test or the condemnation of those who do not understand. Help me to live my life in such a manner that every accusation will prove to be ineffective. In the name of Jesus Christ. Amen.

TODAY'S CHALLENGE: To endure the accusations of my adversaries and not doubt God.

What else is God saying to me today?

What is my response?

DAY TWENTY-FOUR: READ Job 28-31

Job laments his present humiliation and remembers the good times. He longs for the times when he felt God's watchful care over him. He recalls how he handled his blessings and how he was faithful to bless others and not consent to sensual sins.

As if trying to make sense of it all, Job reviews his past behaviors in times of blessings to see if there was something that he had failed to do. He recalls that he did not lust after other women. He was not dishonest. He was fair to those who worked for him. He assisted the poor, the fatherless and the widow. He did not trust in his wealth. He even blessed his enemies. He does not see a reason for his calamity. He continues to ask of God, "Why me?"

PRAYER
Dear Lord,
If my actions were weighed, would my integrity equal Job's? Please let me be conscious that on a daily basis I need to pray: "God deliver me from sensual sins." Help me to not ignore the needs of others, or oppress those who I have authority over. Help me not to put my trust in my wealth, but in You. In the name of Jesus Christ, I pray. Amen.

TODAY'S CHALLENGE: If Satan is watching my life, can God brag about me?

What else is God saying to me today?

What is my response?

DAY TWENTY-FIVE: READ Job 32-34

Elihu, the youngest of Job's friends, is bursting to address Job and the others after waiting in silence for quite a while. He is angry because the others did not have an answer for Job's dilemma, yet, they condemned him. He assures Job that he will not mock him, but, he is appalled that Job would contend with God and state his righteousness before the Almighty.

He points to this behavior as Job's sin. Although he is not as condemning, he too does not have the wisdom of God that is needed in Job's hour of distress. In the end, Elihu, too, accuses Job of adding rebellion to whatever other sins he suspects that Job is concealing.

PRAYER
Dear God,
As I identify with Job's distress, I confess that there are times that I am more like Elihu, Bildad, and Eliphaz, help me to just be more like You. I pray this in the name of Jesus Christ. Amen

TODAY'S CHALLENGE: Without the wisdom of God at work in my life, my wisdom will only cause grief.

What else is God saying to me today?

What is my response?

DAY TWENTY-SIX: READ Job 35-37

Elihu continues to compassionately reprove Job and defend God. The scriptures indicate that Job's righteousness is indeed being tested; but, Elihu's human logic tells him that God is disciplining Job; and he tries to reason with Job to repent: so that God would relent. He reminds Job of God's greatness and power over nature, the elements and all things, and that God is too great for Job to contend with Him.

PRAYER
Dear God,
Certain situations reveal what is in me. Please remove prejudice and judgementalism from me today. I ask this sincerely, in the name of Jesus Christ. Amen.

TODAY'S CHALLENGE: When I encounter "Jobs," to be compassionate; when I encounter people like Job's friend's, to be sure that I am not one of them.

What else is God Saying to me today?

What is my response?

DAY TWENTY-SEVEN: READ Job 38-42

Finally, God speaks to Job out of a whirlwind. God shows Job his utter foolishness in trying to compare man's knowledge with that of the Almighty. As a father instructs a son, God asks Job a series of questions, which are designed to make this point.

Job repents for his lack of understanding; but God is angry at Job's friends for their prejudiced attitudes and for misrepresenting God in their behaviors. God tells them to offer a burnt offering and to have Job pray for them, lest he deal with them for their folly.

After Job prays for his friends, God begins to restore him. He restores Job with double blessings and grants him a long life in which to enjoy his blessings.

PRAYER
Yes Lord!
You alone are the only All-wise, Sovereign, Loving, Omnipotent God. I acknowledge that it is impossible for me to comprehend Your greatness. Thank You for continuously watching over me, though at times You seem far away. I pray for restoration; and long life to enjoy it; for myself and others of Your righteous children, whose dreams seem to have been deferred and whose hope has vanished.

I also pray for anyone who has judged me during my times of testing; and I repent and ask forgiveness for judging anyone who may be going through a time of testing. In the name of Jesus Christ. Amen.

TODAY'S CHALLENGE: To have the faith to believe that God will completely restore me although I may experience severe times of testing.

What else is God saying to me today?

What is my response?

DAY TWENTY-EIGHT: READ Exodus 1-4

In Exodus, we see the birthing of Israel as a distinct nation. The Generation of Joseph and all of his brothers have died. A new king arises in Egypt who does not know Joseph or have any regard for his legacy. Moved by fear, this new Pharaoh oppresses the Israelites, and demands that all Hebrew baby boys be put to death. Through the lineage of Levi, God miraculously and extraordinarily preserves a Hebrew baby boy, Moses, who is found in the river and adopted by Pharaoh's daughter. Consequently, Moses is raised in the household of Pharaoh. Over the years, the oppression of the Hebrews becomes extremely cruel and unbearable. After becoming an adult, Moses rescues a Hebrew slave from an Egyptian oppressor, and kills the Egyptian. When Pharaoh discovers the deed, Moses flees to the desert of Midian to avoid being killed by Pharaoh.

During a forty-year period in Midian, Moses marries Zipporah, the daughter of a priest. It is here, in Midian, that God speaks to Moses out of a burning bush and tells him that in answer to the groans and prayers of the Israelites, he is being commissioned to deliver His people, the children of Israel, out of the hand of Pharaoh, out of Egypt.

Moses argues extensively with God. He does not feel adequate, and feels that both Pharaoh and the people will reject him and questions the identity of his God. When Moses asks God, "who am I to perform this great task and who shall I say sent me?" God replies, tell them "I Am has sent you, and I will go with you."

PRAYER
Dear God,
You are beyond comprehension. My most eloquent words cannot express Your Awesomeness, Majesty and Wisdom. Thank You that You hear the cries of Your children, and You will send deliverance; sometimes through one of Your covenant children—Thank You. When it is my appointment to be an answer to someone else's prayer, help me not to look at my inadequacies, but at Your omnipotence. Help me to not ask, who am I? ; Help me to seek to reveal You, as "I AM." I humbly pray this in the name of Jesus Christ. Amen.

TODAY'S CHALLENGE: When I am faced with a task that is too great for me, to not argue or disobey, but, to look to God, the Great "I AM" for *His* sufficiency!

What else is God saying to me today?

What is my response?

DAY TWENTY-NINE: READ Exodus 5-7

When Moses and Aaron go to Egypt and tell the elders of Israel that the Lord has heard their prayers and looked on their affliction, they believe them and bow in worship.

When Moses and Aaron ask Pharaoh to let the people go and worship God, Pharaoh becomes indignant. Instead of releasing the people, he demands that their labor increase with extra cruelty. This harsh reply causes the spirits of the Israelites to be crushed and their hopes dashed. They cry out to Moses saying, "you have made us abhorrent in the sight of Pharaoh and his servants, to put a sword in their hand to kill us."

Moses cries out to God and God assures him that He is the Lord, Jehovah and He will keep His covenant. He will bring them into the promised land. God recommissions Moses to go again to Pharaoh. Pharaoh hardens his heart as God knew that he would. Consequently, the first miracle is performed, and the first plague is released.

PRAYER
Dear God in Heaven,
Thank You for reminding me through these scriptures that You are Jehovah, the Lord who keeps covenant. Help me to especially remember this when the enemy of my soul afflicts me most viciously. In the name of Jesus Christ. Amen.

TODAY'S CHALLENGE: Lord, help me to believe Your words when the situations that I face seem more powerful and eminent.

What else is God saying to me today?

What is my response?

DAY THIRTY: READ Exodus 8-10

In spite of the first plague, Pharaoh hardens his heart, so God allows him to continue to harden his heart and the plagues continue: the plague of frogs, the plague of lice, the plague of flies, the plague of disease on the animals, the plague of boils on man and animals, the plague of hail, the plague of locusts, and the plague of darkness. Pharaoh continues to harden his heart for so long that God permits his hardness of heart to bring judgment on him and the entire country that he governs.

Contrarily, God points out that His people, the children of Israel, who dwell in Goshen, will not be affected by the plagues. God wants to make sure that both Pharaoh and the Israelites know that God makes a distinction between His people and the people who oppose God.

PRAYER
Almighty God,
Have I seriously considered the consequences of my actions? If any of my actions have negatively affected people in my life, I ask You to please forgive me, and remove any plagues that may have come as a consequence of those actions. When I harden my heart, I invite Your judgment; not only upon myself, but, also upon those whom I love and serve. Please help me to sincerely humble myself, repent and obey when You speak to me. In the name of Jesus Christ, I pray. Amen.

TODAY'S CHALLENGE: To realize that I have more influence than I think that I have. I have the potential to affect millions of lives (or just one) for either good or evil.

What else is God saying to me today?

What is my response?

DAY THIRTY-ONE: READ Exodus 11-13

In the eleventh chapter of Exodus: God brings a final plague on Pharaoh and the Egyptians, the plague of death of the firstborn. God tells Moses that after this horrible judgment, Pharaoh will let them go. He instructs the people to ask for goods from the Egyptians. The fear of God and Moses is upon the Egyptians; so they give generously to the Israelites.

During this time, God institutes the Passover. The blood of slain lambs is placed on the doorposts of the Israelites so that when the death angel strikes at midnight, he will "Passover" those Israelites whose doors are marked by the blood of the lambs.

On that same night, God leads His people, a great multitude, out of 400 years of Egyptian bondage. He charges Moses to tell the elders to continue to celebrate the Passover, year after year, and to tell the testimony of their great deliverance throughout the generations, especially after they entered the promised land.

PRAYER

Dear Heavenly Father,
Thank You for the revelation of Your love that goes to endless measures to find me. Thank You for Your great works of deliverance both historically in the lives of Your people, and personally in my life. Thank You for the blood of the lamb, Jesus the Messiah. I pray for opportunities, especially among my loved ones, to tell of Your great expressions of love and faithfulness in my life. In the name of Jesus Christ. Amen.

TODAY'S CHALLENGE: To stop my trivial complaints and recall the many instances of God's expressions of love to me over the years. Who can I tell right now?

What else is God saying to me today?

What is my response?

DAY THIRTY-TWO: READ Exodus 14-17

Imagine the fearful exuberance that the Israelites must be feeling as they are walking out of Egypt. Although oppressive, it's familiar. They are now walking into the unknown. The people are like abused children who don't know how to recognize or trust in true love. As they try to adapt to trusting in God and His leader, Moses, they vacillate between miracles and murmuring; seeing the vision of a promised land only through the words of the prophet, Moses.

God continues to make Himself known to them as the Lord who hears, the Lord who provides and protects, the Lord who heals, and the Lord who is their Banner.

PRAYER
Dear God,
Teach me Your ways although mine are more familiar to me. Help me to comprehend Your great love for me so that I can trust You completely. I accept You in my life as the Lord who hears me, the Lord who protects and provides for me, the Lord who heals me, and the Lord who is my Banner. In the name of Jesus Christ, I pray. Amen.

TODAY'S CHALLENGE: To think about this: every obstacle in my life is an opportunity to see God reveal himself to me in a different and more delightful way.

What else is God saying to me today?

What is my response?

DAY THIRTY-THREE: READ Exodus 18-20

Moses is met by his father-in-law, the priest of Midian, in the wilderness. When he sees the responsibilities that Moses has; Jethro offers him wise counsel. Moses, the prophet who God speaks to clearly and uses with great signs and wonders, shows incredible humility and respect, and receives Jethro's wise counsel.

It is apparent that Moses does not pretend to know it all simply because he is a prophet. He expresses a humble heart and a servant's spirit. That makes him a great leader. He accepts Jethro's counsel and his ministry is more effective.

God chooses to meet him alone in the mountain and gives him the Ten Commandments, written in stone by the hand of God. What a call, what an opportunity, what a responsibility.

PRAYER
O Lord,
Lead me by Your spirit as well as by wise counsel from Your select servants; including those in my family. Help me to be discerning without being cynical and unteachable. I also pray to be the kind of person who You can trust with Your word and who can accurately and effectively communicate it to others. In the name of Jesus Christ. Amen.

TODAY'S CHALLENGE: May I recognize when God is speaking to me through other people.

What else is God saying to me today?

What is my response?

DAY THIRTY-FOUR: READ Exodus 21-24

God not only gives Moses the Ten Commandments, but other commandments too numerous to count. There are laws concerning virtually every aspect of human existence and relationships; including how to resolve conflicts involving animals.

God is concerned about every detail of human existence and interaction. Although the laws seem overwhelming and too many to remember, it is evident that God wants people to be careful how they treat each other. The Israelites who do not wish to feel the crushing force of the innumerable laws have only to obey the two basic ones, love and obey God and love your neighbor.

PRAYER
Dear Awesome God,

Help me to remember that You love others as much as You love me. Your commandments help me to behave in a manner that will please You and respect other people. In the name of Jesus Christ. Amen.

TODAY'S CHALLENGE: To realize that God's laws are designed to protect my rights as well as the rights of others.

What else is God saying to me?

What is my response?

DAY THIRTY-FIVE: READ Exodus 25-27

God speaks to Moses to construct a tabernacle, a designated place where He will meet with the people, and they will come and worship God. God gives intricate and specific instructions. Moses asks the people who are willing, to bring offerings of gold, silver, and other precious possessions that will be used in the construction of the tabernacle.

God's design has spiritual, natural, eternal and temporal significance. God places special significance on the fellowship between Himself and His people. The tabernacle, with the Ark of the Covenant, all point to a way for fellowship to be restored, and to God preparing a pattern by which his people can enter into His presence.

PRAYER
Heavenly Father,
I thank You for caring for me so much that You made provision for my need to worship. Help me to slow down and be conscious of the awesome privilege that I have to come into Your presence and worship You at will. In the name of Jesus Christ. Amen.

TODAY'S CHALLENGE: If God took such care to design an opportunity for me come into His presence, maybe I should do it more often.

What else is God saying to me today?

What is my response?

DAY THIRTY-SIX: READ Exodus 28-31

God carefully gives intricate instructions for the design of Aaron and his son's garments. The garments of those who will attend to and administer to the things that pertain to worship are important to God. Each detail has prophetic symbolism.

The laws concerning the keeping of the Sabbath are designed to help Israel to stay in harmony and fellowship with God. God in His awesomeness and holiness is very conscious of our humanity, and His great love for us constantly releases grace that closes the gap between our finiteness and His infiniteness; our humanity and His holiness.

PRAYER
Dear Awesome God,
Your mind is incomprehensible. Thank You that nothing escapes Your all-seeing eye. You have carefully designed and constructed Your order in the universe and permitted me to participate in it. I offer my prayer and praise to You as incense. May my worship be pure and holy. In the Jesus of Jesus Christ. Amen.

TODAY'S CHALLENGE: To be dressed properly both mentally and spiritually as I seek to enter into the presence of God?

What else is God saying to me today?

What is my response?

DAY THIRTY-SEVEN: READ Exodus 32-34

The children of Israel who are waiting in the valley at the bottom of the mountain for Moses to return from talking to God become anxious and impatient. They begin to long for what is familiar. They demand that Aaron makes them "gods to go before them." They fashion a molded calf and say, "This is your god O Israel, who brought you out of the land of Egypt!"

In frustration, Moses breaks the Ten Commandments which are written on the stones. Because of their great sin, God's punishment follows. God wants to destroy them, but, Moses intercedes.

Moses asks God to let His presence go with him; then he asks to see God's glory. After forty days and forty nights, in the presence of God, Moses' face is so radiant that the children of Israel cannot look at him; he has to put a veil over his face. He unveils his face, in the presence of God, when he goes to the tabernacle; but, veils his face when he goes before the people. Only Joshua stays at the tabernacle.

PRAYER

Dear Lord God Almighty,
Please help me to not doubt You and turn to idol gods because I don't see Your answers immediately. While God was on the mountain talking to Moses in detail about Aaron, Aaron was in the valley building an idol. Help me to trust You enough to believe that during my valley experiences, You're preparing a special and personal miracle for me. Most of all let me seek Your presence. In the name of Jesus Christ. Amen.

TODAY'S CHALLENGE: Can God trust me when I'm in the valley? Can I trust God when I'm in the valley ?

What else is God saying to me today?

What is my response?

DAY THIRTY-EIGHT: READ Exodus 35-37

Moses gives the children of Israel the laws concerning the Sabbath; then He makes plans to construct the tabernacle and the Ark of the Covenant according to the design that God has given him. He asks for offering from all of those who are willing to give of their possessions for the building of the tabernacle. They give so willingly and so generously that Moses has to tell them not to give anymore. God gives wisdom to the artesian and craftsmen so that everything is constructed according to God's specifications.

PRAYER

Thank You Lord for being merciful. Thank You for restoring and forgiving the people who repented; and allowing them to share in Your glorious work. At points of my rebellion and idolatry, I repent also and ask for forgiveness and restoration. In the name of Jesus Christ. Amen.

TODAY'S CHALLENGE: To trust God to construct my life in a manner that meets his intended specifications.

What else is God saying to me today?

What is my response?

DAY THIRTY-NINE: READ Exodus 38-40

Moses and the craftsmen that he employs follow the Master Architect's plan explicitly. The tabernacle with the Ark of the Covenant, the altars of sacrifice, the laws for cleansing, the court and the clothes for the priest all point to a God who has government, order and majesty.

The words of Exodus burst with excitement as the author describes in detail, the elaborate and intricate design of a breathtakingly beautiful structure. A befitting place in which the King of the Universe chose to manifest His presence.

PRAYER
O Lord,
Your splendor is incomparable. You have a purpose in every thing that You do. I agree with Your plans for my life. I agree with Your design for worship, I agree with Your plan to fellowship with Your children. I welcome Your presence in my life in every way. May something of Your glory and beauty be reflected in my life each day. In the name of Jesus Christ. Amen.

TODAY'S CHALLENGE: To notice that God took care and gave intricate details to the things that pertain to worship. How is my worship?

What else is God saying to me?

What is my response?

DAY FORTY: READ Leviticus 1-4

In the book of Leviticus: God teaches and guides His redeemed people in how to worship a Holy God. The people have been delivered from Egypt, redeemed from bondage and established as a priestly nation. They are now being taught how to offer sacrifices, praise and worship to God, Jehovah.

The burnt offering, the grain offering, the peace offering, the sin offering and the trespass offering all point to a future: when Jesus Christ our great high priest, who Aaron typifies, will fulfill all of the requirements of the law. Instead of bulls, goats, pigeons or grain, we offer the sacrifices of praise and worship and thanksgiving.

PRAYER

Most Holy God,

Thank You for patterns of worship which point to the ultimate sacrifice of the Messiah for the forgiveness of sins. You alone, O Lord, are Holy. Through Jesus Christ, I too have been redeemed; help me to be aware of that and to live accordingly. Today, instead of the burden of animal and grain offerings, I offer You my praise, worship and thanksgiving. In the name of Jesus Christ. Amen.

TODAY'S CHALLENGE: To comprehend the truth that all of the requirements for sacrifices were fulfilled in Jesus Christ.

What else is God saying to me today?

What is my response?

DAY FORTY-ONE: READ Leviticus 5-7

God tells the Israelites how to come before the Lord for both intentional and unintentional sins. He makes provision for repentance and restitution.

He reveals Himself as a just God. Those who can only offer one tenth of an ephah of flour are not required to offer a lamb or a goat. The important thing is that a person who sins confesses his sin and brings an appropriate sacrifice. In confessing sins, God demands that His people be honest with each other. A person who trespasses against his brother is required to make restitution first to his brother, then to bring a trespass offering to God for his sin. God makes provisions for the continual offerings for sins by commissioning Aaron and his sons to keep the fire burning perpetually on the altar of burnt offerings.

PRAYER
Dear Lord,
Thank You so much for making provisions for the forgiveness of sins. Burn into my consciousness the fact that how I relate to other people, directly affects my relationship with You. Help me to not hypocritically make offerings to You, and ignore my responsibility and obligation to make restitution to someone else. I thank and praise You, in the name of Jesus Christ. Amen.

TODAY'S CHALLENGE: If I make an offering to God and ignore my responsibility to other people, does God accept my offerings?

What else is God saying to me today?

What is my response?

DAY FORTY-TWO: READ Leviticus 8-10

These three chapters focus on the consecration of the priests, and the proper way to offer sacrifices. The cleansing, the special garments, the anointing oil, the consecration with blood are all commanded to distinguish the priests as those set apart to make offering to God for the people. God has a divine order in which He is to be approached. Unfortunately, we see the destruction of Nadad and Abihu, Aaron's sons, for offering profane fire before the Lord.

PRAYER
O Most Holy God,
I humbly submit myself spirit, soul and body to Your supreme and superior authority. Please help me to realize that You are not common, You are not a man. Restore my respect for whom You are. Help me to honor You and approach You with reverence. Help me to love You and cultivate intimacy with You without becoming irreverent. In the name of Jesus Christ. Amen.

TODAY'S CHALLENGE: I can only approach God when I accept and do it in the manner that He has ordained. "Just as I am," refers to brokenness and humility, not pride and presumption.

What else is God saying to me today?

What is my response?

DAY FORTY-THREE: READ Leviticus 11-13

God who created the world, the earth and everything therein is also the architect of the human body. After the fall of Adam and Eve the bodies of mankind became susceptible to sickness and disease. God's love is so complete, so personal that He takes special care to teach the Israelites all of the dietary freedoms as well as restrictions that will affect their physical health. God wants his people to be holy, set apart and distinct in every way.

PRAYER

Dear Lord,

I see that You are concerned about what I put into my body for food and how I treat my body because You care for me completely. Thank You. I now attune my ears to You and educate and discipline myself. Help me to overcome bad eating habits and other practices that are detrimental to my health. You made my body and I need Your guidance and strength to care for it properly so that I may glorify You in it. I submit my appetites and craving to You. Help me to correct those things that pertain to my physical well-being. In the name of Jesus Christ I pray. Amen.

TODAY'S CHALLENGE: To glorify God in my eating habits, to treat my body well.

What else is God saying to me today?

What is my response?

DAY FORTY-FOUR: READ Leviticus 14-16

Here we see an interesting juxtaposition which reflects the wisdom, grace and love of an Omniscient God.

God gives instructions to Moses for the children of Israel regarding the detection of contagious, communicable diseases such as leprosy. God simultaneously instructs Aaron the priest on how to offer sacrifices and atonement for the forgiveness of sins and for healing the people of their diseases. God knew that sin brought disease and suffering, but, through the atonement forgiveness and healing are made available.

PRAYER
Dear Holy God,
Please cleanse me and my household from everything that would cause decay in our lives and which would also affect other people. I accept Jesus Christ as the sacrifice for my healing and restoration. In the name of Jesus Christ, I pray. Amen.

TODAY'S CHALLENGE: Is there an outbreak of leprosy (sin) in my life, or my house, that I need to bring before the High Priest, the Lord, Jesus Christ?

What else is God saying to me today?

What is my response?

DAY FORTY-FIVE: READ Leviticus 17-19

In these two chapters, God presents his commandments on key issues of human concern that are unarguable and not to be compromised. He addresses how blood is to be used and prohibits the drinking of it. Symbolically, prophetically and eternally, verse eleven speaks: "For the life of the flesh is in the blood, and I have given it to you upon the altar to make atonement for your souls; for it is the blood that makes atonement for the soul."

God elaborately condemns the sins of incest, homosexuality, bestiality, covetousness, adultery, disrespect and irreverence for parents, improper treatment of the disabled and disadvantaged, dishonesty in business and slander. God condemns the seeking of mediums, psychics or familiar spirits as well as the ill treatment of people from other races or ethnicities. God is just and commands the same for the people whom He calls his own.

PRAYER
Holy God,
May I fear to sin against You or against people. Although I live in a world that is infested with all of the things that You condemn; help me to abhor them as You do and to not engage them with my ears, eyes, or heart. I ask for forgiveness for myself, my family my church and my country for our personal and national sins. May Your word cover the earth, and may people everywhere embrace Your holiness. Thank You for the blood of Jesus which makes atonement for the sins of everyone who confesses their sins, asks Jesus for forgiveness, and repents. In the name of Jesus Christ. Amen.

TODAY'S CHALLENGE: To call holy what God calls holy, to call clean what God calls clean: to call unholy what God calls unholy, and to call unclean what God calls unclean.

What else is God saying to me today?

What is my response?

DAY FORTY-SIX: READ Leviticus 20-23

God's objective is to distinguish the Israelites as a holy people, set apart to serve and worship the True and Living God. He teaches them how to worship Him and how to treat each other. He emphasizes that atonement is through the blood.

God is preparing His people for a promised possession, the land of Canaan, which is presently inhabited by people who defile themselves in abominable ways: child sacrifice to Moloch, consulting familiar spirits, cursing parents, and various sexual sins. God's penalty for most of these abominations is the death sentence. Immediately after we see the penalty for sins, we see God's grace in action. God interjects the convocations and feasts of the Lord: the keeping of the Sabbath, weekly Passover, Feast of unleavened bread, Feast of first fruits, Feast of Pentecost, Feast of trumpets, Day of Atonement and the Feast of Tabernacles.

Innate in mankind is the need to worship. God teaches His people how to have true worship, to a Holy God so that they will not worship and participate in those things that are an abomination and whose end is death.

PRAYER
Most Holy God,
In Your presence my own sense of righteousness is silenced! I have sinned and without Jesus Christ I have no acceptable sacrifice or offering. Thank You, Jesus!

Lord I believe that Your will for me is good. Help me to really know that it is Your love for me that causes You to teach me to choose life and refuse those practices that have the stench of spiritual and physical death attached to them. Some such things are en vogue in my culture; decorated and disguised in order to deceive. May Your truth expose sin for the horrid, despicable thing that it is. Sin hurls mud in the face of God, and brings death in its various forms to all who are affected by it. In the name of Jesus Christ. Amen.

TODAY'S CHALLENGE: To hate sin as God does and to avoid participating in it in any form. To detect its odor and consistently turn away from it.

What else is God saying to me today?

What is my response?

DAY FORTY-SEVEN: READ Leviticus 24-27

God places Aaron, the high priest, in charge of the oil for the lamp that is to burn continually and to be perpetuated throughout the generations.

God continues to give His people laws that will ensure their blessings. He also emphasizes the penalties for disobedience. He explains the laws of the Sabbath year and elaborately highlights the year of Jubilee, a time of restoration. God outlines the penalties for sins and the blessings for obedience. He tells the Israelites: "I have broken the band of your yoke and made you walk upright." Yet they were warned that if they chose to abhor the things of God their bondage would be reinstated. God introduces the role of the kinsman redeemer and teaches the Israelites that when they sin and admit their guilt, He will remember His covenant and restore them.

God teaches the Israelites how to consecrate persons, animals, houses, and fields; and how to devote such things to the Lord. God also gives the laws concerning the tithes. All of these laws God gives to Moses for the good of the people while they are at mount Sinai, before they proceed into the promised land.

PRAYER
Dear Lord,
Your laws are for my good. Help me to choose to obey You and ensure the great blessings and promises that You have in store for me. Thank You for teaching me how to be blessed and how to live in those blessings. I am aware that I have not yet received some of my blessings because You are still preparing me. Dear Lord, consecrate me to Yourself so that I may humbly live in harmony with Your will and purposes. In the name of Jesus Christ. Amen.

TODAY'S CHALLENGE: To not ignore the prerequisites of obedience which precede the blessings and promises of God.

What else is God saying to me today?

What is my response?

DAY FORTY-EIGHT: READ Numbers 1-3

In the first two chapters of the book of Numbers, God speaks to Moses to take a census, to number the people by tribes. The twelve sons of Jacob have greatly increased in number. Each tribe now has tens of thousands of people. The total number of males above the age of twenty who are able to go to war is 603,550.

The Levitical tribe, the family of Aaron, is excluded from the first census because God appoints them to take care of the Tabernacle of the Testimony. God tells Moses that the Levites are His. When He destroyed all the firstborn of Egypt, He sanctified the firstborn of Israel. The Levites become a substitute for the firstborn of each household of Israel. Each of the two hundred and seventy three firstborns were instructed by God, through Moses, to give an offering for their redemption. The redemption money is given to Aaron the priest, and his sons.

God assigns each tribe a position in the assembly and strategically places them there under the standard or banner of the family name. The Levites He tells to camp around the Tabernacle of the Testimony and to keep charge of it.

PRAYER
Dear Lord,
In Your wisdom You placed each tribe of the Israelites in the position that You knew was properly suited for them. You knew their areas of weakness, strength, gifts and talents. You had a position and a purpose for each tribe member.

I humbly ask You to take Your all-seeing eye, examine me in all of my areas of strengths and weaknesses, and strategically position me in Your perfect will, so that I can be an asset to Your eternal plan. I am aware that You have a place for me in a plan that is far greater than I can fathom. You are my redeemer. I await Your instructions. In the name of Jesus Christ. Amen.

TODAY'S CHALLENGE: To understand that God knows exactly where I am best suited to serve.

What else is God saying to me today?

What is my response?

DAY FORTY-NINE: READ Numbers 4-6

Each of the families of the tribe of the Levites are given specific assignments as it pertains to the service of the Tabernacle of the Testimony. In all there are 8,580 who are given various tasks.

God then gives Moses instructions on how to handle unclean persons, persons who sin, and those suspected of adultery. These are to be dealt with outside of the camp in a manner that God details to Moses.

Those who would take the Nazarite vow are also given specific instructions. God then gives instructions to Moses for Aaron to bless the children of Israel in this manner.

"The Lord bless and keep you, the Lord make His face shine upon you and give you and be gracious to you; the Lord lift up His countenance upon you and give you peace."

PRAYER
O Dear Lord,
As I continue to be sensitive to Your voice so that I may know my position in Your Kingdom, help me to avoid those behaviors that cause me to be outside of Your will. I pray Lord that You will bless me and keep me, make Your face shine upon me and be gracious to me. Lord lift up Your countenance upon me and give me peace. I pray this in the name of Jesus Christ. Amen.

TODAY'S CHALLENGE: May I be still until God tells me what to do.

What else is God saying to me today?

What is my response?

DAY FIFTY: READ *Numbers 7-10*

After Moses erects the tabernacle, he anoints and sanctifies it. Then the leaders of all of the tribes make offerings which include covered carts, silver platters, silver bowls, incense and many such valuables.

In an elaborate, yet solemn ceremony, God instructs Moses to consecrate the Levites and present them as a wave offering before the Lord. He reiterates that the Levites belong to Him; that they were sanctified on the night that He struck Egypt's firstborn.

Then the children of Israel keep the Passover at the appointed time. After that a cloud appears and covers the Tabernacle. The cloud becomes their navigator and guide. When the cloud moves, they move, when it stays they stay. Even if the cloud rests for a long time, the camp does not move. At night the cloud appears as fire; providing a lighted pathway for the Israelites.

PRAYER
Dear Lord,
Sanctify me and set me apart for the work that You have for me to do in Your Kingdom and in this world. I want to offer You my best. Help me to be sensitive and obedient to Your leading. In the name of Jesus Christ. Amen.

TODAY'S CHALLENGE: To move with the cloud (God's presence) being willing to move when He moves, and stay when He stays.

What else is God saying to me today?

What is my response?

DAY FIFTY-ONE: READ Numbers 11-14

Moses has organized the people, strategized them for advancement into the promised land and is moving them forward. The people become frustrated and begin to murmur and complain. This displeases the Lord and he sends fire to consume some of them.

They complain about the manna, and begin to complain about what God provided for them. They begin to crave meat. God allows them to have meat; but a plague breaks out among them while they are still consuming the flesh.

Miriam and Aaron begin to complain against Moses because he married an Ethiopian woman. Miriam is stricken with leprosy because of her sin. Aaron asks for mercy and Moses asks God to please heal her. Miriam remains stricken for seven days, and the assembly does not move forward until she is healed. Then the camp moves forward.

As they near Canaan, Moses sends twelve men to spy out the land. Among them are Caleb and Joshua. After forty days the men return and ten of them give a very dismal report, so dismal that the people lose hope. Some of them weep all night. Some rise up and ask for a new leader who will take them back to Egypt! Only Moses and Joshua believe that the Lord will give them the land as He promised. Because the ten spies bring back such an evil report and caused the heart of the people to faint, God sentences them to death; and because of the people's unbelief, they are sentenced to forty years of wandering in the desert, a year for each day that the spies were in the promised land.

PRAYER
Dear Lord,
Please forgive me for complaining and murmuring. Help me to be thankful for Your provisions, even if they don't seem exciting at the moment. Help me not to forget that You have indeed blessed me and I am thankful. Help me to believe Your promises in spite of what I see. In the name of Jesus of Jesus Christ. Amen.

TODAY'S CHALLENGE: To not murmur or complain.

What else is God Speaking to me today?

What is my response?

DAY FIFTY-TWO: READ Numbers 15-17

God tells Moses when the children of Israel come into the promised land that they are to give a thanksgiving offering. Instructions are given for offerings for unintentional sins; however there is no offering for intentional sins.

Three men Korah, Dathan and Abiram, lead a rebellion against Moses and Aaron and question their positions of leadership. God destroys Korah and his followers in an unusual manner. The ground opens up and swallows them while they are alive, then closes up again. Instead of fearing God, the congregation gathers against Moses and Aaron and accuses them of killing the people. They turn toward the tabernacle of meetings and suddenly the cloud covers it. God speaks to Moses to get away from the people so that he can consume them in a moment. Moses and Aaron fall on their faces. Moses instructs Aaron to quickly get a censor and take fire from the altar and make atonement for the people. A destructive plague has already broken out among the people and some have died. Aaron takes the censor with incense and stands between the living and the dead and the plague is stopped.

God confirms the call of Moses and Aaron through another miracle. He instructs Moses to have each leader of the twelve tribes to bring a rod with their names on it. Aaron's rod is included. Moses places the rods before the Lord in the Tabernacle of witness. The next day the rod of Aaron, from the tribe of Levi, has produced blossoms and yielded ripe almonds. Moses brings all of the rods to the children of Israel so that they can see the distinction of Aaron's rod. God instructs Moses to keep Aaron's rod in the tabernacle as a testimony against the rebels.

PRAYER
Most Holy God of all creation,
You are patient, kind and just. You are also just when You mete out punishment against rebellion. Please remove from me any traits of the rebels in these accounts, so that I will not invite Your wrath into my life. I am aware that I may not always agree with Your choices in Leadership. Help me to not murmur against those whom You have called. In the name of Jesus Christ, Amen.

TODAY'S CHALLENGE: To be close enough to know the heart of God so that I can fight against His enemies, not His friends.

What else is God saying to me today?

What is my response?

DAY FIFTY-THREE: READ Numbers 18-20

The Lord tells Moses and Aaron that He gave the Levite the priesthood as a gift for service. God tells Aaron that he and his sons should receive a portion of the heave offering and the first fruits of the people. God says: "Behold I have given the children of Levi all the tithes in Israel as an inheritance in return for the work which they perform, the work of the tabernacle of meeting."

Other events include the purification of the red heifer and the death of Miriam. The children of Israel begin to complain and murmur against Moses and Aaron and against God because there is no water. God instructs Moses with Aaron to call the people together and speak to a rock and He would cause water to spring from it. They call the assembly, and instead of speaking to the rock as God had commanded, Moses strikes the rock twice; indicating that He and Aaron performed this miracle. Because of his disobedience and failure to hallow God in front of the people, God tells Moses that he and Aaron will not enter the promised land.

God instructs Moses to go up to Mount Hor in the sight of the congregation. He strips Aaron of His garments and places them on Aaron's son Eleazar. Aaron dies there on top of the mountain. They all mourn for Aaron for thirty days.

PRAYER
O Lord,
You are wonderful, and You are Holy. Help me and Your people to submit humbly to Your authority and respect and obey Your commands. Help me to be more sensitive and willing to give to those who work in Your service. As Your servant, Please help me to follow Your instructions without variations. In the name of Jesus Christ. Amen.

TODAY'S CHALLENGE: God has a purpose behind all of his laws and directives whether I know what it is or not.

What else is God saying to me to today?

What is my response?

DAY FIFTY-FOUR: READ Numbers 21-24

The king of Arad of the Canaanites takes some of the Israelites as prisoners. God gives Moses permission to conquer the city. As they continue their journey the people become very discouraged. They ask Moses, "Why have you brought us up out of Egypt to die in the wilderness? For there is no food and no water, and our souls loathe this worthless bread."

The Lord sends fiery serpents among them. Many are bitten and die. The people repent and God instructs Moses to erect a bronze serpent on a pole and to tell the people that those who will look up will live.

The people move on, conquering Sihon and Bashan. They camp in the plains of Moab. Balak, the King of the Moabites has heard of the defeat of his neighbors and he and his people are in great fear. He sends his people to bring Balaam to speak curses on the children of Israel. God tells Balaam that he should not go with Balak's men. They offer him great sums of money. He refuses to go and curse the Israelites. They beseech Balaam again and he goes with them. While en route his donkey refuses to go forward. He strikes the donkey who then speaks to him. In the process, Balaam sees an angel with his sword drawn. His donkey has saved his life. He continues on the trip to meet Balak. Once there Balak tries to get Balaam to curse Israel from various positions, but Balaam can only bless Israel. He says. "Behold I have received a command to bless; He has blessed and I cannot reverse it."

PRAYER
O Most Holy and Wise God,
Your word reminds me of Your Sovereignty. You forgive me when I sin, and protect me when I'm under attack. As indicated in the account of Balaam, when You have blessed me, no one can reverse it. I thank You in the name of Jesus Christ. Amen.

TODAY'S CHALLENGE: To find the balance between aspiration and complaining, to thank God for blessing me and for nullifying the curses of my enemies.

What else is God saying to me today?

What is my response?

DAY FIFTY-FIVE: READ Numbers 25-27

The Israelites remain in an area called Acacia Grove and there begin to commit harlotry with the women of Moab. They make sacrifices and bow down to their gods. Twenty-four thousand Israelites die of a plague because of their sin against God. Phinehas, the son of Eleazar destroy the offenders and is rewarded by God for making atonement for the people and the plague stops.

God tells Moses and Eleazar to take another census; counting the men, age twenty and up, who are able to go to war. The total number is 601,730. God tells Moses how to divide the land by tribes, including the inheritance of daughters when they have no brothers.

God also tells Moses that none of the old generation, except Caleb and Joshua, will enter the promised land. God tells Moses that he too will die without going into the promised land just as Aaron had because of his sin when he struck the rock and did not hallow the name of the Lord before the people. Moses asks God to appoint another leader. God chooses Joshua and tells Moses to lay his hands on Joshua, give him some of his authority, and inaugurate him in front of Eleazar, the priest, and the people.

PRAYER
Dear Lord,
Help me to remember that You are a God of love and justice even if I don't understand Your ways. As much as You love people, You also hate sin and the propagation of it. Help me to obey You more out of love, gratitude and reverential fear rather than out of fear of punishment. In the name of Jesus Christ, Amen.

TODAY'S CHALLENGE: To see that God's love and mercy are balanced with his holiness and righteousness.

What else is God saying to me today?

What is my response?

DAY FIFTY-SIX: READ Numbers 28-30

God tells Moses to caution the children of Israel to make their offering at the appointed times. They include: daily offerings, weekly offerings; and on the fourteenth day of the first month they were to celebrate Passover; and on the fifth day the feast of unleavened bread for seven days. God also institutes the observance of the Firstfruits, the blowing of trumpets and the convocation of Tabernacle.

God also gives detailed instructions on the making of vows to God.

PRAYER
Dear God,
You gave the Israelites many instructions for observances and offerings and holy days to help remind them to continue to worship You in the land of promise. I sense in all of them Your love and desire for Your people to obey You so that they would not commit the wickedness of the former inhabitants and lose their blessing. I pray for myself and Your people today. When You hear our cries and answer our prayers, help us to continue to obey You. Also when we make vows in the valley of desperation, help us to not forget them on the mountain of manifestation. I pray sincerely in the name of Jesus Christ, Amen.

TODAY'S CHALLENGE: To love, worship, serve and obey God when I have everything that I need.

What else is God saying to me today?

What is my response?

DAY FIFTY-SEVEN: READ Numbers 31-33

God instructs Moses to take vengeance on the Midianites. He is instructed to take a thousand men from each tribe, twelve thousand men. They prevail over Midian, but, Moses is angry at them for keeping alive the women of such as caused sin and destruction at Peor. Moses and Eleazar instruct the officers to purify everything and Moses distributes the spoils. Half are given to the men who took part in the war and the other half to all of the congregation. Moses is instructed by God to give a portion to the Levites.

The tribes of Reuben and Gad have a multitude of livestock and decide to settle in a region prior to the crossing of the Jordan. Moses warns them not to arouse God's anger by settling comfortably in their land while their brothers go to war. They promise Moses that they would leave their livestock and cities and little ones, but, they themselves will be armed and ready to go to war with their brothers. Moses sternly warns them to keep their vow.

Moses speaks to the congregation, reminding them that God has brought them from Rameses to the plains of Moab. They are now prepared to enter the promised land. God speaks to Moses to tell the children of Israel to drive out the inhabitants, destroy their places of pagan worship, dispossess the inhabitants and dwell in the land for God has given it to them to possess. God warns them that if they allow the inhabitants of the land to remain they will be an irritant, a thorn in their sides, and will harass them; moreover God would do to the children of Israel what he planned to do to the wicked inhabitants.

PRAYER
O Lord,
Thank You for Your loving kindness and patience with Your people. When there are people, places and things that You command me to not associate with it is for my protection because of the evil influence that they will have upon me. Please help me to obey You, especially when the situations are attractive and enticing. In the name of Jesus Christ. Amen.

TODAY'S CHALLENGE: To destroy without regret, every relationship and situation that would cause me to sin against God.

What else is God saying to me today?

What is my response?

DAY FIFTY-EIGHT: READ Numbers 34-36

God tells Moses the boundaries of Israel's inheritance. With these instructions one elder from every tribe will divide the land. The Lord commands the children of Israel to give cities to the Levites from their inheritance and possession. God also gives instructions for cities of refuge. Due to the situation of the daughters of Zelophehad, God tells Moses that daughters who receive an inheritance must marry within their tribe so that every tribe will keep its own inheritance. All of these instructions, warnings and commandments are given to the children of Israel in the plains of Moab before entering the promised land.

PRAYER
Dear God,
Thank You for being a God who enters into human affairs. Thank You for being a father who instructs His children, and commands obedience for their own protection and blessing. You have made provisions for every human need and Your wisdom is available whenever we ask Your counsel. I pray to always respect, honor, love and reverence You. This should always prompt me to say, "yes Lord." In the name of Jesus Christ. Amen.

TODAY'S CHALLENGE: To respect the wisdom of God by seeking and obeying His counsel.

What else is God saying to me today?

What is my response?

DAY FIFTY-NINE: READ Deuteronomy 1-3

Moses explains the laws of God and reminds the people of God's covenant to Abraham, Isaac and Jacob. The people are now 'as the stars of Heaven' in multitude just as God promised Abraham, and his descendants are now entering the promised land.

Moses reminds the Israelites of the faithfulness of God to deliver their enemies into their hands, yet those who sinned will not enter the promised land. Moses himself will not be allowed to enter the promised land because he did not hallow God at the rock. He charges them to encourage Joshua for he will cause them to inherit the land. He charges them to respect the boundaries of Esau and Moab. He also charges them to not possess their portion of the inheritance and forget about their brothers but to help them to also possess their possession.

PRAYER
Dear Lord God of promise,
I humbly bow before You in awe of Your faithfulness and righteousness. I respect Your wisdom, even when You say no or when You mete out just punishment for sin. Have mercy upon me and those who call themselves Your people. Help us to obey You, respect the boundaries that You have established, and move forward together into Your promise. In the name of Jesus Christ. Amen.

TODAY'S CHALLENGE: To fear God, and know that neither His love for me nor my service to Him exempts me from the consequences of my sins.

What else is God saying to me today?

What is my response?

DAY SIXTY: READ Deuteronomy 4-6

Moses summarizes the covenant so that the Israelites can obey God and thereby live and possess the land which God is giving them. He especially warns them to not forget how they actually heard the voice of God in Horeb when God gave them the Ten Commandments. He instructs them to teach them to their children.

Moses cites many examples of how God chose to display His power on behalf of this nation; reminding them that He alone is God. He warns them to disassociate from all that is idolatrous lest they lose their inheritance. He then rehearses the covenant and charges them to keep it, and to convey it to their children so that they too will continue in the blessings of God and remember that it was God who brought them into the land that was promised to their forefathers.

PRAYER
Dear God,
I acknowledge that You are one God. Please help me to keep my heart and mind from idols. Not only were You faithful to Israel; I have personal testimonies of Your faithfulness to me. Help me to read Your word daily and pass it on to others. I know that Your desire is to bless. In the name of Jesus Christ. Amen.

TODAY'S CHALLENGE: To remember Your covenant and to obey Your word.

What else is God saying to me today?

What is my response?

DAY SIXTY-ONE: READ Deuteronomy 7-9

God commands the Israelites to totally destroy the Canaanites, to not intermarry because they will cause them to seek other gods and God would destroy them.

Moses tells the Israelites that God chose them because He loves them and because He will keep the oath that He swore to their fathers.

He encourages them to not be afraid of the sizes or numbers of their enemies for 'God, the Great Awesome God is among you.' They are not to covet any of the accursed silver or gold that adorns their gods. God will bless them above all of the nations of the earth. They are also charged to remember God when they obtain their blessings and that it is God who gives them power to obtain wealth that He may establish His covenant. Moses reminds the Israelites that it is not because of their goodness that God is giving them the promised land; but because of His promise to Abraham and because of the wickedness of the inhabitants there.

PRAYER
Dear Lord,
You are a good God. When I look at the possessions of the wicked, You call their wealth accursed. Forgive me for envying them. I want Your blessings, so help me to not covet their silver or gold, but to be submissive and obedient to You, knowing that You give me the power to obtain wealth that You may establish Your covenant with me as a descendant of Abraham through faith. In the name of Jesus Christ. Amen.

TODAY'S CHALLENGE: To not covet accursed wealth.

What else is God saying to me today?

What is my response?

DAY SIXTY-TWO: READ Deuteronomy 10-12

Moses makes a compassionate plea to the children to remember how merciful God has been to them throughout their journey. He reminded them of times that God would have destroyed them, but, he interceded for them and God chose not to destroy them. Moses knows that he will die soon, so he pleads with them to love God with all of their hearts, to fear and obey Him so that they will win their battles and be blessed above all nations before them.

He reminds them that they went into Egypt as seventy (70) persons, and are now as the stars of Heaven in multitude. He extols the Lord God; reminding them that He is the Mighty Awesome God, their praise, the one who has done these great things.

Moses sets before them a blessing and a curse, a blessing for obedience, a curse for disobedience. He instructs them to utterly destroy the places where the other nations served their gods, and seek God's place of worship for themselves. They were sternly warned to not practice any of the evil things that the other nations did such as burning their children to their gods and various other forms of idolatry.

PRAYER
O Lord, it is sometimes hard to see the wicked prosper and not envy them, or not be tempted by the evil that they practice in order to obtain wealth. I pray for the faith to see that Your blessings are far greater and eternal, and that true prosperity comes as a result of loving You and obeying Your commandments. Help me to run the race of life without looking back or around me, to not compare myself with others, but, to look straight ahead at the goal of running with my eyes on You. In the name of Jesus Christ I pray. Amen.

TODAY'S CHALLENGE: To run the race without looking back or comparing myself to others.

What else is God saying to me today?

What is my response?

DAY SIXTY-THREE: READ Deuteronomy 13-16

Moses warns the people against false prophets and dreamers who will entice them to serve other gods. He reminds them that God redeemed them out of bondage and even if a brother, son or mother entices them to serve other gods that they should not follow them. God tells Israel that they are a chosen people, a holy nation set apart to serve God.

God gives dietary guidelines; distinguishing the clean from the unclean animals, birds and seafood. He also emphasizes that the people are to tithe to the Levites and designate some of their increase for the strangers, the fatherless and the widows.

At the end of every seven years, the Israelites are told to release any brother from any debts owed and the Lord would bless them greatly. He admonishes them to open their hand wide to the poor and needy in the land. This release also applies to the release of slaves. They are to also observe the law of firstborn, and Passover. They are told to appoint judges and officers for the administration of justice.

PRAYER
Dear Lord,
Please forgive me for not always studying Your word and giving it first place in my life. Help me to change that habit, and to encourage others to do the same. I need Your strength and wisdom in order to abhor the wickedness in my environment and to daily choose a path of blessing. Thank You for Your love. I realize that every law of God, every admonition to obedience is for my blessing and protection. Help me to obey Your directions in spiritual matters, dietary practices, business practices, social interactions and in all aspects of my life.
In the name of Jesus Christ. Amen.

TODAY'S CHALLENGE: To humbly realize that I NEED to read God's word everyday.

What else is God saying to me today?

What is my response?

DAY SIXTY-FOUR: READ Deuteronomy 17-19

God gives Israel many commandments for the purpose of helping them to continue to be blessed in the land of promise. He tells them how to make sacrifices, and how to treat intentional and unintentional sins. They are to respect the decision of the Levites and judges and to establish cities of refuge. He tells them how to select a king when they come into the land of promise.

He reminds them that the Levites have no inheritance, but their offerings and provisions are to come from the people. All of these commandments are given so that the Israelites can be blessed in their land of promise, enjoy good health, treat each other justly, and not commit idolatry.

PRAYER
Dear Lord,
Thank You that You make every provision for Your people to live blessed lives. Sometimes I have worshiped and praised You, then figuratively sat You in a corner while I live my life; not realizing how much I need Your wisdom and guidance in absolutely every aspect of my life on a daily basis. I invite You to be my constant friend companion, consultant, confidant, Lord and King. In the name of Jesus Christ. Amen.

TODAY'S CHALLENGE: To realize that God has an answer for *everything.*

What else is God saying to me today?

What is my response?

DAY SIXTY-FIVE: READ Deuteronomy 20-22

Moses continues to give the people God's laws to live by. In times of battle, he encourages them to not be afraid because the Lord will fight for them. The law of unknown murder is to be atoned for by elders from the city closest to the place where the crime was committed. He gives guidelines for marriage and how to treat a rebellious stubborn son. He teaches them how to handle their brother's property and how to handle misconduct in marriage.

PRAYER

Dear Lord,

You alone know the hearts of all human beings because You alone are the Creator. At times when we don't understand Your ways, we can always pray and have access to Your wisdom. I need Your courage when I face life's battles. When I'm not sure how to conduct myself in any interpersonal matter, show me Your path of righteousness and give me the strength and integrity to walk in it. In the name of Jesus Christ, I pray. Amen.

TODAY'S CHALLENGE: Integrity in all interpersonal relationships.

What else is God saying to me today?

What is my response?

DAY SIXTY-SIX: READ Deuteronomy 23-25

God is establishing a standard of holiness among His people. He gives intricate laws pertaining to acceptance into the congregation. He does not allow anything which will bring defilement or which will perpetuate sin. He expects harmonious fellowship in the nation and for laws of moral and physical cleanliness to be strictly adhered to. He teaches them how to treat strangers, the fatherless and widows and He tells them which enemies to destroy and how to treat lawbreakers within their nation. God's ideal for the nation of Israel is for His chosen people to be distinct, holy and blessed.

PRAYER
Dear Holy God,
I can never measure up to Your standards of holiness on my own. Thank You that in all that You did in the past, You paved a way for a redeemer who would be my ultimate sacrifice. Thank You for seeing that Your laws must be written within my heart. Thank You for Your great provision for my inadequacies and shortcomings. In the name of Jesus Christ, I pray. Amen.

TODAY'S CHALLENGE: To marvel at the fact that within all of God's laws is a redemptive clause.

What else is God saying to me today?

What is my response?

DAY SIXTY-SEVEN: READ Deuteronomy 26-28

Moses instructs the children to observe the tithe of the third year by bringing their Firstfruits to the priest with a speech that acknowledges their bondage and deliverance in Egypt. The tithes are to be given to the Levites, the widows, the fatherless and the strangers in their midst and the blessings of the Lord are to be asked upon them. God promises to bless them for obeying this command.

Moses instructs the Israelites to set up stones on Mount Ebal after they cross the Jordan and erect stones and build an altar to the Lord. Moses and the priests call the people to attention and tell them that after crossing the Jordan, certain priests would stand on Mount Gerizim to bless the people, and certain priests would stand on Mount Ebal to curse the people. He outlines the acts of disobedience which will bring curses. The people are told that, if they obey God's commandments, all of the proclaimed blessings would come upon them. He outlines the acts of obedience that will bring God's blessings. The blessings are bountiful, generous and awesome and include blessings of possessions, victory over enemies, health, children, work, business, honor, promotion and more. The curses, however, are unbearable. They include failure, confusion, defeat by enemies, unfaithfulness in marriage, extraordinary and prolonged plagues and sicknesses.

PRAYER
O Blessed Lord,
Please forgive me for all acts of disobedience. Please remove any curses and open my eyes to Your truth. Thank You so much for Your mercy. I choose obedience which brings Your great blessings. Thank You for the power to obey You. In the name of Jesus Christ. Amen.

TODAY'S CHALLENGE: I have the power to choose: disobedience to God which brings curses or obedience to God which brings blessings.

What else is God saying to me today?

What is my response?

DAY SIXTY-EIGHT: READ Deuteronomy 29-31

Moses calls the Israelites into covenant giving a strong warning to those who would be disobedient and say in their hearts that they will still be blessed. He warns that they will be cursed.

Moses tells the people that they are accountable for what is revealed to them; the secret things belong to God. He sets before them life and death, blessing and cursing, urging them to choose life.

At this juncture, Moses is 120 years old. He will soon die; but he encourages the hearts of Joshua and the people, telling them to be strong and courageous and to not be afraid, for the Lord is with them. He commands them to keep the Feast of Tabernacles and read the law to each generation so that they may fear God and keep His commandments.

God then calls Moses and Joshua into the tabernacle of meetings. He tells Moses that he is about to die and instructs him to inaugurate Joshua as the new leader. God also tells Moses that the people will break His covenant after his death, after they enter into the promise land. Moses writes a song as a witness against the people and teaches it to them.

PRAYER
Dear Heavenly Father,
Please help me to take heed to Your warning and learn to daily walk in obedience to You. Help me to not be so presumptuous as to assume that You will bless me even if I'm disobedient. With Your help I can walk a path of obedience which will lead to incredible blessings. This day I choose life, I choose blessings. In the name of Jesus Christ. Amen.

TODAY'S CHALLENGE: To keep my end of my covenant with God.

What else is God saying to me today?

What is my response?

DAY SIXTY-NINE: READ Deuteronomy 32-34

Moses writes a prophetic song which tells the story of Israel's bondage, deliverance, blessing and disobedience, which will bring disaster to them; but, in the end, God will provide atonement for His land and for His people.

On the same day that he writes the song and teaches it to the people, God directs him to go up to Mount Nebo and there he will die. God reminds Moses that because he trespassed against God and did not hallow him at the waters of Meribah Kadesh, he will be allowed to see the promise land but not to enter into it. Before he dies, Moses blesses Israel tribe by tribe.

Moses then goes up to Mount Nebo. There God shows him all of the land which he swore to Abraham, Isaac and Jacob. Then Moses, the servant of the Lord dies there in the land of Moab. God buries him and no one knows where his grave is. "Never has Israel known a prophet like Moses whom the Lord knew face to face."

PRAYER
Dear Lord,
Thank You for the life of Your servant Moses whose testimony speaks until this day. Thank You for his meek spirit, and his heart of intercession. Thank You for revealing so many of Your mighty miracles through that chosen vessel. Thank You for his place of honor in Your kingdom. In spite of Your great and magnificent work through him, You still allow us to see his human frailty, his tendency to sin just as all human beings have. Help me to learn from his life and testimony. In the name of Jesus Christ. Amen.

TODAY'S CHALLENGE: To live in obedience to God so that I may not only see, but, enter into the promised land of God's blessings for my life; and to know that my relationship as God's servant does not exempt me from being punished for my sins.

What else is God saying to me today?

What is my response?

DAY SEVENTY: READ *Joshua 1-3*

After the death of Moses, God commands Joshua to arise and go over Jordan into the promise land. He admonishes Joshua to not let the Book of the Law, depart from his mouth, but, to meditate in it day and night, do what is written in it, and he would have good success. He strengthens Joshua with these words. "Be strong and of good courage." He assures Joshua that He will be with him just as He was with Moses and no man will be able to stand before him.

Joshua sends two spies into Jericho. They lodge at the home of a harlot, Rahab, who has heard of their God. She proclaims him as 'the Lord who is God in Heaven above and earth beneath.' She hides the spies from the men of Jericho who are pursuing them. In return, she asks that the Israelites spare her life and the lives of her family when they take over the city. The spies agree and instruct her to hang a scarlet thread from her window and all who are in her house will be saved.

God magnifies Joshua in front of the people by performing an awesome miracle. God stops the waters of the Jordan River, which overflowed its banks at that time of year, and which were flowing downstream, and caused the Levites to cross over with the Ark of the Covenant and the multitude of the Israelites to follow on dry ground.

PRAYER
O Awesome God,
I am breathless as I contemplate the greatness of Your Majesty and Power and Wisdom and Might. How refreshing to see You at work in the lives of Your people; fighting for them, directing them, performing miracles as only You can. Wholeheartedly, I welcome and embrace You as my God of miracles who will do great things for me and among Your people in this present hour also. In the name of Jesus Christ. Amen.

TODAY'S CHALLENGE: To often remember that the God who I serve is capable of performing great feats.

What else is God saying to me today?

What is my response?

DAY SEVENTY-ONE: READ *Joshua 4-6*

After the people cross over the Jordan, God instructs Joshua to have twelve men, one from each tribe, to chose a stone from the bottom of the Jordan and to place them as a memorial in Gilgal as a testimony for future generations.

All of the Canaanites hear of this miracle and fear Israel to the point that their hearts grow faint. God then instructs Joshua to circumcise all of the males of the younger generation. This is symbolic of the rolling away of the reproach of Egypt. In Canaan the manna ceases and that year the people eat corn and the produce of the land of Canaan.

When Joshua is near Jericho he has an angelic visitor, the commander of the army of the Lord. God gives unusual instructions for the conquering of Jericho. The priests and the army of Israel march around the impenetrable wall of Jericho once a day for six days. On the seventh day they march around seven times. On the seventh time around, at the blowing of the trumpets, Joshua commands the people to "shout." The walls of Jericho fall flat. Israel's army defeats the city, saving only Rahab and those in her household according to the promise that they had made to her. The people were strictly warned to not take any of the accursed things.

PRAYER
Lord of Hosts,
Only You have the Wisdom to defeat my enemies. Thank You that You have specific strategies, divine directives, and a myriad of methods to give me the victory. I ask You to chose my battles and defeat the enemies of my soul with Your methods. In the name of Jesus Christ. Amen.

TODAY'S CHALLENGE: To wait for God's instructions when facing adversity.

What else is God saying to me today?

What is my response?

DAY SEVENTY-TWO: READ *Joshua 7-9*

After the defeat of Canaan, Joshua sends men to defeat the city of Ai; but, instead Israel is defeated. Joshua tears his clothes and cries out to the Lord for the reason for this defeat. God tells Joshua that Israel has sinned and transgressed His covenant by taking of the accursed things and stolen and deceived and put it among their own stuff; therefore, they could not stand before their enemies.

It is discovered that Achan, of the tribe of Judah, had taken accursed items from Jericho and hidden them in the earth in his tent. His penalty is death by stoning for himself and his family. All that he possesses is set on fire. Then Israel defeats Ai.

Joshua builds an altar in Mount Ebal and reads the Law of Moses before all the congregation of Israel. The inhabitants of Gibeon hear how Joshua has defeated the surrounding cities and they are afraid. They devise a scheme and present themselves as vagabonds from a far country and ask to be joined with the Israelites. The rulers of Israel make a covenant with them without seeking the Lord. When their deception is realized, Joshua curses them, sentencing them all to slavery, to serve the Israelites as wood cutters and water carriers for the house of the Lord.

PRAYER
O Lord,
Help me to avoid the temptation to partake of things that may be appealing to me, but, are considered accursed by You. Help me to not hide things within myself that will ultimately bring defeat and destruction. I also pray that I will be alert to deception. Please remind me to consult You even before I do what looks like a good deed. I bow before You in reverence and humility in the name of Jesus Christ. Amen.

TODAY'S CHALLENGE: To avoid those things that I know are sinful and to seek God's counsel in all of my decision making.

What else is God saying to me today?

What is my response?

DAY SEVENTY-THREE: READ Joshua 10-12

Adoni-Zedek, King of Jerusalem hears about the defeat of his neighboring kings and that the inhabitants of Gibeon have made peace with Israel. Gibeon is a great city and the king becomes very fearful. He summons help from four other kings in order to attack Gibeon.

God tells Joshua to not be afraid. He will deliver them into his hands. Joshua's army defeats them and God also sends hailstones, which kills more of them than Israel's army. During this battle, God gives Joshua power and he commands the sun and moon to stand still until the enemy is defeated. The sun does not go down for a whole day. The Lord fights for Israel.

The five kings are found hiding in a cave. Joshua has them brought out. He calls his captains of war to come near and put their feet on the necks of the kings. He encourages them to not be afraid because this is what God will do to all of their enemies with whom they will fight. Joshua and the children of Israel conquer the territory of thirty-one kings and their kingdoms in addition to the kings that Moses defeated.

PRAYER
Dear Lord,
When I am outnumbered by adverse circumstances and situations, I thank You that You will defend me and defeat my enemies. Help me to not be afraid as I rely on your Strength, Wisdom and Power. I thank You that through You I have power to defeat my enemies. In the name of Jesus Christ. Amen.

TODAY'S CHALLENGE: To believe that if necessary, God will work a miracle in my life such as has never been seen before.

What else is God saying to me today?

What is my response?

DAY SEVENTY-FOUR: READ *Joshua 13-15*

After Joshua becomes an old man, there is still unconquered territory in parts of Canaan. God tells Joshua to divide the territory by tribes. Each tribe receives their inheritance by lot as the Lord commanded Moses. However, Caleb reminds Joshua that because he had brought back a good report when they spied out the land, Moses had promised him Hebron because he had wholly followed the Lord. Caleb proclaims that although forty-five years have passed, he is just as strong and his eyesight just as good as they were on the day that Moses sent him out. He asks for the choice land of Hebron for himself and his descendants. Joshua blesses him and grants his request.

PRAYER

Dear Lord,

I thank You for the faith of a man like Caleb. I too ask for a mind that will believe You and wholly follow You even if the majority says the contrary. Thank You that You reward the faithful and strengthen them to inherit their promises. I offer these prayers and thanksgiving, in the name of Jesus Christ. Amen.

TODAY'S CHALLENGE: To believe that I can still obtain my promise though I may have to wait a while.

What else is God saying to me today?

What is my response?

DAY SEVENTY-FIVE: READ *Joshua 16-18*

Joshua continues to divide the territory by lot with each tribe's boundaries defined. The entire congregation of Israel assembles at Shiloh and sets up the Tabernacle of Meetings there.

Seven tribes have not yet received their inheritance. Joshua challenges them to possess their promised land. He selects three men from each tribe to survey the land. He casts lots before the Lord to decide the boundaries.

PRAYER
Dear Lord,
Help me not to become complacent, but, to do all that You have directed me to do in order to help to establish Your kingdom. I trust Your Wisdom in deciding what I should do and when and how. In the name of Jesus Christ. Amen.

TODAY'S CHALLENGE: To realize that God's vision for me often encompasses much more than I feel able to obtain.

What else is God saying to me today?

What is my response?

DAY SEVENTY-SIX: READ Joshua 19-21

The second lot came out for Simeon; however, Judah's inheritance is so great that the tribe of Simeon is established within Judah. Boundaries are established, also, for the tribes of Zebulun, Issachar, Asher, Napthali and Dan.

After dividing the land, the children of Israel give an inheritance to Joshua. They give him whatever cities he asks for. God instructs Joshua to have the people appoint cities of refuge for anyone who might accidentally kill another.

The Levites also are given land from among the people for themselves and their livestock as Moses had commanded. The settlement of Israel is now completed and God gives them rest.

PRAYER

Dear Lord Almighty,

Thank You for being watchful over all of Your children. I see that the experiences of the Israelites are reflections of my own need to look to You as a trusting child looks to a loving father for provision and direction. I invite You to lead me. I am Your child also and I submit to You in all areas of my life. In the name of Jesus Christ. Amen.

TODAY'S CHALLENGE: To trust in God as a wise Heavenly father who does not forget to provide for his children.

What else is God saying to me today?

What is my response?

DAY SEVENTY-SEVEN: READ *Joshua 22-24*

The Reubenites, the Gadites and half the tribe of Manasseh had left their inheritance on the other side of the Jordan. They kept their vow to continue to help their brothers obtain their inheritance, so Joshua blesses them and sends them on their way.

On their way back, they erect a great altar as a witness, between them and their brothers, that the Lord is God. The leaders of the other tribes, not understanding at first, set out to make war against them because they thought that their brothers were erecting an altar in order to sacrifice to idols. Phinehas, the priest and the elders investigate the matter and discover that the other tribes are not committing idolatry and the matter is settled. They called the altar Witness.

Joshua speaks to the leaders of Israel and reminds them of God's faithfulness to fulfill all of the good things that He has promised. He warns them that God will be just as faithful to bring harmful things if they transgress the covenant.

Joshua reviews the covenant that God made with Abraham, which has now culminated in their possessing the promise land. He makes his immortal challenge and declaration: "Choose ye this day who you will serve. As for me and my house, we will serve the Lord." The people all agree to serve the Lord, also. Joshua places a large stone near the sanctuary. He tells the people. "This stone shall be a witness to us for it has heard all the words of the Lord which He spoke to us."

After these things, Joshua, the son of Nun, the servant of the Lord dies. He is one hundred and twenty years old.

PRAYER
God of Heaven and Earth,
You are the Beginning and the End. Evidenced in these accounts is the fact that You not only make promises to Your children, but, you accompany them with Your presence in the process. I praise You for Your faithfulness. As for me and my house we will serve the Lord! In the name of Jesus Christ. Amen.

TODAY'S CHALLENGE: To live in harmony with God and man.

What else is God saying to me today?

What is my response?

DAY SEVENTY-EIGHT: READ Judges 1-4

After the death of Joshua there is still unconquered territory. The Lord directs Judah to go up first against the Canaanites. The tribes of Benjamin, Joseph, Zebulum, Asher, Napthali and Dan fail to drive out the inhabitants but allow them to dwell among them.

The Angel of the Lord comes to Bochim and rebukes the people for making covenants with the inhabitants. Because of their disobedience, the Lord does not drive the inhabitants out, but allows them to stay as a thorn in their sides. The people repent and offer sacrifices to the Lord.

After the death of Joshua and the elders, the younger generation begin to do evil and serve the Baals and Ashtoreths, the gods of the people around them. Because of their disobedience they are enslaved to the King of Mesopotamia for eight years. They cry out to God and he raises up Othniel, Caleb's younger brother. They rest for forty years. After Othniel's death the children begin to do evil again. Then they are in bondage to Eglon, King of Moab, for eighteen years.

Later the children of Israel sin and are enslaved to Jabin King of Canaan. The commander of his army is Sisera. Deborah, a prophetess, is judging Israel at this time. At the word of the Lord, Deborah calls for Barak to go up and fight against Jabin and Sisera. Barak said that he will not go to war unless Deborah goes with him. She agrees, but tells Barak that he will receive no glory in this war, that Sisera will be defeated by a woman. During the heat of the battle, Sisera flees and came to rest in the tent of Jael, a Kenite woman. She kills him by driving a tent peg through his head while he is asleep.

PRAYER
Dear Lord, please help me to live a life of continuous obedience to You and Your word so that I will not be in bondage to the enemy. I pray that Your presence in my life will not be only because I need deliverance, but more to strengthen me to move forward in Your will and plan for my life. In the name of Jesus Christ. Amen.

TODAY'S CHALLENGE: To effectively teach the younger generation to fear God and obey Him.

What else is God saying to me today?

What is my response?

DAY SEVENTY-NINE: READ Judges 5-8

After the death of Sisera and the defeat of Jabin, King of Caanan, Deborah and Barak sing a song of God's deliverance and blessings. The land rests for forty years.

After this time, the children of Israel begin to do evil in the sight of the Lord again. God delivers them into the hands of Midian for seven years. Because of the Midianites, the children of Israel make caves and strongholds in the mountains. They are impoverished because the Midianites destroy their crops, their animals, and their land. God sends a prophet and reminds them of their disobedience.

The Angel of the Lord visits Gideon, son of Joash and commissions him to deliver the Israelites miraculously. Gideon, after several confirmations, takes 300 men, whom God chooses and defeats the army of the Midianites. The country is quiet for forty years. Gideon, also called Jerubbaal, goes to dwell in his own house. He is the father of seventy sons by his many wives, and one son, Abimelech by a concubine in Shechem. As soon as Gideon dies, the people sin again. They do not remember God who delivered them nor Gideon's family. They make Baal Berith their god.

PRAYER
Dear Merciful God,
I ask for Your forgiveness for my sins and the sins of the people in the land in which I live. You have been faithful to bless us, but, we have grossly sinned against You. I pray that we will listen to Your prophets and repent. Forgive us for the many gods that we as a people worship instead of You. May Your spirit fall upon me and many others as it did upon Gideon so that we may be instruments of Your deliverance in this hour of spiritual impoverishment. In the name of Jesus Christ I pray. Amen.

TODAY'S CHALLENGE: To not repeat the sins of the past and to faithfully communicate my faith to the next generation.

What else is God saying to me today?

What is my response?

DAY EIGHTY: READ Judges 9-12

Abimelech, the son of Jerubbaal, (Gideon), speaks to his mother's family in Shechem and he persuades them to make Abimelech their leader. He goes to his father's house in Ophrah and kills all of his seventy brothers except Jotham, the youngest who hides himself. The men of Shechem make Abimelech king. When Jotham hear the news, he goes up to mount Gerizim and pronounces a curse upon Abimelech. He chides the people for dishonoring his father. Abimelech reigns over Israel for three years, then God sends a spirit of ill-will between him and the people of Shechem. During an attack, Abimelech is killed when a woman drops a millstone from a window and crushes his skull. After Abimelech's death Tola, then Jair, judge Israel. Then the children of Israel begin to sin in the sight of the Lord. They serve the Baals and the Ashtoreths. God sells them into the hands of the Philistines and the people of Ammon who oppress and harass them for eighteen years. Ammon makes war with Israel and the leaders of Gilead begin to look for a man who will go to war against Ammon and become the leader of Gilead.

A man named Jepthah, a mighty man of valor, is a Gileadite; but his mother is a harlot so he is rejected by his brothers and thrown out of their father's house. Jepthah flees from his brothers, and dwells in the land of Tob. He bands with worthless men and goes about raiding. The elders go to Jephthah and ask him to fight Ammon on their behalf and they will make him their leader. Jepthah goes with the elders. The Spirit of the Lord comes upon Jepthah. He promises God, "If you will indeed deliver the people of Ammon into my hands, I will make a burnt offering of whatever comes out of my house to meet me when I return." God grants his request. Upon his return, his only child, Mizpah comes out to meet him with timbrels and dancing. When he sees her, he tears his clothes in sorrow. They both agree that Jepthah must keep his vow to God. Mizpah must remain a virgin.

Dear Lord God
Help me not to reject my brothers and sisters in the family of God because they are somehow different from me. Help me to remember that their gift might be essential to my deliverance. If I am rejected, help me to not be so hungry for approval and acceptance that I make vows which I will later regret. In the name of Jesus Christ, I pray. Amen.

TODAY'S CHALLENGE: To accept God's approval and reject man's rejection.

What else is God saying to me today?

What is my response?

DAY EIGHTY-ONE: READ *Judges 13-15*

The children of Israel sin again and the Lord allows them to be captives of the Philistines for forty years. The Angel of the Lord appears to the wife of Manoah of the Danites. She is barren, but the Lord tells her that she will conceive and bear a son. He instructs her to not drink wine or similar drinks nor eat any unclean thing. This son will be a Nazarite to God from the womb. No razor shall come upon his head. God tells her that this son will begin to deliver Israel out of the hands of the Philistines. She conceives a son and names him Samson. The child grows and is blessed of the Lord.

Samson meets a woman in Timnah whom he desires as his wife. One day, while journeying with his parents to Timnah, a young lion attacks him. The spirit of the Lord comes upon Samson mightily and he tears the lion apart with his bare hands. He does not tell his parents. While in Timnah during the wedding feast, Samson is provoked to anger and kills thirty Philistines. Later in the year, he takes a trip back to see his wife who remained in her father's house. However, her father has given her to Samson's friend who was his best man at his wedding. Samson burns the grain fields of the Philistines. In retaliation, the men burn Samson's wife and father-in-law to death. The men of Judah come to arrest Samson. While being taken back with the men of Judah, Samson is attacked by the Philistines. He breaks free from his ropes with ease, finds the jawbone of a donkey and single-handedly kills a thousand Philistines.

PRAYER
O Lord God of Wisdom,
Thank You that You hear the cries of Your people even when it is our own sin that has produced our bondage. I not only cry out for deliverance; I cry also consecrate me and make me a deliverer. Let Your spirit come upon me and empower me to perform great feats in Your name and for the fulfillment of Your purpose in the world that I live in. In the name of Jesus Christ, I pray. Amen.

TODAY'S CHALLENGE: To dare to believe that God can choose me for his special purposes.

What else is God saying to me today?

What is my response?

DAY EIGHTY-TWO: READ Judges 16-18

Samson sees a harlot in the city of Gaza and goes in to her. When the Gazites try to capture him, Samson takes hold of the doors of the gate of the city and the two gateposts, pulls them up and carries them to the top of a hill.

He later falls in love with Delilah from the valley of Sorek. The lord of the Philistines offer Delilah a great sum of money if she can find out and divulge to them the source of Samson's great strength. After several unsuccessful attempts, Delilah continues to pester him daily to the point that his soul is "vexed to death." He finally acquiesces and tells her his secret. Delilah lulls Samson to sleep and has his head shaved. When he arises his strength is gone. The Philistines take him captive, put out his eyes and take him to Gaza where he works there in prison.

On a certain day, the lords of the Philistines gather to offer a great sacrifice to their god, Dagon and to praise him for delivering Samson into their hands. Over three thousand Philistines are on the palace roof. When their hearts are merry they send for Samson so that he can entertain them. Meanwhile Samson's hair has begun to grow back while he is in prison. Samson prays. "O Lord God, remember me, I pray! Strengthen me, I pray, just this once. O God, that I may with one blow take vengeance on the Philistines for my two eyes." Samson takes hold of the two middle pillars which support the temple. He says, "Let me die with the Philistines!" He pushes with all of his might and the temple with all of the lords of the Philistines falls. He kills more Philistines at his death than he had in life. His family recovers his body and buries him.

A man named Micah from the mountains of Ephraim demonstrates how the children of Israel commit personal idolatry. The Danites, who eventually take Micah's shrine and household idols, are an example of how Israel commits tribal idolatry.

PRAYER
O Lord,
Thank You for Your special gifts that are given to Your people in order to fulfill Your purposes. Please help me to be careful where I go and what I feast my eyes upon. Please give me Your divine wisdom in all of my interpersonal relationships so that my anointing will not be sabotaged. In the name of Jesus Christ. Amen.

TODAY'S CHALLENGE: To establish relationships with people who serve the same God that I do.

What else is God saying to me today?

What is my response?

DAY EIGHTY-THREE: READ Judges 19-21

During this time, there is no king in Israel. A certain Levite takes a concubine from Bethlehem in Judah. She goes back to her father's house for four months. When the Levite goes to the father-in-law's house to bring her back, he is entertained well and encouraged to stay for five days. The Levite leaves with his concubine. As nightfall approaches, they seek lodging among the Benjaminites, but, no one will give them lodging. Finally an old man takes them in.

As they are getting settled in, the perverted men in the city begin pounding at the door, seeking to lie with the man. His host begs them to not commit such wickedness. The Levites gives his concubine to the men who sexually abuse her all night until morning and leave her dead at the front door.

The Levite cuts her up into twelve pieces and sends a piece of her to the leaders of the twelve tribes of Israel and demands justice. The children of Benjamin refuse to give up the perverted men so that they can be brought to justice. The children of Israel therefore go to war with the tribe of Benjamin and defeat them.

The other tribes of Israel swear to never give their daughters in marriage to a Benjaminite. The people later grieve this decision and seek wives for the Benjaminites. They take four hundred women from Jabesh Gilead through war, but, this is not enough. They devise a scheme whereby the Benjaminites kidnap women from Shiloh and take them as their wives. "In those days there was no king in Israel; everyone did what was right in his own eyes."

PRAYER
Dear Lord!
Please help me not to do what is right in my own eyes! In the name of Jesus Christ, I pray. Amen.

TODAY'S CHALLENGE: To let God be King.

What else is God saying to me today?

What is my response?

DAY EIGHTY-FOUR: READ Ruth 1-4

Ruth, a Moabitess, is the daughter-in-law of Naomi who is the wife of Elimilech, an Ephrathite. Misfortune befalls Naomi while in the country of Moab. Her husband dies, and about ten years later her two sons die, also. She is left with her two daughters-in-law: Ruth and Orpah. Naomi decides to return to her home in Bethlehem, Judah. She encourages the two young women to go back to their mother's home and find new husbands. Orpah does so, but Ruth vows to go with Naomi and take the God of Naomi as her God, also.

Upon their arrival in Bethlehem, Judah, Naomi tells her friends that her name is not Naomi, but, Mara, because of her misfortune. Ruth works in the grain fields to take care of Naomi. She happens to glean in the field of Boaz, a wealthy man who is also a kinsman of Elimelech, Naomi's deceased husband. Naomi instructs Ruth on how to interact with Boaz. Ruth finds favor in the eyes of Boaz and he soon becomes her kinsman redeemer and husband. Ruth and Boaz have a son, Obed, who brings incredible joy and comfort to Naomi. Obed becomes the grandfather of King David through whose lineage the Messiah comes.

PRAYER
Dear Lord,
Thank You for being my Redeemer. You redeem Your people from physical, emotional and financial bondages, indeed from bondages of all kind. Thank You. In the name of Jesus Christ. Amen.

TODAY'S CHALLENGE: To choose the best thing even when there is no expectation of reward.

What else is God saying to me today?

What is my response?

DAY EIGHTY-FIVE: READ I Samuel 1-3

For a period of time, the children of Israel have no leader or king or judge. Each man does what seems right in his own eyes. The word of the Lord is rare in those days.

During this time, a woman named Hannah is married to Elkanah who is from the mountains of Ephraim. Hannah is barren, but for years she earnestly prays for a male child. Elkanah's other wife bears him children and provokes Hannah. Finally, she prays and weeps in anguish, vowing to God that if He will give her a male child she will give him to the Lord, all the days of his life, and no razor will come upon his head. One day while praying at the house of the Lord in Shiloh, Eli the priest, tells her that God has granted her request.

Hannah bears a son and names him Samuel, meaning 'asked of God.' As soon as she weans him, she takes him to Eli, the priest, so that he can minister there before the Lord all of his life.

Meanwhile, Eli's two sons are committing abominable acts at the door of the tabernacle. This greatly displeases God. One night God calls young Samuel while he is lying down to sleep. Thinking that Eli called him, Samuel goes in to Eli twice, saying, "Here I am." By the third time that this occurs, Eli perceives that it is the Lord who is calling Samuel. He instructs him to answer the Lord by saying "Speak Lord for your servant hears." God speaks to young Samuel and tells him of impending judgment against Eli and his house because he did not rebuke or restrain his sons. Eli demands that Samuel tells him all that the Lord said. Samuels tells him. Samuel grows in stature and favor with God and man. All Israel knows that Samuel has been established as a prophet of God.

PRAYER
Dear Lord,
Thank You for never leaving Your people alone. Through the ages, whoever has sought You has found You. I understand that You also are seeking people to whom You can entrust gifts and responsibilities. Please forgive me for ways in which I may have taken my ministry assignment lightly. Help me to take more seriously my God-given responsibilities. In the name of Jesus Christ. Amen.

TODAY'S CHALLENGE: To not be passive about the things that displease God.

What else is God saying to me today?

What is my response?

DAY EIGHTY-SIX: READ I Samuel 4-7

Israel goes out to battle the Philistines and loses. They then bring the Ark of the Covenant into the camp thinking that this will bring them victory. Upon the arrival of the Ark, the people shout so loudly that the earth shakes; but the Philistines encourage themselves and fight more fiercely. They defeat the Israelites and capture the Ark of the Covenant.

Samuel's prophecy is fulfilled. Eli's two sons, Hophni and Phinehas are killed in the battle. When Eli hears that his two sons are dead, he too falls dead; ending his forty year reign as a judge in Israel. All of these distresses cause Phinehas' wife, who is pregnant, to go into labor. She bears a son, whom she names Ichabod, meaning 'the glory has departed,' she then dies also.

The Philistines take the Ark of God and sits it in the house of their god, Dagon. The next morning, Dagon has fallen on its face before the Ark of God. The people set Dagon upright again. The next morning they find that Dagon has fallen before the ark again, this time with its head and hands broken. In Ashdod, and in each city wherein the Ark is sent, the people are stricken with a deadly destruction. The Ekronites plead with the lords of the Philistines to send the Ark away. The Philistines call for the diviners and priests to ask them how they should send the Ark back to the Israelites. Instructions are given.

The Ark is returned and brought into the house of Abinidab. Eleazar, his son, is appointed to keep it. The Ark remains in the city of Kirjath Jearim for twenty years. Samuel tells the people that if they will return to the Lord with all of their hearts and put away the foreign gods He will deliver them from the hands of the Philistines. They obey and subdue the Philistines. They have no more war with them all of the days of Samuel's life.

PRAYER
Dear Lord,
Thank You for a prophet such as Samuel who was 'asked of God.' Hannah wanted a son; and You needed a servant. When the prayers of Hannah on earth synchronized with the will of God in Heaven, a miracle happened. As I pray my selfish prayers, I ask You to refine my motives and divinely edit my petitions so that my answered prayers may harmonize with Your will and bring You glory and honor. In the name of Jesus Christ, I pray. Amen.

TODAY'S CHALLENGE: To pray the will of God.

What else is God saying to me today?

What is my response?

DAY EIGHTY-SEVEN: READ I Samuel 8-10

Samuel is old. He appoints his sons as judges; however they are dishonest and unacceptable to the people. The Israelites tell Samuel that he is old, and his sons are inadequate. They ask Samuel to give them a king like the other nations around them have. Displeased with their request, Samuel prays to God about the matter. God tells Samuel that it is really God that the people are rejecting, not him; and to grant their request. They did not want God to reign over them. Although Samuel warns the people of the unpleasant things that a king will do to them they still insist.

God chooses Saul, a tall, handsome man from the tribe of Benjamin. Through a series of events Saul and Samuel meet. Samuel invites Saul to eat with him. Afterwards he pours a flask of oil on Saul's head and tells him that God has chosen him to be commander over His inheritance. Samuel tells Saul that the Spirit of the Lord will come upon him and he will prophesy, this will be a sign to him of God's appointment. These things come to pass and Saul returns home.

Samuel calls the tribes together at Mizpah. He announces to the people that they have rejected God who delivered them out of all of their tribulations and asked for a king. He presents the reluctant Saul to them. The people shout, "Long live the King." Some rebel and reject Saul.

Samuel explains the behavior of royalty to the people, writes it in a book and lays it before the Lord.

PRAYER
Dear God,
Help me to never be embarrassed to have You alone as my God. In the name of Jesus Christ, I pray. Amen.

TODAY'S CHALLENGE: To not be blinded by the gods of this world.

What else is God saying to me today?

What is my response?

DAY EIGHTY-EIGHT: READ I Samuel 11-13

The men of Jabesh Gilead are threatened by Nahash and the Ammonites in a cruel and unusual way. When Saul hears the news, the Spirit of the Lord comes upon him and his anger is greatly aroused. He assembles the people and destroys the Ammonites.

The people are so impressed with Saul's performance that they want to put to death the people who had earlier questioned his ability to rule as their king. Saul forbids them. The people make a sacrifice of peace offering before the Lord and they all rejoice greatly with Saul.

Samuel asks the people if he has been dishonest or defrauded anyone in any way. They all testify that he has not. Samuel proceeds to remind them that each time that they have called upon God to deliver them, He has sent a deliverer, beginning with Moses and ending with Samuel. He tells them that they have done wickedly by asking God for a king to rule over them. However, he admonishes them to not turn from God. He tells them, that if they are obedient to God, they and their king will do well. If they do not obey, the hand of the Lord will be against them.

During the second year of Saul's reign, he becomes anxious because the people are afraid and Samuel does not come to offer supplication before the Lord at the expected time. Saul offers the burnt offering himself. Samuel comes immediately afterwards. He rebukes Saul strongly and announces to him, that because he has not kept the commandment of the Lord, his kingdom will not continue and that God has sought a man after His own heart.

PRAYER
Dear Lord,
When You bless me, help me not to become big in my own eyes to the point of disobeying Your ordinances and stepping out of my God-assigned position. I ask You for Wisdom, and Humility, recognizing that any thing extraordinary that I do that is good is because of Your Spirit working in me. In the name of Jesus Christ. Amen.

TODAY'S CHALLENGE: To never take matters into my own hands.

What else is god saying to me today?

What is my response?

DAY EIGHTY-NINE: READ I Samuel 14-16

Without telling his father; Jonathan, Saul's son, takes his armor bearer and attacks a garrison of the Philistines. God causes the earth to tremble and the Philistines begin to retreat. When he is weary in the battle, Jonathan touches the tip of his rod on a honey comb and takes a little honey to refresh himself. He does not know that his father has issued a curse against anyone who eats on this day. When Saul discovers that Jonathan has eaten the honey, he swears to put him to death. The people intervene on Jonathan's behalf and refuse to allow Saul to kill him. Saul establishes his sovereignty and fights against all of the people in the land. There is fierce war with the Philistines. When Saul sees any strong or valiant man, he takes him for himself.

Samuel tells Saul that God says to utterly destroy Amalek; all of the people and all of the animals. Saul gathers his people together and attacks. However he only destroys what he deems worthless and spares the king and the best of the animals. Samuel rebukes him and declares. "Behold, to obey is better than sacrifice." He further announces: "Because you have rejected the Word of the Lord, He has also rejected you from being king." Samuel does not visit Saul again, but, continues to mourn for him. The Lord regrets that He made Saul king over Israel.

The Lord sends Samuel to the house of Jesse, a Bethlehemite, to anoint the new king that He has chosen. After seeing all of Jesse's sons, God reveals to Samuel that He has chosen David, the youngest. Samuel takes the oil and anoints David. Meanwhile, the Spirit of the Lord departs from Saul and a distressing spirit troubles him. One of the servants recommends David to play music for Saul in order to relieve the distressing spirit. Saul sends for David.

PRAYER
Dear Lord,
I pray that You will never regret blessing or promoting me. Please help me to remain 'little in my own eyes.' Remove from me all rebellion, pride, stubbornness and idolatry, and help me to be obedient to Your Word. In the name of Jesus Christ, I pray. Amen.

TODAY'S CHALLENGE: To not try to impress God with my righteousness, but to be obedient to His Word.

What else is God saying to me today?

What is my response?

DAY NINETY: READ I Samuel 17-20

The Philistines gather their armies against the Israelites. A champion of the Philistines, Goliath, stands over nine feet tall and challenges the Israelites to send a man to fight with him. Saul and the Israelites are greatly dismayed and afraid. On a certain day, David, the son of Jesse, is sent by his father to take supplies and to inquire of the welfare of his older brothers, who are at the battle site. Goliath appears issuing the same challenge. The men of Israel convey the news that the king will give great riches and his daughter to be the wife of any man who will prevail against Goliath.

David persuades Saul to allow him to fight Goliath. David faces Goliath with only a sling and five smooth stones. When Goliath advances toward David, he runs to meet him, puts a stone in his sling and strikes Goliath in his forehead. Goliath falls on his face to the ground. David runs and stands over Goliath and uses the Philistine's own sword with which to behead him. Saul begins to ask who David is. David answers, "I am the son of your servant Jesse the Bethlehemite."

As David speaks, the heart of Jonathan, Saul's son is knit to him. Jonathan and David make a covenant. David meanwhile goes wherever Saul sends him and behaves very wisely. He is accepted by all of the people and by Saul's servants. One day as David returns from battle, the women sing, "Saul has slain his thousands, and David his ten thousands." Saul becomes very angry and he is suspicious of David from that day.

When the distressing spirit comes upon Saul again, he tries to kill David with a spear. Saul subsequently makes many attempts to kill David, but he is not successful. Finally Jonathan warns David that he must flee because Saul has become *determined* to kill him. Sorrowfully, Jonathan and David make a covenant between themselves and their descendants and depart.

PRAYER
Dear God,
Thank You, when my mountain seems much bigger than I, that I can prevail, in the Name of the Lord. When others seek to harm me, I ask for Your protection and Wisdom. In the name of Jesus Christ, I pray. Amen.

TODAY'S CHALLENGE: To avoid being jealous when God chooses to bless someone else.

What else is God saying to me today?

What is my response?

DAY NINETY-ONE: READ I Samuel 21-24

David comes to Nob, to Ahimelech, the priest. He gives David and the men with him holy bread to eat. Doeg, an Edomite, one of Saul's herdsmen, is also there. Ahimelech also gives David Goliath's sword because he had no weapon. David flees from there and finds himself before Achish, the king of Gath. Perceiving that Achish plans to harm him, David feigns madness and Achish releases him.

He flees to the cave of Abdullah where about 400 men join him. He asks the King of Moab to protect his parents. A prophet of God encourages David to go to the land of Judah.

When Saul hears that Jonathan has made a covenant with David he is furious. He intimidates his servants and asks why no one has informed him about David's actions. Doeg tells Saul of Ahimelech's kindness to David. Saul has Ahimelech brought to him and commands his servants to kill him. The servants refuse. Saul tells Doeg to kill him. He kills Ahimelech and a total of eighty-five of the Lord's priests. He also destroys the city of Nob: the city of the priests. Only Abiathar, one of Ahimelech's sons escapes. He finds David and tells him what happened. David is distraught, he tells Abiathar to remain with him and he'll be safe.

David and his men take refuge in the recesses of the cave of En Gedi. Saul enters the cave and David has opportunity to kill him; but only cuts off the edge of his robe. David chooses to not avenge himself, but, to allow the Lord to judge between himself and Saul. David shows himself to Saul, with the piece of his robe, and assures him that he means him no harm. Saul weeps and blesses David. They depart and go their separate ways.

PRAYER
Dear Lord
When trials, distresses, and afflictions come simply because of Your anointing on our lives, it's very puzzling and hard to bear. In those times, please give me Your Strength, Wisdom and Protection and help me to remember Your faithfulness and love toward me. In the name of Jesus Christ, I pray. Amen.

TODAY'S CHALLENGE: To allow God to avenge me when some one does me wrong.

What else is God saying to me today?

What is my response?

DAY NINETY-TWO: READ I Samuel 25-28

Samuel dies and the Israelites lament for him and bury him at his home in Ramah. David goes down to the wilderness of Paran.

Nabal, a very rich man in Maon of the house of Caleb, live there with his wife, Abigail, a beautiful woman of good understanding. When David hears that Nabal is shearing his sheep, he sends young men to tell Nabal that he has not harmed his sheep and to ask for provisions for himself and his men. Although Nabal's men tell him how David assisted them, Nabal refuses to help David. David prepares to kill every male that belongs to Nabal. Abigail hears the report and intercedes. She prepares food for David and his men; comes and bows before David and honors him as God's anointed. She tells David that Nabal is, as his name, a fool. The next day Abigail tells Nabal what happened. His heart turns to stone within him. About ten days later God strikes Nabal and he dies. David sends and asks Abigail to be his wife.

David has opportunity to kill Saul again in the wilderness of Ziph, but, only takes his spear and his jug of water that is by his head. David feels that Saul is determined to kill him, so he decides to escape to the land of the Philistines. When Saul hears, he stops pursuing David. Achish the king of Gath gives him the city of Ziglag in which to dwell. During those days the Philistines gather together to make war with Israel. Samuel is dead and God does not answer Saul when he inquires of him. Saul takes two men, disguises himself and visits a woman in En Dor, who is a medium. Saul asks her to call Samuel from the dead. Samuel rebukes Saul and announces to him that God will deliver Israel into the hands of the Philistines and Saul and his sons will die the next day.

PRAYER
Dear Lord,
Help me to live my life in the consciousness that You are Sovereign and that You judge the thoughts, intentions and actions of mankind. Thank You for being a just God. Please give me a heart to repent when I sin so that I will not persist in foolish, destructive pride. In the name of Jesus Christ. Amen.

TODAY'S CHALLENGE: To make sure that I live in such a manner that God will answer when I pray.

What else is God saying to me today?

What is my response?

DAY NINETY-THREE: READ I Samuel 29-31

When the Philistines gather to go to war with Israel, David is in the rear with Achish. Fearing that he might turn against them in battle, the lords of the Philistines insist that David returns home and not take part in the battle. Upon his return to Ziglag, David and his men find that the city has been attacked and all of the wives, children and possessions have been taken. The men want to stone David; but he strengthens himself in the Lord. He asks God if he should pursue. God tells him to go up against the enemy and he will recover all.

The Philistines fight against Israel and pursue Saul and his sons. They kill all three of Saul's sons. Saul is severely wounded by the archers. He tells his armorbearer to draw his sword and kill him so that he will not be abused by the Philistines. The armor bearer refuses, so Saul falls upon his own sword and dies. The Philistines cut off his head and strips him of his armor.

PRAYER
O Dear Lord,
Whatever the enemy has taken, please give me the strength to recover all. In the name of Jesus Christ, I pray. Amen.

TODAY'S CHALLENGE: To look to God for strength in the midst of utter confusion and despair.

What else is God saying to me today?

What is my response?

DAY NINETY-FOUR: READ I Samuel 1-4

After the death of Saul, and after David has recovered all from the Amalekites and returned to Ziglag, a young man tells David that Saul and his sons including Jonathan are dead. Apparently thinking that he will find favor with David, the young man, an Amalekite tells David that he killed Saul. David has him executed. David laments Saul's death and writes a song called The Song of the Bow. David inquires of the Lord and He directs him to go to Hebron. The men of Judah come there and anoint David king over the house of Judah. But Abner, commander of Saul's army, makes Ishbosheth, Saul's son, king over all of Israel.

There is a long war between the houses of Saul and David. Saul's house grows weaker, and David's grows stronger. Six sons are born to David while he is in Hebron. Ishbosheth accuses Abner of lying with his father's concubine. Abner becomes extremely angry and vows to transfer the kingdom of Israel into the hands of David. Abner encourages certain tribes of Israel to make David their king. Abner contacts David. David makes a feast and meets peacefully with Abner who promises to gather all Israel for David to reign over them as king. However, Joab does not trust Abner and he wants to avenge his brother's death, so he finds Abner and stabs him to death without David's knowledge.

Upon discovering what has happened, David laments Abner's death publicly, and tells his servants that Abner was a great man and a prince. His words and behavior prove to the people that he had no intention of killing Abner. This pleases the people.

Two men of Saul's troops kill Ishboseth and take his head to David. Instead of rewarding them, David executes them. Meanwhile a nurse escapes with Jonathan's young son Mephibosheth. In the process of fleeing, she falls and Mephibosheth becomes lame.

PRAYER
Dear Lord,
In the midst of the clouds of human error and self-will, I pray, that the reign of Your Sovereign Will be done in my life and in my world. In Jesus name. Amen.

TODAY'S CHALLENGE: To not rejoice when God's judgment falls on one of his people.

What else is God saying to me today?

What is my response?

DAY NINETY-FIVE: READ II Samuel 5-8

All of the tribes of Israel come to David at Hebron, affirm him as their brother, and anoint him king over Israel. David establishes the city of David and becomes great. The Lord God of hosts is with him. Hiram king of Tyre sends messengers and builds David a house. David takes more concubines and wives and has eleven additional children.

When the Philistines hear that David has been anointed king over Israel they search for David. He goes down to the strong hold. He asks the Lord if He will deliver the Philistines into his hands? The Lord's answer is affirmative. David goes to Baal Perazim and defeats the Philistines. David exclaims, "The Lord has broken through my enemies before me, like a breakthrough of water!"

David arranges for the Ark to be brought to the city of David. The trip is intercepted when a man, Uzzah dies after touching the Ark to keep it from falling. The Ark is instead taken to the house of Obed-Edom whose house God greatly blesses. Upon hearing this David brings the Ark into the city in a procession. David dances and rejoices before the Ark with all of his might. His wife Michal, Saul's daughter, despises him. She therefore never bears children. David desires to build a house for God, but God tells him that his seed will build a house for him. God promises David that his house and his kingdom will be established forever. David goes and sits before the Lord and praises his greatness, faithfulness and mercy. He asks God too bless his house forever. David goes on to conquer many of his enemies around him. He reigns over all Israel and administers judgment and justice to all the people.

PRAYER
Dear Lord,
Thank You that You fulfill Your promises to Your people in spite of how long it takes or what circumstances they may endure, Thank You that as You were faithful to David, so will You be to me. I, like David, praise You with all of my heart and thank You for Your greatness, faithfulness and mercy. In the name of Jesus Christ. Amen.

TODAY'S CHALLENGE: To unashamedly praise God in public.

What else is God saying to me today?

What is my response?

DAY NINETY-SIX: READ II Samuel 9-12

David inquires as to whether there is any one left from the house of Saul so that he can show him kindness for Jonathan's sake. Zeba, A former servant of Saul, informs David that Mephibosheth, Jonathan's lame son, is living in Lo Debar. When Mephibosheth sees David he prostrates himself. David tells him not to fear, that he would show him kindness for his father, Jonathan's sake. David restores all of the land of Saul to Mephibosheth and appoints Zeba and his family to work for him. "As for Mephibosheth," said the king, "he shall eat at my table like one of the king's sons." David seeks to render a similar kindness to Hanun, the son of the king of Ammon. Hanun does not trust David's motives and soon there is a battle. Israel defeats all those who come out against them.

In the spring of that same year, when kings go out to battle, David sends Joab and his servants, but, he remains in Jerusalem. One evening, from his roof, he sees a beautiful woman bathing. David inquires about the woman and is told that she is the wife of Uriah the Hittite. David sends messengers and takes her and he lays with her. After a while, the woman sends word to David that she is with child.

David treacherously tries to cover his sin by sending for Uriah to come home; hoping that he will lay with his wife and think that the child is his. Uriah is so noble that he refuses to be comforted while his fellow servants are in battle. David sends a letter to Joab, by the hand of Uriah, instructing Joab to arrange for Uriah to be killed in battle. After Uriah is dead David marries his wife. This thing of course displeases the Lord. God sends Nathan the prophet to confront David. David repents, but Nathan declares that God has said that because of his treachery the sword will never depart from David's house, his son will die, and his wives will be taken from him and given to his neighbor. God strikes the child born of adultery and it dies. David goes in to comfort Bathsheba. She conceives again and bears Solomon. God loves him.

PRAYER
Dear God,
It's hard to understand the dichotomy of King David's behavior. He is so noble that he seeks Jonathan's son and restores him; yet he's so treacherous that he steals Uriah's wife and has him killed! Dear God help me to not be so blinded by my passions that I fall into a pit of sin which erupts and spills its penalty into my and my family's lives forever. In the name of Jesus Christ, I pray. Amen.

TODAY'S CHALLENGE: If I sin, to throw myself on the mercy seat of God immediately.

What else is God saying to me today?

What is my response?

DAY NINETY-SEVEN: READ II Samuel 13-16

Absalom, David's son, has a lovely sister Tamar. Amnon, her brother, becomes obsessed with desire for her. Prompted by his friend Jonadab, Amnon pretends to be sick and asks his father David to have Tamar cook for him. He rapes Tamar and instantly hates her and sends her away in humiliation. She remains desolate in her brother Absalom's house. Two years later Absalom finds the opportunity to kill Amnon as he had purposed when Amnon first defiled his sister. Absalom flees to Talmai and stays there for three years.

At the request of Joab, through a wise woman, King David sends for Absalom to come home, but, the king refuses to see him at first. Finally, at Absalom's insistence the king sees him and kisses him. After this Absalom begins to stand at the gate. He begins to steal the hearts of the people. After forty years Absalom leads a rebellion against his father to overthrow his throne. David and his people flee, except for ten of his concubines which he leaves to keep the house. David begins wandering. Shimei, from the house of Saul comes out and curses David. Zeba, the servant of Mephibosheth brings provisions for David and his people but Miphibosheth stays in Jerusalem. David gives all that Miphibosheth owns to Zeba and his family. Meanwhile, in Jerusalem, Absalom asks counsel of Ahitophel who advises him to sleep with his father's concubines on the top of the house in the sight of all Israel.

PRAYER

Dear Lord,
We can see the sad consequences of David's sins and the sorrow that they bring to him and his household. I pray for grace, mercy and strength to resist sin so that I and my loved ones may live a life of peace, prosperity, fruitfulness and blessings. In the name of Jesus Christ, I pray. Amen.

TODAY'S CHALLENGE: To trust God during times of intense persecution.

What else is God saying to me today?

What is my response?

DAY NINETY-EIGHT: READ II Samuel 17-19

Ahitophel advises Absalom to pursue David on a particular night. Absalom calls also Hushai who gives different advice than Ahitophel. Absalom likes Hushai's counsel better. David is warned of the impending attack and flees across the Jordan. The battle takes place in the woods of Ephraim. The people of Israel are overthrown by the servants of David. The mule on which Absalom is riding takes him underneath a big terebinth tree. His long hair gets caught in the boughs of the tree; his mule goes from under him leaving him hanging in the air. Someone tells Joab who returns and stabs him with three swords. Ten of his young men surround Absalom and kill him. When David receives the news he goes into his chamber and mourns deeply. Joab rebukes him and tells him that he will lose the loyalty of the people if he does not go and address them immediately. David addresses the people and is restored as king.

PRAYER
O, Dear Lord,
The Creator of Heaven and earth, please take from me all tendencies of Absalom which include pride, betrayal, deceit and lack of wisdom. In the name of Jesus Christ, I pray. Amen.

TODAY'S CHALLENGE: To forgive the people who are disobedient to God and seek to harm me, even those I care about.

What else is God saying to me today?

What is my response?

DAY NINETY-NINE: READ II Samuel 20-21

Sheba, a Benjaminite, rebels against David and all of Israel deserts David except the house of Judah. David sends Amasa, whom he had appointed to take Joab's position after Joab killed Absalom, to assemble the men of Judah. Amasa delays longer than the set time that David has given him. Joab and his men go after him and also to pursue Sheba. Joab overtakes Amasa and kills him. He continues to pursue Sheba. They besiege him in a city called Abel, and proceed to destroy the city. A wise woman intercedes and Joab tells her that they only want Sheba. She promises him that Sheba's head will be thrown over the wall to them. The woman goes to all the people and they cut off Sheba's head and throw it over to Joab. Joab blows the trumpet signaling everyone to return to his tent. He goes back to Jerusalem. He is once again in charge over the army of Israel.

Israel experiences a famine for three years. When David inquires of the Lord for the reason for it, God tells him it is because of how Saul treated the Gibeonites. David asks the Gibeonites how he can make atonement so that they can bless God's inheritance. They ask for seven of Saul's descendants so that they can hang them.

When the Philistines are at war again with Israel, Ishbi-Benob, one of the sons of the giant, tries to kill David, but, Abishai comes to his aid. David's men insist that he remain in the city and not go out to war anymore. The four sons of the giant are killed by David and his servants.

PRAYER
Dear Heavenly Father,
You are the only wise God, the One who intervenes in the affairs of mankind. I ask You to intervene when my enemies would over throw me. Thou I have often failed, I still remain Your child and Your servant. In the name of Jesus Christ. Amen.

TODAY'S CHALLENGE: To dare to ask God the reason for the famine.

What else is God saying to me today?

What is my response?

DAY ONE-HUNDRED: READ II Samuel 22-24

David speaks thanksgiving in the words of a beautiful song. He praises God for being his strength, his fortress and deliverer and for giving him victory over his enemies. David speaks last words of wisdom as he reflects upon the responsibilities of rulers.

Honorable mention is made of all of David's mighty men of valor who defended him, fought with and for him, and risked their lives for him.

Later, God's anger is aroused against Israel and he moves David to count the number of inhabitants of Israel and Judah. When David acknowledges that he has behaved foolishly, he repents. Gad, the prophet tells David that God is offering him a choice of one of three penalties. The penalty for David's transgression culminates in a plague that kills seventy thousand men. David purchases land from Araunah in order to offer burnt offerings and peace offerings to the Lord and the plague is withdrawn from Israel.

PRAYER
Dear Lord,
Thank You that Your wisdom is not to be compared. You know secrets that lurk in the deep recesses of men's hearts, including mine. I humbly submit my will to You so that I will not sin. Dear Lord, please purify my heart. In the name of Jesus Christ, I pray. Amen.

TODAY'S CHALLENGE: To realize that God knows everything about situations that I only see a very small part of.

What else is God saying to me today?

What is my response?

DAY ONE HUNDRED AND ONE: READ PSALM 1-3

INTRODUCTION

Although not all of the Psalms were written by David, the majority of them have been ascribed to his authorship. David's Psalms reflect various experiences and encounters that he had with God. First as a shepherd boy, then an anointed king who was forced to live in caves and strongholds as the deranged king Saul hunts him down to kill him. When David is finally crowned king of Israel, he commits a horrendous crime of adultery and murder, which starts a chain-reaction of heartache and heartbreak especially as it concerns his children. It is at various points during these various segments of his life that David pens the passionate words of the Psalms which through generations have expressed both the anguish of our souls and the optimism of our spirits. In order to get the maximum benefit of the Book of Psalms, as you read, **make each Psalm a personal prayer.**

The Lord blesses whoever rejects ungodly counsel and meditates in the word of God day and night. A person who does this shall be firm and fruitful and established like a tree that is planted by the water; and whatever he does shall prosper.

The Lord laughs at those who take counsel together against the Lord and his anointed. God will reward his children. Kings and judges of the earth should serve the Lord with fear. The Psalmist declares: "God is a shield for me, my glory and the one who lifts up my head."

PRAYER

O Lord God,

Thank You for Your word. Help me to look to Your word for wisdom and counsel so that I and my work will be established and sure. I thank You that You protect me and lift me out of depression. In the name of Jesus Christ. Amen.

TODAY'S CHALLENGE: To get my counsel from God and His word.

What else is God saying to me today?

What is my response?

DAY ONE HUNDRED AND TWO: READ *Psalms 4-6*

David implores the Lord to hear him when he calls, recalling that in the past, God has been faithful. He speaks to himself to be angry at his enemies without sinning. This can be done by meditating in his heart and holding his peace. He comforts himself with the knowledge that only God can keep him safe so he can sleep in peace.

In his observation of the co-existence of both good and evil in his world, David emphatically states that God abhors evil and rebellion, but, He will bless the righteous and surround them with favor as a shield. The Psalmist cries out for mercy and deliverance and assures himself that God has heard his prayer and his enemies will be turned back and ashamed.

PRAYER
Dear Merciful Lord,
You alone are the one who can keep me safe from all harm and all evil. I submit myself to You so that I can have peace even when dangers of various kinds surround me. I love You and I do remember Your past faithfulness to me. I ask You to continue to surround me with favor as a shield. I ask You Lord to fight against my enemies for me. In the name of Jesus Christ, I pray. Amen.

TODAY'S CHALLENGE: To trust in God's deliverance and protection in the midst of adversity.

What else is God saying to me today?

What is my response?

DAY ONE HUNDRED AND THREE: READ Psalm 7-9

David draws near to God, declaring that his trust is in God alone. He asks for deliverance from those who persecute him. Open to divine examination, David asks God to judge his behavior and punish him accordingly. Assured of his own integrity in the matter, David emphatically prays for God's judgment upon the wicked. He declares praises to the name of the Lord, Most High.

David extols the majesty of God, exclaiming the Excellency of the Lord's name in all the earth. Considering the awesomeness of God, the Psalmist finds it incredible that God has so highly esteemed man. He declares that he will sing and praise the God of Heaven with his whole heart. God does not forget the cry of the humble. David prays that God will not allow the will of man to prevail, but that the nations will fear God and know that they are but men.

PRAYER

O Lord God,
You alone are God; Unique, Distinct, Holy, Ubiquitous. When I face conflict, I pray that my heart is pure before You so that I can expect You to defend me. O Lord, how excellent is Your name. I ask for a stronger desire to draw closer to You. I pray that the nations will extol You as God; that leaders of nations will fear You and know that they are only men. In the name of Jesus Christ, I pray. Amen.

TODAY'S CHALLENGE: To consistently acquiesce my finite will and wisdom to the infinite, just and perfect will and wisdom of God.

What else is God saying to me today?

What is my response?

DAY ONE HUNDRED AND FOUR: READ Psalm 10-12

The Psalmist intercedes for the helpless and the poor. He outlines the ways of the wicked and pleads to God for justice. The wicked plot evil and think that God does not see. But, God will rain coals upon them. He describes the arrogance of those who disregard God's word; however the Psalmist compares the words of the Lord to silver tried in a furnace of earth.

PRAYER
Dear God,
I know that You see the actions of those who disregard You and Your word. I ask You to please direct me around the plots of the wicked and cause me to be a recipient of the blessings that come form honoring You and Your word in every area of my life. In the name of Jesus Christ, I pray. Amen.

TODAY'S CHALLENGE: To ignore the boasting of the wicked and trust in the words of God.

What else is God saying to me today?

What is my response?

DAY ONE HUNDRED AND FIVE: READ Psalm 13-15

David's soul cries out to the Lord for deliverance from the oppression of his enemy. He tells God that he has trusted in His mercy. He says, "The fool has said in his heart, there is no God." All such people have become corrupt.

He contrasts this with the works of the righteous who do no evil to his neighbor, and does not backbite, but, honors and fears the Lord. Such people David says, "shall never be moved."

PRAYER
Dear Lord,
Often we do not see the reward of the wicked administered, and it seems that the suffering of the righteous is prolonged. At such points in my life, I pray for Your grace that will enable me to always say as David did, "My heart shall rejoice in Your salvation. I will sing to the Lord." In the name of Jesus Christ, I pray. Amen.

TODAY'S CHALLENGE: To believe that God the just judge, punishes the wicked and rewards the righteous although I may not be a witness when he pronounces the verdict.

What else is God saying to me today?

What is my response?

DAY ONE HUNDRED AND SIX: READ *Psalms 16-18*

David asks God for preservation and affirms that his soul has declared the Lord as his God. He rejoices in the good inheritance that he has in the Lord. The Psalmist treasures his fellowship with God as expressed in this phrase. "In your presence is fullness of joy; at Your right hand are pleasures forevermore."

"Let my vindication come from Your presence," he prays. He continues to thank God for all the benefits of being a child of God. He describes God as his Rock, Fortress, Deliverer, and Strength. His praises culminate in the declaration. "The Lord lives, blessed be my Rock, let the God of my salvation be exalted!"

PRAYER
Dear God,
I need Your protection in ways that I am unaware. My enemy might be a natural disaster or an accident or an invasive disease. I exalt You over all of my enemies and ask You to be my Rock, my Fortress, Deliverer and Strength. In the name of Jesus Christ, I pray. Amen.

TODAY'S CHALLENGE: To find my vindication in the presence of the Lord.

What else is God saying to me today?

What is my response?

DAY ONE HUNDRED AND SEVEN: READ Psalms 19-21

The wonderful handiwork of God is proclaimed in these verses. "The heavens declare the glory of God." The Psalmist uses allegory, giving human abilities to nature, to describe how nature itself expresses the glory of God. As he continues to extol the Purity and Holiness of God, he prays that the meditations of his heart and the words of his mouth would be acceptable to God.

David contrasts the foolishness of trusting in human deliverance with trusting in the Lord of hosts. He prays that the King will grant our petitions, defend us, help us, and grant our heart's desires. He thanks God for granting his heart's desires and devouring his enemies.

PRAYER
Dear Lord,
May You answer me in the time of trouble; defend me, send me help from the sanctuary and strengthen me out of Zion. May You remember all of my offerings, grant my heart's desires and fulfill all my purpose and petitions. In the name of the Lord Jesus Christ, I pray. Amen.

TODAY'S CHALLENGE: To submit all my petitions to God; careful to tell him my *real* heart's desires and trust that He will divinely edit what is unwise.

What else is God saying to me today?

What is my response?

DAY ONE HUNDRED AND EIGHT: READ *Psalm 22-24*

The Psalmist cries out. "My God, my God, why have You forsaken me?" He further elaborates the anguish of his soul, describing his heart as "melting within him, and his strength as dried up as a potsherd." In the same division, he appears to shake his soul into consciousness as one would shake a hysterical person out of delirium. He then begins to praise God as his soul experiences crucifixion and ultimate resurrection.

The twenty-third Psalm, perhaps the most widely quoted passage in all of scripture, is timeless in its poetic beauty and ability to bring comfort and consolation. The Psalmist begins by saying. "The Lord is my shepherd." The entire Psalm gently compares God's care for David as a master shepherd who lovingly guides, protects, and cares for his sheep.

Psalm twenty-four recognizes that the earth and everything therein belongs to God, and that He is the King of Glory!

PRAYER
Dear Lord,
Thank You that You do not leave my soul impoverished, that for every instance of crucifixion, through faith in You, there is a resurrection. Thank You that You are my shepherd who faithfully protects and cares for me. Thank You that You own the earth and Your ultimate will shall be done. In the name of Jesus Christ, I offer this thanks. Amen.

TODAY'S CHALLENGE: Remembering that Resurrection follows crucifixion, as day follows night.

What else is God saying to me today?

What is my response?

DAY ONE HUNDRED AND NINE: READ Psalms 25-27

David expresses his complete trust in God. There is no indication that he has any other reliable source. He reminds himself that God is good. He asks God for forgiveness of his sins and transgressions and for mercy. He realizes that only God can bring him out of his distresses and deliver him from his enemies.

He comforts himself with the assurance that God will guide, prosper, bless the descendants of, and show His covenant to those who fear and reverence Him. David confesses his integrity and prays that God will make a distinction between him and those who are bloodthirsty and hypocritical.

Psalm twenty-seven is a resolve to trust in God and in His deliverance and salvation. He knows that God will not allow him to fall. In the time of trouble, God will hide him in the secret place. The beginning of the chapter is its message. "The Lord is my light and salvation; whom shall I fear?"

PRAYER
Dear Lord,
You alone are my help, my refuge, my comfort, my strength. My hope for safety and deliverance rests in Your faithfulness. When I am afraid and confused, may these words rise up within me; and as water extinguishes fire, may they extinguish my fears and dissipate my confusion: "The Lord is my light and my salvation; whom shall I fear? In the name of Jesus Christ, I pray. Amen.

TODAY'S CHALLENGE: To trust in God alone.

What else is God saying to me today?

What is my response?

DAY ONE HUNDRED AND TEN: READ *Psalms 28-30*

David extols God as his Rock, the solid foundation on which he rests. Although circumstances, at times, made him feel as if he were being punished as the wicked, the Psalmist declares that his heart trusted in God. Acknowledging that it is God who blesses and gives refuge, the Psalmist admonishes everyone to "Give unto the Lord the glory due to His name." His Greatness and Power are to be extolled.

The Psalmist rejoices because God healed him and delivered him from his enemies. He declares that God has "turned his mourning into dancing." He also makes this frequently embraced declaration, "Weeping may endure for a night, but, joy comes in the morning."

PRAYER
Dear Lord,
It is true, unless You deliver us, we are in bondage, unless You protect us, we are defenseless. Even the power and strength that we exercise comes from You. I bow before You, worship and extol Your Greatness. Please remove anything from me that will obscure the reality that You indeed are Lord of all. During the hard times, please remind me that joy comes in the morning. In the name of Jesus Christ. Amen.

TODAY'S CHALLENGE: To not allow the tears of my trials to wash away my hope for future deliverance.

What else is God saying to me today?

What is my response?

DAY ONE HUNDRED AND ELEVEN: READ Psalms 31-33

Many times our sins or even unwarranted slander cause us to feel ashamed. David unhesitatingly expresses the anguish of his soul to his God. He does not deny his feelings of grief, lack of strength, and brokenness. He hears the slander and feels the shame. He does not defend himself, but, calls upon the Lord and asks for mercy.

David acknowledges the Lord's forgiveness. He says, "He who trusts in the Lord, mercy shall surround him. Our soul waits for the Lord; He is our help and our shield." Ultimate victory is the culmination of hope.

PRAYER
Dear Heavenly Father,
There are times when my sins and mistakes cause me to feel ashamed. There are times when the persecution from others cause me pain. I ask You to judge my heart. I confess that these feelings sometimes beat against my soul as the sea against the shore, and at times threaten to overwhelm me. Please let Your mercy surround and shield me so that I will be sustained and emerge victoriously. In the name of Jesus Christ, I pray. Amen.

TODAY'S CHALLENGE: To confess my sins, and trust in God's faithfulness to restore me.

What else is God saying to me today?

What is my response?

DAY ONE HUNDRED AND TWELVE: READ Psalms 34-36

David has discovered that praise to God is appropriate, at all times. Praise to God has the capability of lifting us from despair to a God-perspective, so that we can see that the Lord hears the cry of the righteous and delivers them and he is near to all those whose hearts are broken.

Psalm thirty-five is considered an imprecatory Psalm (a call for judgment on one's enemies). It contains David's cry for God to vindicate him, not David pronouncing a curse on them. David asks God to draw out his weapons and stop those who pursue him. He asks how long will they be allowed to rejoice over him. He concludes with an exaltation of God who extends lovingkindness and mercy to those who know Him.

PRAYER
Dear Heavenly Father,
I find the power of praise to be an amazing medicine; capable of curing many of my emotional ills. We need medicine, when we least feel like taking it. Dear Lord, when my soul is sick from grief, pain, anguish or despair, give me the strength to take a healthy dose of praise. I too ask You to fight those who fight against me. Meanwhile let me rejoice in Your mercy and lovingkindness. In the name of Jesus Christ, I pray. Amen.

TODAY'S CHALLENGE: To avoid speaking judgment on my enemies and trust God to vindicate me.

What else is God saying to me today?

What is my response?

DAY ONE HUNDRED AND THIRTEEN: READ Psalms 37-39

Psalm thirty-seven is an admonition to rest in the Lord. David's comforting words assures the fretful soul that it can be at peace; committing everything to the Lord, and delighting in Him. He details the destruction of evil doers. Phrases such as "The steps of a good man are ordered of the Lord" and "I have not seen the righteous forsaken, nor his descendants begging bread," are among the most faith-provoking of all scriptures.

PRAYER
Dear Lord,
When I see the wicked boast in their arrogance, and the righteous seem to suffer long, please help me to remember Psalm thirty-seven. I pray to not fret, to rest in the Lord, and delight myself in Him. I believe that You will give me the desires of my heart. I trust in You, Dear Lord. In the name of Jesus Christ. Amen.

TODAY'S CHALLENGE: To *rest* in the Lord.

What else is God saying to me today?

What is my response?

DAY ONE HUNDRED AND FOURTEEN: READ *Psalms 40-42*

The Psalmist, praises God for being faithful to him. Instead of vindicating himself, he waited for the Lord and the Lord heard his cry for help. He calls the man "blessed" who makes the Lord his trust. He finds delight in doing God's will. He also speaks of the blessings that come from remembering the poor. They will be blessed, healed and find mercy from God.

The Psalmist compares his desire for God's presence with that of a deer which pants for the water brooks. He tells his soul to fret not but to "Hope in God."

PRAYER
Oh Dear Lord,
It is hard to wait for You sometimes, but, the alternatives are futile and foolish. I ask You to order my steps, take vengeance on my enemies and help me to wait for Your answers. Be merciful to me, O Lord, and You raise me up. In the name of Jesus Christ, I pray. Amen.

TODAY'S CHALLENGE: To not allow my adversities to cause me to neglect the poor and others who may need my assistance.

What else is God saying to me?

What is my response?

DAY ONE HUNDRED AND FIFTEEN: READ Psalms 43-45

During the confusion of the reign of the enemy, the Palmist pleads for God's vindication. He asks for God's light and truth to lead him. The Psalmist tells God how he has heard of the great deeds that He performed for his forefathers. He declares. "You are my King, O God; command victories for Jacob." He tells God that His people have become a scorn and reproach, yet they have not forgotten the name of the Lord. He tells God that if they did evil He would punish them, so he cries out for deliverance because of their righteousness.

PRAYER
O Dear God,
In times of confusion, help me to remember that You are just. Help me to see the rewards of serving You and walking in integrity. I believe that You will vindicate me as I walk in Your righteousness. In the name of Jesus Christ, I pray. Amen.

TODAY'S CHALLENGE: To believe that God is just as faithful to reward my righteousness, as He is to punish my wickedness.

What else is God saying to me today?

What is my response?

DAY ONE HUNDRED AND SIXTEEN: READ Psalms 46-48

Whether the Psalmist is speaking to himself, an army, a family, or friends, the confidence that "God is our refuge and strength, a very present help in trouble," inspires hope. He ends the litany with an admonition to "be still and know that He is God" and "the Lord of hosts is with us."

God is exalted, as the King, to whom praises are due. "Great is the Lord and greatly to be praised." God is distinguished as the Almighty who gives victory to His people. When the other kings assembled together they were in terrible fear as they witnessed the awesomeness of the God of Israel.

PRAYER
Dear Lord of hosts,
Thank You for the protection that the Lord of hosts provides for me. Dear Lord, I need You to fight and win the wars in my life, most of which I cannot see. Help me to not be paralyzed by the fear that accompanies trouble; but to hold onto the fact that "The Lord of hosts is with me." In the name of Jesus Christ, I pray. Amen.

TODAY'S CHALLENGE: To be still and know that God is God.

What else is God saying to me today?

What is my response?

DAY ONE HUNDRED AND SEVENTEEN: READ *Psalms 49-51*

The Psalmist makes an announcement to all of the inhabitants of the world, both high and low, rich and poor. The gist of his message is that riches and wealth have no power to redeem one from the pit. The Psalmist establishes the fact that God needs no one because He owns everything and is the judge of all people.

Psalm fifty-one is an expression of the brokenness and contriteness of David's soul after he sinned with Bathsheba and was confronted by the prophet Nathan. It is a befitting prayer for anyone who comes face to face with their sin. In it David asks God to have mercy, blot out his transgressions, and to wash him thoroughly. He did not deny his transgression but acknowledges his sinful nature. He prays for restoration and appeals to the mercy of God.

PRAYER
You, O Lord, are in a distinct class. You alone are God. Although my sin may not be of the magnitude of David's, in this instance, I acknowledge that at times I sin because of the carnal nature within me. I ask You to please cleanse me, restore me and give me opportunities to tell of Your goodness. In the name of Jesus Christ, I pray. Amen.

TODAY'S CHALLENGE: To realize that only God has the power to forgive my transgressions and redeem me from destruction.

What else is God saying to me today?

What is my response?

DAY ONE HUNDRED AND EIGHTEEN: READ Psalms 52-54

David warns the man who devises evil and strengthens himself in his wickedness. The end of that man shall be destruction. But those who trust in God will flourish. He calls the man who says there is no God, a fool.

David calls upon the Lord to vindicate him from such oppressors and to repay his enemies for their evil. He vows to praise the name of the Lord for his deliverance.

PRAYER

Dear Lord,

When the oppressors of my life, who do not know You, confront me, please vindicate me and I will praise Your Name. I realize that whatever the nature of my challenge, You are the Lord Almighty, You are completely able to defend me. In the name of Jesus Christ, I pray. Amen.

TODAY'S CHALLENGE: To make God my strength.

What else is God saying to me today?

What is my response?

DAY ONE HUNDRED AND NINETEEN: READ Psalms 55-57

David laments the pain of the betrayal of a brother or friend. He describes the reward of the wicked and the steadfastness of the righteous. David proclaims that he will trust God when he is afraid. Unsure who are his enemies and who are his friends, at times, the Psalmist resolves to put his total trust in God alone. He describes being with men as if his soul is among lions. He sings. "Be exalted O Lord above the heavens, let Your Glory be over all the earth."

PRAYER
Dear Heavenly Father,
Betrayals hurt, especially when they come at a time when oppression of the enemy is already overwhelming. At such times, help me to draw closer to You and know that You are forever faithful. In Jesus name, I pray. Amen.

TODAY'S CHALLENGE: God will deliver me out of all my trouble.

What else is God saying to me today?

What is my response?

DAY ONE HUNDRED AND TWENTY: READ Psalms 58-60

The Palmist prays for mercy. Perhaps while hiding in a cave, being pursued by Saul, unable to match the physical strength of Saul's army, he calls upon the Lord to "Break out the fangs of the young lions." He prays for God's deliverance from his enemies, describing the fierceness and unrelentlessness of the pursuit.

They are like serpents, cobras, bloodthirsty men who lie in wait for his life. But David sings of God's power to deliver, defend, and tread down the enemy.

PRAYER
Dear Lord,
I don't face Saul's physical army, but, there are issues that I face which are monumental. My strength alone is too small. I pray Lord, magnify Yourself on my behalf, tread down the enemies of my soul. I too shall sing of Your deliverance and salvation. In the name of Jesus Christ, I pray. Amen.

TODAY'S CHALLENGE: To always exalt the Lord above my challenges.

What else is God saying to me today?

What is my response?

DAY ONE HUNDRED AND TWENTY-ONE: READ Psalms 61-63

One can almost hear the strings of His instrument as David sings: "Hear my cry, O God; attend to my prayer, from the end of the earth, I will cry to You." Perhaps he has a moment of respite from the hot pursuit of his enemies. He praises God for hearing his vows and being a shelter and strong tower.

David further vows to wait for the Lord's salvation. He chooses to not trust in people or in riches, but, to trust the Lord at all times. God's lovingkindness is better than life, He is worthy to be blessed and praised.

PRAYER
Dear Lord,
Thank You for the times of being refreshed in Your presence. Thank You for the peace that comes when I find my refuge in You alone. Forever be my Strong Tower, my Shelter, I pray. In the name of Jesus Christ. Amen.

TODAY'S CHALLENGE: To wait *silently* for God.

What else is God saying to me today?

What is my response?

DAY ONE HUNDRED AND TWENTY-TWO:
READ Psalms 64-66

Words can sometimes pierce as arrows, and are often the pivot from which war erupts. David asks God to stop those who talk of laying a snare for him. "They sharpen their tongues like a sword. He says, but, God shall shoot them down like an arrow."

As if to drown out the words of the adversary, David talks about the praise that awaits God. He blesses God for His awesome deeds and the manifestation of His power in nature. He commands all the earth to shout to God. He praises God for what He has done. David did not regard iniquity in his heart and God heard his prayers.

PRAYER
Dear Heavenly Father,
Thank You that You can cause adversarial words and plans against me to be powerless. I ask You to fight my unseen battles and confuse every plot of the adversary that seeks to devour my soul. Purify my heart, from all iniquity, so that I may rejoice in answered prayer. In the name of Jesus Christ. Amen.

TODAY'S CHALLENGE: To so fill my ears with my own praises to God that I am unable to hear the words of my enemies.

What else is God saying to me today?

What is my response?

DAY ONE HUNDRED AND TWENTY-THREE:
READ Psalms 67-69

"When all the people praise the Lord, the earth shall yield her increase," says the Psalmist. The beginning of Psalm sixty-eight shouts, "Let God arise and his enemies be scattered." In praises and songs David expresses the greatness and mercies of God who is "a father to the fatherless, a defender of widows." He blesses the Lord who daily loads us with benefits, but, wounds the head of the enemy.

In Psalm sixty-nine we feel David's anguish of soul as he feels that he is sinking and that the floods are overflowing him. He prays for salvation, and expresses praise to God, because he knows that the Lord will hear him. All praise is due to God.

PRAYER
Dear Lord,
When I feel like the floods of adversity are overwhelming me, may I express hope in Your deliverance, and see Your salvation. You are faithful and I know that You will hear my prayers. Thank You for all of the benefits that I have in You. In the name of Jesus Christ. Amen.

TODAY'S CHALLENGE: To meditate on the daily benefits that God provides instead of the daily hassles that come my way.

What else is God saying to me today?

What is my response?

DAY ONE HUNDRED AND TWENTY-FOUR:
READ Psalms 70-72

When oppression seems eminent, David cries. "Make haste, O God to deliver me!" The Psalmist seems almost frantic as he calls upon the Lord to make those who pursue him ashamed and confused. He expresses that his trust is in God and asks to never be put to shame. The Psalmist expresses the many ways in which he needs the Lord. He calls God: his Rock, his Fortress and his Trust, from youth. Now, that he is aged, he prays, "God do not forsake me, until I declare Your Strength to this generation; Your Power to everyone who is to come."

Psalm seventy-two is a Psalm of David's son, Solomon. He prays for wisdom to judge the people righteously. He speaks of the magnificence of the ultimate King who will command worship from all of the kings of the earth. This prophetic Psalm speaks of the whole earth being filled with the glory of God.

PRAYER
O Lord,
When disaster seems certain, somehow, You intervene and Your grace is poured out. I gratefully thank You for Your watchful and loving care for me and my loved ones. Wherever we are, You are Lord of all. I pray for grace and life and health that I may declare Your Strength to my generation. In the name of Jesus Christ, I pray. Amen.

TODAY'S CHALLENGE: To know that God cuts through deadlines.

What else is God saying to me today?

What is my response?

DAY ONE HUNDRED AND TWENTY-FIVE: READ Psalms 73-75

The Psalmist confesses that he almost slipped because he looked at the illusion of the prosperity of the wicked. The wicked have no pangs of death. Their eyes bulge with abundance. They speak against the heavens and disregard God. They are ungodly, yet, they increase in riches. He elaborately describes the actions of the enemy. They damage the sanctuary, defile the dwelling place of God's name and blaspheme it. The Psalmist thought that he was living righteously to no avail.

The Psalmist says, "It was too painful for me-until I went into the sanctuary of God; *then* I understood their end." He humbly resolves to continually praise God who is a righteous judge.

PRAYER

Dear Lord,

Please forgive me also for the times that I have been puzzled at what appears to be the prosperity of the wicked and the suffering of the righteous. At times, when it seems that You are ignoring the obvious, and my service to You seems to be in vain, lead me into the sanctuary of Your presence, so that I can know Your truth and continue in pure fellowship with You. In the name of Jesus Christ, I pray. Amen.

TODAY'S CHALLENGE: To diligently seek answers from God before I judge him.

What else is God saying to me today?

What is my response?

DAY ONE HUNDRED AND TWENTY-SIX: READ Psalms 76-78

The Psalmist, Asaph, praises God for victory in battle. He praises God for hearing his cries and complaints. In Psalm seventy-eight, Asaph proclaims the faithfulness of God throughout the generations. He recalls God's testimony in Jacob and all of his descendants. He recalls the miracles of the Egyptian exodus and the crossing of the Red Sea. He recalls the rebellion of the children of Israel, yet the mercies of God prevailed. Although they broke covenant, God "shepherded them according to the integrity of His heart."

PRAYER
Dear Lord,
Thank You for being a God who keeps covenant and extends mercy to Your children. I ask You to please help me when I tend to complain. Help me to relax in the knowledge that You will remain faithful to Your promises. In the name of Jesus Christ. Amen.

TODAY'S CHALLENGE: To recall the faithfulness of God to me in the past, and know that He does not change.

What else is God saying to me today?

What is my response?

DAY ONE HUNDRED AND TWENTY-SEVEN:
READ Psalms 79-81

Asaph intercedes for Jerusalem. He describes the desolation and destructions. He prays for God to not remember their former iniquities. He prays. "Stir up your strength and come and save us!" He prays to God for restoration. In Psalm eighty-one, Asaph speaks the voice of God to the people. He tells them to put away their foreign gods, and worship the God who delivered them out of Egypt. If the people will heed the voice of God, He will subdue their enemies.

PRAYER
Dear Holy God,
Like the Israelites, I cry for deliverance when I'm in trouble. Please help me to not ignore the fact that my troubles are sometimes caused by my own sin. I ask You to show me any areas of my life that might produce bondage and prevent the full display of Your deliverance. I ask You to remove it, so that I may be restored to Your purpose for my life. In the name of Jesus Christ, I pray. Amen.

TODAY'S CHALLENGE: To not just pray for freedom from bondage, but also freedom from the things in my life that produce bondage.

What else is God saying to me today?

What is my response?

DAY ONE HUNDRED AND TWENTY-EIGHT:
READ Psalms 82-84

Asaph rebukes the unjust judges in Israel who show partiality to the wicked. He tells them to give justice and attention to the poor and fatherless, the poor and needy. He prays for God to arise and judge the earth.

The Psalmist pleas for God to destroy Israel's enemies. He implores God to destroy those who hate him and who have consulted together against His people.

Psalm eighty-four is a reflection on the goodness of being in the house of God and in the presence of God. "For a day in your courts is better than a thousand. I would rather be a doorkeeper in the house of my God than dwell in the tents of wickedness. For the Lord God is a sun and shield; The Lord will give Grace and Glory; no good thing will he withhold from those who walk uprightly."

PRAYER
Dear Lord God,
I do need You to be my sun and shield. Protect me from the coldness of a cruel world. Shield me from the attitudes and actions that do not reflect Your Glory. And I pray for a release of those things into my life that are good for me. In the name of Jesus Christ, I pray. Amen.

TODAY'S CHALLENGE: To realize the joy of being in the presence of God.

What else is God saying to me today?

What is my response?

DAY ONE HUNDRED AND TWENTY-NINE:
READ Psalms 85-87

The psalmist speaks of the favor of the Lord. He delivers from captivity and brings revival to His people. "The Lord will give what is good; and our land will yield its increase. Righteousness will go before Him and shall make His footsteps our pathway."

"Save Your servant who trusts in You," is the cry of David. He also desires for God to teach him the ways of the Lord. "Unite my heart to fear Your name." Praises go forth for Zion for the Most High Himself shall establish her.

PRAYER
Dear Lord,
I surrender all of my life to You, with a desire to do Your will. I ask for Your favor and goodness. Please give me what is good and unite my heart to fear Your name. In the name of Jesus Christ. Amen.

TODAY'S CHALLENGE: To hear what the Lord speaks.

What else is God saying to me today?

What is my response?

DAY ONE HUNDRED AND THIRTY: READ Psalms 88-90

The Psalmist feels the weight of affliction and cries out to God to incline his ear. He describes his condition as distraught and afflicted. In Psalm eighty-nine, we see the writer making a decision to praise God and claim His promises in spite of circumstances. He says, "O Lord of hosts, who is mighty like You, O Lord? Your faithfulness also surrounds You."

Psalm ninety is a Psalm of the servant of God and the first leader of Israel, Moses. He identifies God as our dwelling place before the earth and worlds were formed. "Even from everlasting to everlasting, You are God." He prays for God to have compassion on His servants, make our day glad, and establish the works of our hands.

PRAYER
Lord,
You are still my dwelling place. When I feel the weight of affliction, help me to still praise You. Have compassion on me, I pray, and establish all the works of my hands that You have ordained. In the name of Jesus Christ, I pray. Amen.

TODAY'S CHALLENGE: To hold on to God's promises in spite of circumstances.

What else is God saying to me today?

What is my response?

DAY ONE HUNDRED AND THIRTY-ONE: READ Psalms 91-93

One of the most beloved Psalms, is Psalm ninety-one. It comforts us to know that we can dwell in the secret place of the most high. (Take time now and meditate on Psalm ninety-one as you read it aloud.)

Psalm ninety-two admonishes us to give thanks to the Lord and sing praises to Him. The intensity of the praise reflects the depths of the appreciation that the Psalmist has for God's lovingkindness and faithfulness. He further declares the majesty of God who reigns.

PRAYER
Dear Lord,
Thank You for the secret place of Your presence. In the name of Jesus Christ. Amen.

TODAY'S CHALLENGE: Because I have made the Lord my habitation no evil will befall me.

What else is God saying to me today?

What is my response?

DAY ONE HUNDRED AND THIRTY-TWO: READ Psalms 94-96

The Psalmist realizes that vengeance belongs only to God. He appeals to God, who is the judge of the whole earth, to shine forth and punish the proud. God will stand up for us against the workers of iniquity and cut them off.

The people are called to worship God because He is Great. He created everything in nature and is the Maker of all mankind. "The Lord is Great and greatly to be praised." The people sing to the Lord and bless His name.

PRAYER
Dear Lord,
Thank You for being a just and righteous judge. You are omniscient and the possessor of all wisdom. I kneel before You and worship You as the God above all gods. In the name of Jesus Christ, I offer this thanks. Amen.

TODAY'S CHALLENGE: To trust God to defend me.

What else is God saying to me today?

What is my response?

DAY ONE HUNDRED AND THIRTY-THREE:
READ Psalms 97-99

When the enemy's wrath has been fierce and the Lord gives His people the victory: dancing, singing and praises erupt. The Psalmist declares that above the enemies, above adversity, and above all gods, "The Lord reigns."

He revealed Himself in righteousness, faithfulness, and victory. "Exalt the Lord!"

PRAYER
I join in with all of those who know the goodness of God; I exalt the Lord and worship at His Holy Hill. In the name of Jesus Christ. Amen.

TODAY'S CHALLENGE: To give extensive thanks to God daily.

What else is God saying to me today?

What is my response?

DAY ONE HUNDRED AND THIRTY-FOUR:
READ *Psalms 100-102*

Psalm one hundred is an encouragement to "Make a joyful shout to the Lord!" He is to be praised for being our Creator and our Shepherd. He is to be thanked and praised for He is Good. David in Psalm one hundred and one commits to walk with a perfect heart and not know wickedness.

The prayer of the afflicted contains pleas for safety, healing and peace. The Lord is praised as the one who remembers through the generations. Because of God's faithfulness, we can always expect God to strengthen His servants.

PRAYER
Dear Holy God,
At all times, You are worthy to be praised. Although the clouds of distress may darken the sky of my expectation; You are still God with All Power to break through and cause the light of Your favor to shine upon me. In the name of Jesus Christ, I pray. Amen.

TODAY'S CHALLENGE: To walk with a perfect heart.

What else is God saying to me today?

What is my response?

DAY ONE HUNDRED AND THIRTY-FIVE:
READ Psalms 103-105

David commands his soul to bless the Lord and remember Him as the Forgiver of iniquities, the Healer of all our diseases and Our Redeemer. He also blesses the Lord who is the God of all creation. He is the Divine Architect of the waters, the earth, the valleys the tress and all living things.

He is remembered as a God who keeps covenant from generation to generation. Wherever His people wandered, although He tested them, God did not forsake them. Praise the Lord.

PRAYER
Dear Lord,
I accept You as the One who forgives my iniquities, as my Healer, and Redeemer. I am awed at Your creations and bless Your name forever. Thank You that You are a Covenant-Keeping God. In the name of Jesus Christ, I pray. Amen.

TODAY'S CHALLENGE: As I look for future answers to prayer, to not forget the great things that God has done for me in the past.

What else is God saying to me today?

What is my response?

DAY ONE HUNDRED AND THIRTY-SIX: READ Psalms 106-108

The Psalmist remembers the enduring mercy of God and the sinfulness of the people. He recalls the journey and sinfulness of the Israelites who rebelled at the Red Sea, in the wilderness and with the calf at Horeb. He traces their journey and confesses the rebellion of his forefathers all the way into the land of Canaan.

God is to be thanked for his enduring mercy. Whenever the people cried out to God, He delivered them out of their distresses. The acts of God are innumerable. "Whoever is wise will observe these things and they will understand the loving kindness of the Lord."

David sings that his heart is steadfast. "I will sing and give praise, even with my glory." He vows to praise God with the lute and harp and praise God at dawn. God is exalted above the heavens, His glory above all the earth.

PRAYER
Dear Lord God,
Should I remember my many transgressions, I would be overwhelmed. I ask You to forgive and blot them out, every one. Let the memory of them be only as a testimony of Your Goodness and Faithfulness. I exalt You above the Heavens, and earth, and over every area of my past, present and future. In the name of the Lord Jesus Christ. Amen.

TODAY'S CHALLENGE: To remember my past only as a reflection of the goodness of God.

What else is God saying to me today?

What is my response?

DAY ONE HUNDRED AND THIRTY-SEVEN:
READ Psalms 109-111

David calls to God's attention the accusations of the wicked. He asks God to reward them for their unwarranted attack. The Lord will judge the nations and rule over all of His enemies.

The Psalmist praises the Lord with his whole heart for his great works. He remembers His covenant with His people. "Holy and awesome is His name. The fear of the Lord is the beginning of wisdom."

PRAYER
Dear Lord,
I thank You that You are my defense when I am misunderstood or when false accusations are made. I thank You that Your righteous reign will endure forever. In the name of Jesus Christ, I pray. Amen.

TODAY'S CHALLENGE: To Allow God to protect me from slander and betrayal.

What else is God saying to me today?

What is my response?

DAY ONE HUNDRED AND THIRTY-EIGHT:
READ Psalms 112-114

The Psalmist praises God and calls the man blessed who fears God and delights in his commandments. His descendants will be mighty on earth and wealth and riches will be in his house. God's name is to be praised from sunrise to sunset. It is God who raises the poor and remembers the barren women. God delivered His people out of Egypt and commanded the Red Sea and the Jordan. He brought water from the rock.

PRAYER
Dear Lord,
When I face a situation that looks impossible, please help me to reflect for a few minutes on the power of the God that I serve. Help me to remember that when I pray to You, I am praying to the God who delivered the Israelites out of Egypt, who opened the Red Sea, parted the Jordan, and brought water from a rock! In the name of Jesus Christ. Amen.

TODAY'S CHALLENGE: To fear God and delight in His commandments.

What else is God saying to me today?

What is my response?

DAY ONE HUNDRED AND THIRTY-NINE:
READ Psalms 115-118

Those who worship idols do not see our God because He is in Heaven. Their idols have eyes, ears, and mouths but cannot see, hear or speak. God will bless His people and their children. To His name be the glory.

Psalm one hundred and sixteen is a personal Psalm of love, worship and thanksgiving for the deliverance and salvation of the Lord.

Psalm one hundred and eighteen outlines the many reasons to thank the Lord. Among them are thanks for His mercy, for answered prayer, for his help, for power over death. "Give thanks to the Lord for He is good."

PRAYER
Thank You Lord for being a King who lives forever. Thank You for being the Cornerstone. "This is the day that the Lord has made; I *will* rejoice and be glad in it." In the name of Jesus Christ. Amen.

TODAY'S CHALLENGE: To have complete trust in a God who I cannot see.

What else is God saying to me today?

What is my response?

DAY ONE HUNDRED AND FORTY: READ *Psalms 119*

Psalm one hundred and nineteen expresses the heart and desire of one who has chosen to esteem God's Word, His precepts and His laws as the ultimate guide for life. Adherence to God's Word will keep one from sin, and provide wise counsel. God's Word will provide strength and provide understanding, and revive in righteousness. The Psalmist asks for God's mercies and that God would not take His Word out of his mouth. He loves the commandments of the Lord. This Psalm should be prayed meditatively by all who desire to be more committed to studying and living by God's word.

PRAYER
Dear Lord,
May I love Your word and keep Your word before my eyes and within my heart always, in the name of Jesus Christ. Amen.

TODAY'S CHALLENGE: To pray all of Psalm 119 as my personal prayer.

What else is God saying to me today?

What is my response?

DAY ONE HUNDRED AND FORTY-ONE: READ Psalms 120-123

When in distress the Lord will hear us. When we encounter contentious people, the Lord will help us. All efforts of salvation and deliverance apart from God are futile. The Psalmist pens this poetic song of trust and expectation from God. "I will lift up my eyes to the hills from whence comes my help. My help comes from the Lord, who made heaven and earth." The Psalmist speaks of the Lord's power to keep us from evil.

David speaks of his pleasure in going to the house of the Lord. He finds the house of God as a place of refuge. The Psalmist speaks of how completely he needs the mercy of the Lord.

PRAYER
Dear Lord,
I thank You that from the darkness of human distress and confusion, I can lift up my eyes to the hills from whence comes my help, My help comes from the Lord. I solicit Your help for my life, for my family, for Your people all over the world. I thank You for the places of worship that have been set aside to honor You and pray to You. I thank You for Your great mercy, in the name of Jesus Christ. Amen.

TODAY'S CHALLENGE: To believe with all of my heart that the Lord is my keeper.

What else is God saying to me today?

What is my response?

DAY ONE HUNDRED AND FORTY-TWO:
READ Psalms 124-126

David praises the Lord who is on our side and in whose name our help is found. He compares those who trust God to mount Zion, immovable. He implores God. "Do good to those, O Lord, to those who are good." The Psalmist rejoices when God restores the captives. "Those who sow in tears shall reap in joy."

PRAYER
Dear Lord,
Thank You for being on my side. Thank You that You did not allow the waters of adversity to overwhelm me. In areas of my life that have been devastated by various life circumstances, I pray for Your divine restoration. In the name of Jesus Christ, I pray. Amen.

TODAY'S CHALLENGE: To believe that what I sow in tears, I'll reap in joy.

What else is God saying to me today?

What is my response?

DAY ONE HUNDRED AND FORTY-THREE:
READ Psalm 127-129

The words of comfort found in Psalm one hundred twenty seven silences anxiety and fear. All of human effort and labor is in vain unless the Lord establishes it. The blessings of God on the family come where the fear of the Lord is. Those who persecute God's people will not be able to prevail against them.

PRAYER
Dear Lord,
I pray that You will build my house. I pray that You will bless my family and my children. Help me to walk in Your ways and enjoy Your blessings. In the name of Jesus Christ, I pray. Amen.

TODAY'S CHALLENGE: To relax and let the Lord build my life.

What else is God saying to me today?

What is my response?

DAY ONE HUNDRED AND FORTY-FOUR:
READ Psalms 130-132

The Psalmist finds himself in the depths, he cries out to the Lord. He expects forgiveness and waits for the Lord's deliverance. He encourages himself to hope in God.

David prays to God to remember him in all of his afflictions. He vows not to go to sleep until he finds a place for the Lord. He implores God to not turn away the face of His anointed. He calls upon the Lord to remember His promises to the house of David.

PRAYER
O Dear Lord,
When I cry out from the depths of fear, or the depths of a broken heart, or the depths of need, or the depths of affliction, I know that You will hear my cry. I thank You for Your faithfulness. In the name of Jesus Christ, I pray. Amen.

TODAY'S CHALLENGE: To hope in God's word and wait for the Lord.

What else is God saying to me today?

What is my response?

DAY ONE HUNDRED AND FORTY-FIVE: READ Psalm 133-135

When brethren dwell in unity, the Lord commands blessings. The Psalmist commands the servants of the Lord to bless the Lord.

The servants of the Lord are encouraged to praise the Lord, because He is good. He is great. He is Lord over nature. He defeated Israel's enemies and gave them the promise land. The Psalmist speaks of the folly of serving idols. All of Israel is admonished to bless the Lord.

PRAYER
Dear Lord,
Thank You for Your goodness and Your love which enables us to live in unity with other believers. I praise You, as Lord of all creation, King of kings and God of gods. In the name of Jesus Christ. Amen.

TODAY'S CHALLENGE: To strive to dwell in unity with others of the faith.

What else is God saying to me today?

What is my response?

DAY ONE HUNDRED AND FORTY-SIX: READ Psalm 136-138

The cadence of Psalm one hundred thirty-six resounds in the soul as you read the words, "Oh give thanks to the Lord, for He is good! His mercy endures forever." He does great wonders, He created earth, the sun, the moon, and the stars. He delivered Israel from Egypt and into the promised land."

In exile, in a foreign land, the children of Israel are challenged to sing songs of Zion. David vows to praise God before the gods. He details many reasons to praise God. He glorifies God for His Greatness and answers to prayers.

PRAYER

Thank You Lord for You are great, You are good, Your mercy endures forever. I welcome Your great wonders, Your deliverance, and the fulfillment of Your promises in my life. In the name of Jesus Christ, Amen.

TODAY'S CHALLENGE: To give thanks to God for more than sixty-seconds.

What else is God saying to me today?

What is my response?

DAY ONE HUNDRED AND FORTY-SEVEN:
READ Psalms 139-141

Psalm one hundred thirty-nine humbly acknowledges the omniscience of God both as overseer of the universe and the one who knows each person intimately. The Psalmist praises God for also knowing him and forming him in his mother's womb. He realizes that he is wonderfully and fearfully made and that God's thoughts toward him are precious and too many to count. The Psalmist submits to God, asking Him, "Search me, O God, and know my heart; try me and know my anxieties; and see if there is any wicked way in me and lead me in the way everlasting."

A prayer for deliverance from violent and wicked men and that God would not grant the desires of the wicked.

PRAYER
Thank you Lord,
I know that You know every thing about me. I ask for You to search me and take out everything that You find unloving and unuseful for Your purposes in my life. In the name of Jesus Christ, I pray. Amen.

TODAY'S CHALLENGE: To be honest and naked before God.

What else is God saying to me today?

What is my response?

DAY ONE HUNDRED AND FORTY-EIGHT:
READ Psalms 142-144

The Lord hears our cry and He is our refuge. He is our deliverer from persecutors. David suffered years of persecution. At times, his soul was in great anguish. He cries out, "answer me speedily, O lord my spirit fails!" He resigns himself to the care of God's shelter, trusting Him to destroy those who afflict his soul. He extols the great God who is his Rock. He marvels at the care of God for His people and is awed at the greatness of God. He lauds the people who trust in him.

PRAYER
Dear Lord,
When my soul is in anguish, I will cry out to You. Deliver me from those who persecute me. Help me to always make You my refuge and my shelter. In the name of Jesus Christ, I pray. Amen.

TODAY'S CHALLENGE: To resign myself to God's care.

What else is God saying to me today?

What is my response?

DAY ONE HUNDRED AND FORTY-NINE:
READ Psalms 145-147

The Psalmist declares that he will bless the Lord's name every day. He speaks of the greatness of the Lord. What an awesome laudation and tribute to the wonder and glorious splendor of His majesty. He speaks of God's compassion, His mercy, His power, His majesty, and His dominion. All praises belong to God. It is good to sing praises to God.

PRAYER
O Dear Lord,
You are so great, so awesome, words cannot express the greatness of Your power, majesty, and dominion. Thank You for being in my life. In the name of Jesus, I pray. Amen.

TODAY"S CHALLENGE: To bless the Lord's name every day.

What else is God saying to me today?

What is my response?

DAY ONE HUNDRED AND FIFTY: READ Psalms 148-150

All of creation is commanded to praise the Lord. In the heights, all the angels, all His hosts, sun and moon, stars of light, heavens and even the waters. His name alone is to be exalted and praised. He is the Creator of all things.

The people are extolled to praise the Lord. They are encouraged to rejoice, dance, sing, play instruments and sing aloud on their beds. "Let everything that has breath praise the Lord."

PRAYER
O Dear Lord,
I praise You; praise You, for You are so great. I exalt Your name forever. You are the Creator of all things. I take this moment to rejoice here in Your presence. In the name of Jesus Christ. Amen.

TODAY'S CHALLENGE: To rejoice in the Lord in creative ways.

What else is God saying to me today?

What is my response?

DAY ONE HUNDRED AND FIFTY-ONE: READ Proverbs 1-3

King Solomon writes the proverbs in order to provoke young men to receive the instruction of wisdom, justice, judgment and equity. "The fear of the Lord is the beginning of knowledge, but, fools despise wisdom and instruction." He admonishes young men to hear the instruction of the father and mother, and to avoid the corruption that comes from association with sinners. He personifies wisdom and assigns her a voice that cries out. Simple ones and scorners eat the fruit of their foolishness.

He describes wisdom, understanding and discernment as treasures to be sought. The keeping of these commandments will bring long life and peace, favor and high esteem. The message is captured in these much-quoted verses. "Trust in the Lord with all your heart, and lean not on your own understanding; in all your ways acknowledge Him and He shall direct your paths."

PRAYER
Dear God of all wisdom,
I ask for a deeper revelation of the "fear of the Lord," so that I can avoid corruption and deception. Help me to hold fast to the Godly teachings of fathers and mothers of the faith; as well as in the natural. I answer wisdom's cry and ask her to be my companion in all of life's affairs. I acknowledge You Lord in all of my ways, and I sincerely ask You to direct my paths. In the name of Jesus Christ, I pray. Amen.

TODAY'S CHALLENGE: To seek wisdom as a treasure above silver or gold.

What else is God saying to me today?

What is my response?

DAY ONE HUNDRED AND FIFTY-TWO: READ *Proverbs 4-7*

Children are called to hear the wise instructions of their fathers. Solomon tells us that His father, David, gave him good doctrine which he is now passing on. He says emphatically, "Get wisdom! Get understanding!

He warns again against entering the path of the wicked and walking in the way of evil. He also outlines the perils of adultery and sexual sins. He warns that the ways of a man are before the Lord and his own iniquities will entrap him and catch him in the cords of sin. It is dangerous to be the guarantor for a friend, and one should make great effort to free himself from such pledges. He warns against laziness and lack of planning for the future. One should avoid wicked men with perverse mouths. Wisdom should be embraced as a sister and the harlot must be avoided because her house is the way to Hell.

PRAYER
Dear Heavenly Father,
There is not an earthly father who has all wisdom. I ask You to teach me what only a Heavenly Father can. Only You are omniscient. I ask You to impart to me divine wisdom and understanding. Guard my life against all sexual sins, laziness and all forms of perversity. I pray this in the name of Jesus Christ. Amen.

TODAY'S CHALLENGE: To embrace wisdom and avoid the path of the wicked.

What else is God saying to me today?

What is my response?

DAY ONE HUNDRED AND FIFTY-THREE: READ Proverbs 8-11

Solomon poetically describes the role of wisdom who stands on the top of the hill and cries at the gates to be heard for her voice is one of excellence, and to be coveted above silver, gold or rubies. "The fear of the Lord is the beginning of wisdom, and the knowledge of the Holy One is understanding."

"A wise son makes a glad father, but a foolish son is the grief of his mother;" is the beginning of a list of proverbs that addresses the plight of the wicked, and the inheritance of the righteous; and the differences between the wise and the foolish.

The sayings of Solomon address virtually every topic that affects human experience and behavior and concludes that both the righteous and the ungodly will receive their just recompense upon the earth.

PRAYER
Most Holy God,
Thank You for Your words through King Solomon. I ask You to seal the truth of these words within my heart. I worship You and ask You to please help me to spend the appropriate time in Your word and in Your presence. In the name of Jesus Christ, I pray. Amen.

TODAY'S CHALLENGE: To believe that God Himself will reward both the wicked and the righteous.

What else is God saying to me today?

What is my response?

DAY ONE HUNDRED AND FIFTY-FOUR: READ Proverbs 12-14

Proverbs twelve calls the person stupid who hates correction. He speaks of favor coming to the righteous. He extols the virtue of an excellent wife. Solomon's strong admonitions to live righteously and shun evil are presented from various angles and perspectives in order to stress the importance of his message. He condemns laziness, lying lips, deceitfulness, and anxiety, "But diligence is man's precious possession."

He talks about the virtues of proper speech, truthfulness and the absence of pride. Poverty and shame are promised to those who disdain correction. "A wise woman builds her house, but the foolish pulls it down with her hands." He compares the prudent with the simple, the fool with the wise.

PRAYER
Dear Lord,
I submit to Your correction. I submit to Your righteousness. I submit to the virtue that comes from knowing You. I reject laziness, lying, deceitfulness and anxiety. I ask for Your help in proper speech and maintaining diligence. In the name of Jesus Christ, I pray. Amen.

TODAY'S CHALLENGE: To maintain diligence as a precious possession.

What else is God saying to me today?

What is my response?

DAY ONE HUNDRED AND FIFTY-FIVE: READ Proverbs 15-18

Solomon counsels one to use a soft answer to turn away wrath, but, wrath stirs anger. He reminds us that the eyes of the Lord are every place. He speaks on many subjects including; discipline, a merry heart, the refining pot of God and children. He speaks on how to walk in love by covering another's transgression, not gossiping, not taking vengeance and being a true friend.

Each proverb is a subject of meditation within itself. The folly of isolation and the safety in a multitude of counselors, the name of the Lord is a tower, finding a wife is a good thing, and many other sayings all encase the great wisdom that God gave to Solomon.

PRAYER

Dear Lord,

Thank You for the proverbs. May I commit many of them to memory. Thank You that Your eyes are in every place. Thank You so much that You are my strong tower and through You, I can walk in perfect love. In the name of Jesus Christ, I pray. Amen.

TODAY'S CHALLENGE: To avoid wrath which stirs up anger.

What else is God saying to me today?

What is my response?

DAY ONE HUNDRED AND FIFTY-SIX: READ *Proverbs 19-21*

In these verses, Solomon addresses issues of wealth and riches, explaining that they do not satisfy; and admonishes one to have pity on the poor. He also cautions self-sufficiency and pride. He gives advice on drinking wine, conduct toward kings, and the blessings of being and finding a friend who is righteous. The virtues of justice and fairness in business is admirable. "The king's heart is in the hand of the Lord, like the rivers of water; He turns it wherever He wishes," has been a point of hope for many who find themselves praying for favor with man.

PRAYER

Dear Holy God,

You are my source of life and wisdom. I pray for friends who are righteous and I pray to be a righteous friend. Help me to take time to have pity on the poor. I choose to not be self-sufficient, but to rely on You. When I need favor from man, I trust You to turn their heart so that I may be able to fully perform Your will in my life. In the name of Jesus Christ. Amen.

TODAY'S CHALLENGE: To be a righteous friend and cover other's transgressions with love.

What else is God saying to me today?

What is my response?

DAY ONE HUNDRED AND FIFTY-SEVEN:
READ Proverbs 22-24

"Train up a child in the way he should go and when he is old, he will not depart from it," says King Solomon. He continues his teachings on how to treat the poor, the wisdom of avoiding angry men, eating modestly with kings and not overworking to be rich, but, being zealous for the fear of the Lord.

He warns against drunkenness, envying the wicked, showing partiality, and laziness.

PRAYER
Dear Lord,
I pray to be the kind of child that will not depart from right teaching, regardless of my age. Help me to train up my children or influence other children in a way that indelibly imprints them with God's truths and His love. In Jesus name I pray. Amen.

TODAY'S CHALLENGE: To treat the poor in a way that will please my father, God.

What else is God saying to me today?

What is my response?

DAY ONE HUNDRED AND FIFTY-EIGHT:
READ Proverbs 25-28

Solomon teaches on how to live harmoniously with kings, neighbors, rulers, enemies and the necessity of being able to rule over one's own spirit.

He discusses the folly of trying to honor a fool. "As a dog returns to his own vomit, so a fool repeats his folly."

He warns against presumption, greed, and pride and encourages the righteous to be diligent and faithful for they will abound with blessings.

PRAYER
Dear Lord.
Please whisper to me the secrets of wisdom so that I may live harmoniously with people from all walks of life. Help me to rule over my own spirit and not act foolishly. Help me to be faithful to Your word so that I may receive Your blessings. In the name of Jesus Christ, I pray, Amen.

TODAY'S CHALLENGE: To conduct myself properly wherever I go.

What else is God saying to me today?

What is my response?

DAY ONE HUNDRED AND FIFTY-NINE: READ Proverbs 29-31

Solomon's proverbs carry a consistent theme; wisdom versus folly, righteousness versus evil, honor versus dishonor, diligence versus indolence, purity versus adultery, temperance versus violence, lies versus truth.

Proverbs thirty-one is the famous proverb of the virtuous woman whose price is placed far above rubies and whose children rise up and call her blessed and whose husband praises her.

PRAYER
O Dear Lord,
It is easy to read Your word and agree with it. It is sometimes much harder to live out its message in daily interpersonal relationships. As I have completed the book of proverbs, I ask You to help me to read it again and again so that I may live its truths, heed its admonitions and embrace its wisdom. In the name of Jesus Christ, I pray. Amen.

TODAY'S CHALLENGE: To be a virtuous person.

What else is God saying to me today?

What is my response?

DAY ONE HUNDRED AND SIXTY: READ Ecclesiastes 1-3

The preacher in this book concludes that all of human wisdom and labor is vanity because life is a continuum. "That which has been is what will be, that which is done is what will be done." He concludes that human wisdom is vanity and increases sorrow.

He also finds that there is vanity in sensual pleasure, in accomplishments, indulgencies and wealth. All attempts at fulfillment are like grasping for the wind. None of this has permanent value to the preacher.

In chapter three, he concludes that there is a time and season for everything under the sun, and that God makes everything beautiful in its time.

PRAYER
Dear Lord,
All of life is vain without Your purpose being fulfilled in it. Help me to not pursue those things that are like "grasping for the wind," but, rather to seek those things that have eternal purpose and value. Help me to discern each season of my life and trust You to make it beautiful in its time. I ask this in the name of the Lord Jesus Christ. Amen.

TODAY'S CHALLENGE: To not invest in things and activities that are empty.

What else is God saying to me today?

What is my response?

DAY ONE HUNDRED AND SIXTY-ONE: READ Ecclesiastes 4-6

The preacher observes the oppression of the poor and has no comforter. He compares their plight with the dead and concludes that never having existed is better. He also observes the vanity of selfish toll and the blessings of a friend. "Two are better than one."

He observes also that popularity is vanity and grasping for the wind. He admonishes one to walk prudently in the house of God and not utter anything hastily before God.

He concludes that it is good and fitting for one to eat and drink and enjoy his labor, this is his heritage from God. He sees futility in having wealth only to lose it and to labor and not be satisfied.

PRAYER
Dear Lord,
These sayings reflect the frustration of a life that accomplishes everything and still is futile. I thank You that this does not have to be so. God is able to give design, purpose, and direction to one's life. I pray for a life that is both blessed and fulfilling. In the name of Jesus Christ, I pray. Amen.

TODAY'S CHALLENGE: To sift through all that is vanity and select that which is good.

What else is God saying to me today?

What is my response?

DAY ONE HUNDRED AND SIXTY-TWO: READ Ecclesiastes 7-9

The preacher states that a good name is superior to precious ointment and observes that seeing another's death might have an effect on the living so that they will think about their own life.

He admonishes one to seek wisdom, and to obey civil as well as divine authority. He observes that because the wicked are not punished immediately, they set their hearts to do evil; but wisdom is superior to folly and better than strength.

PRAYER
O Lord, You observe the righteous and the wicked at all times. You also control life and death. I pray that my days on earth will bring You glory and not be spent foolishly. I pray to not compromise with sin, but, to understand that Your mercy and grace do not prevent You from punishing the wicked. In the name of Jesus Christ, I pray. Amen.

TODAY'S CHALLENGE: To value each moment of my life.

What else is God saying to me today?

What is my response?

DAY ONE HUNDRED AND SIXTY-THREE:
READ Ecclesiastes 10-12

The preacher juxtaposes folly and wisdom through various scenarios. He also gives advice on investing as well as charitably giving. He admonishes the young to seek God in their youth and put away youthful fleshly desires.

The preacher uses allegory to encourage young people to serve God while they are young. It is vain to think that youth will last. His conclusion of the whole matter is this. "Fear God and keep His commandments for this is the whole duty of man, for God will bring every work into judgment, including every secret thing, whether good or evil."

PRAYER
O Dear Lord,
I seek Your wisdom in all of life's affairs. I pray for Your guidance and direction and the strength to resist folly and make wise choices. Help me to serve God with my whole heart while I have health, strength, and vitality. I also pray that my works, even the secret things, will bring glory and honor to You. In the name of Jesus Christ, I pray. Amen.

TODAY'S CHALLENGE: To serve God wholly while I have strength.

What else is God saying to me today?

What is my response?

DAY ONE HUNDRED AND SIXTY-FOUR:
READ SONG OF SOLOMON 1-4

INTRODUCTION
Called the Song of Songs, this book contains much allegory and is written like a one-act drama. The characters are: The Shulamite, (the bride) the King, (the groom) and the Daughters of Jerusalem.

The bride speaks to her beloved, as well as the daughters of Jerusalem. She is inviting his affection. She takes inventory of her own beauty, dark, but lovely, tanned by the sun. There is dialog between the bride and groom as they express their mutual attraction and admiration.

The Shulamite tells the daughters of Jerusalem of her experiences in the house of her beloved. She then relates his visit to her house.

The Shulamite tells of a dream that she has. The groom praises the bride's beauty in detail and the wedding is consummated.

PRAYER
Dear Lord,
Thank You for the beauty of romantic love, and for the institution of marriage; which is a type of God's relationship with His people. I pray for Your love to be modeled in marriages that You have ordained. May we also see that You love Your people and desire to have intimate fellowship with us. I welcome and invite that fellowship with You, Dear Lord. In the name of Jesus Christ. Amen.

TODAY'S CHALLENGE: To freely express my love to God and to those who are close to me.

What else is God saying to me today?

What is my response?

DAY ONE HUNDRED AND SIXTY-FIVE:
READ Song of Solomon 5-8

The groom speaks, then the Shulamite sleeps, but, says that her heart is awake. The daughters of Jerusalem question her undivided devotion and enthrallment of her beloved. What makes him so special? She describes the virtues that she cherishes in him, both physically and spiritually.

The Beloved (groom) praises his bride's beauty. He describes her as more beautiful than Tirzah, more lovely than Jerusalem. Although there are many others available to him, he says that she is the perfect one, the only one.

PRAYER
Dear Lord,
What a beautiful love story! I pray for myself and those of Your children who desire such to have a renewed appreciation for the love that You created between husband and wife. In the name of Jesus Christ. Amen.

TODAY'S CHALLENGE: To pray for marriages.

What else is God saying to me today?

What is my response?

DAY ONE HUNDRED AND SIXTY-SIX: READ I Kings 1-4

King David is very old, and cannot be comforted. His son, Adonijah, the son of Haggith exalts himself saying. "I will be king!" Certain men follow him. Nathan, the prophet informs Bathsheba and tells her to tell King David and to remind him that the throne was promised to her son, Solomon. Upon hearing the news, King David commands Zadok the priest to anoint Solomon and bring him to Gihon. There Solomon is seated on David's throne.

Adonijah and his followers hear the news and are terrified. The followers flee and Adonijah goes and takes hold of the horns of the altar. Solomon tells him that he will not be harmed if he is found worthy and sends him home.

King David charges Solomon, "Be strong therefore and prove yourself a man."He gives Solomon certain instructions and after a forty year reign David rests with his fathers and is buried. Solomon's takes the throne and his kingdom is firmly established. He has Adonijah executed after he asks for his father's concubine, Abishag. Joab and Shimei are also executed and Abiathar is exiled.

Solomon marries a daughter of the Pharaoh of Egypt. God appears to Solomon and says, "Ask! What shall I give you?" Solomon humbly asks for an understanding heart, to judge God's people and to discern between good and evil. God commends Solomon for his request and promises him unparalled wisdom. He also promises to give Solomon what he did not ask for, both riches and honor like no king before or after him.

Solomon's wisdom is displayed in a dispute between two women and a child who died. His fame spreads throughout Israel. God gives him wisdom above all the men of the East and of Egypt. Men of all nations come to hear the wisdom of Solomon. Israel and Judah dwell safely all the days of Solomon's reign.

PRAYER
Dear God In Heaven,
Thank You for remembering and honoring Your promises to Your children as David remembered and honored his promise to Solomon so that Your will was done. When it seems like the promises that You have made to me are being taken away or intercepted, help me to run to You so that You can restore what is rightfully mine. I also ask You for an understanding heart, and the ability to discern what is good and evil. In the name of Jesus Christ, I pray. Amen.

TODAY'S CHALLENGE: To only pray for wisdom today.

What else is God saying to me today?

What is my response?

DAY ONE HUNDRED AND SIXTY-SEVEN: READ I Kings 5-7

Solomon informs Hiram, King of Tire, a friend of his father David, that he plans to build a house for the name of the Lord. Solomon buys cedar and cypress logs from him. In exchange he gives him wheat and oil.

King Solomon also raises up a labor force from among the Israelites. All the materials are gathered to build the temple. God speaks to Solomon and promises to dwell among them if they keep His commandments and walk in them.

The temple is elaborately and intricately designed according to Solomon's specifications. It is completed in seven years. Solomon then builds his house with the judgment hall, elaborate fixtures and great rooms. It takes thirteen years to build Solomon's house.

PRAYER
Dear Lord,
May whatever I do for You be of the best quality that I can offer. I pray that You will be pleased to manifest Your presence with me and the work that I desire to do for You. I pray for the wisdom and discipline to keep Your commandments and walk in them so that my work does not become a substitute for my intimate fellowship and relationship with You. In the name of Jesus Christ, I pray. Amen.

TODAY'S CHALLENGE: To get God's design for my ministry and fulfill it.

What else is God saying to me today?

What is my response?

DAY ONE HUNDRED AND SIXTY-EIGHT: READ I Kings 8-10

After the temple is completed with all of its decorations and elaborate fixtures and furnishings, Solomon calls an assembly with all of the elders of Israel. The priests take the Ark into the Holy Place. When they come out, the cloud of God fills the house of the Lord and the priests cannot continue ministering because the Glory of the Lord fills the house of the Lord.

Solomon blesses the entire congregation. He then blesses the Lord for honoring his father, David. He stands before the altar of God, in the presence of the congregation, spreads out his hands toward heaven and prays. He then rises and blesses the congregation. The people bring sacrifices before the Lord and rejoice. Solomon holds a feast for fourteen days. God appears to Solomon a second time and acknowledges that he sanctifies His house. He admonishes Solomon to walk in integrity of heart and uprightness.

Solomon also builds a fleet of ships and builds other cities. The queen of Sheba visits Solomon and is breathless at his splendor. She says, "Your wisdom and prosperity exceed the fame of which I heard." She gives him unique gifts also. King Solomon surpasses all the kings of the earth in riches and wisdom.

PRAYER
Dear God,
I pray for Your blessings and presence as I strive to follow Your plan and complete my divine assignments. I welcome Your presence to fill my life so that I can only rejoice in You. I pray for You to use my life, gifts and talents so that their excellence will bring glory to You. In the name of Jesus Christ, I pray. Amen.

TODAY'S CHALLENGE: To seek God's approval on what I build.

What else is God saying to me today?

What is my response?

DAY ONE HUNDRED AND SIXTY-NINE: READ I Kings 11-13

Solomon intermarries with many foreign women who God had forbidden the Israelites to marry. In his old age, his wives turn his heart to other gods. Solomon does evil in the sight of the Lord. Therefore God tells him that He will tear the kingdom away from him and give it to his servant. Only one tribe will remain for the sake of his father, David, and for Jerusalem. The Lord raises up adversaries against Solomon; among them is his servant, Jeroboam. The prophet, Ahijah, tells Jeroboam that God will tear ten tribes of Israel out of the hand of Solomon and give it to him. Solomon seeks to kill Jeroboam, but, he flees to Egypt and remains there until the death of Solomon.

After Solomon's death, Rehoboam, Solomon's son, goes to Shechem to be inaugurated as king. The children of Israel send for Jeroboam. Together they speak to Rehoboam, asking him to make their tax burden lighter. Rehoboam rejects the counsel of the elders who advise him to deal kindly with the people. He follows the advice of his younger peers who advise him to speak harshly to the people. The people refuse to follow Rehoboam. Instead they make Jeroboam king over them.

Jeroboam does evil in the sight of the Lord. He leads the people into idolatry and makes priests of anyone who desires the office. One day a man of God begins to prophesy to the altar as a witness against Jeroboam and the ungodly priests. Jeroboam stretches out his hands to have the man arrested. His hand withers and freezes in place. He cries out to the man of God to intercede for him and his hand is restored. He still does not repent. As a result, God promises to exterminate and destroy the house of Jeroboam from the face of the earth. Sadly, the prophet who brought the word of God to Jeroboam is deceived by another prophet, who cause him to disobey God and he is killed by a lion.

PRAYER
Dear Lord,
How could Solomon, who possessed such wisdom and favor turn away from You? How many practices and people are there in my life that may be slowly eroding my faith in You and my dedication to You. Please cleanse my heart and life and help me to follow You wholly. In the name of Jesus Christ, I pray. Amen.

TODAY'S CHALLENGE: To obey God fully.

What else is God saying to me today?

What is my response?

DAY ONE HUNDRED AND SEVENTY: READ I Kings 14-16

Jeroboam's son becomes ill. He tells his wife to disguise herself and go and ask the prophet whether the child will live. God tells the prophet, Abijah, who she is and he tells her that God will bring disaster upon the house of Jeroboam and the child will die because of all of the evil that Jeroboam did before the Lord.

Rehoboam reigns for seventeen years in Judah and does evil in the sight of the Lord. He dies and his son, Abijam reigns as king of Judah. He also does evil in the sight of God. After his death, his son, Asa reigns. He does right in the sight of the lord and reigns for forty-one years. Meanwhile Israel has five Kings, the fifth being Zimri. After his death the people of Israel are divided. Half of them follow Omri, half follow Tibni. Omri quickly defeats Tibni and he alone reigns as the sixth king of Israel. He perpetuates Jeroboam's evil and does worse than all who were king before him.

In the thirty-eighth year of Asa's reign, Ahab, the son of Omri becomes king over Israel. He reigns for twenty-two years. Ahab does more evil than all of the kings before him to provoke the Lord's anger. He adds to his rebellion, the marriage of a staunch worshipper of Baal, Jezebel.

PRAYER
Dear Lord,
Thank You for giving us a choice to either follow good or evil. We are not destined to follow the evil of those before us. This day, I submit myself to You and Your will for my life. I pray that what I pass on to others will be a testimony of continued faithfulness to God. In the name of Jesus Christ, I pray. Amen.

TODAY'S CHALLENGE: To resist the sin of rebellion.

What else is God saying to me today?

What is my response?

DAY ONE HUNDRED AND SEVENTY-ONE:
READ I Kings 17-19

During the wicked rule of Ahab and Jezebel, God raises up one of history's most powerful prophets, Elijah, the Tishbite from the region of Gilead. Elijah enters the scene with a challenge to the god, Baal, whose followers believe control the weather. Elijah declares to Ahab. "There shall not be dew nor rain these three years except at my word." God then directs Elijah to go to the brook, Cherith, where he is sustained and fed by ravens. After the brook dries up, God directs Elijah to the house of a widow who needs a miracle. After making Elijah a cake first, her food is miraculously sustained. Sometimes later, the woman's son dies and is raised up by the prophet.

After three years, the Lord sends Elijah back to Ahab. God promises Elijah that he will now send rain to the earth. Upon their meeting, Elijah tells Ahab to gather all of the children of Israel at Mount Carmel. There, in a spectacular display of power, Elijah publicly challenges the prophets of Baal and defeats them. He challenges the children of Israel to choose whom they will serve. They begin to proclaim God as the Lord. Elijah commands them to seize the prophets of Baal and four hundred and fifty are executed. Elijah tells Ahab to hurry home before the rain overtakes him. The spirit of the Lord comes upon Elijah and he makes it to the entrance of Jezreel where Ahab lives before Ahab and his chariots arrive.

When Ahab tells Jezebel what Elijah has done, she issues a death threat to Elijah. Elijah runs for his life. He rests in the wilderness under a broom tree and prays. "It is enough! Now Lord, take my life." He sleeps, but is awakened by an angel who feeds him. He sleeps again. The angel of the Lord returns and tells him to eat. The food sustains him for forty days and nights. He goes to Mount Horeb where God speaks to him in a 'still small voice.' God tells Elijah to go to Damascus. On his way he is to anoint Hazael as king over Syria and Jehu king over Israel. He is to anoint Elisha, the son of Shephat as prophet in his place.

PRAYER
Dear Lord,
Thank You that in the midst of evil, You always raise up someone who will speak Your word. When I become weary in warfare as Elijah did, please sustain me and complete the work in me that You have begun. In the name of Jesus Christ, I pray. Amen.

TODAY'S CHALLENGE: To understand that obedience to God might bring reprisal.

What else is God saying to me today?

What is my response?

DAY ONE HUNDRED AND SEVENTY-TWO:
READ I Kings 20-22

Ben-Hadad, King of Syria gather forces with thirty-two kings and make war against Samaria. They send a challenge to Ahab. A prophet tells Ahab that God will give victory over the Syrians. After the Syrians are defeated, they suppose that Israel's God is God of the hills, but, if they battle the Israelites in the valley, they will win. God gives Israel victory to show them that He is God of the mountain and God of the valley. Ahab makes a treaty with Ben-Hadad. A prophet tells Ahab,"Thus says the Lord: 'Because you have let slip out of your hand a man whom I appointed to utter destruction, therefore your life shall go for his life and your people for his people.'" The king goes home sullen and displeased.

Ahab covets the vineyard of Naboth, a Jezrelite. Naboth will not relinquish it because it was a family inheritance. When the countenance of Ahab fell because of this, Jezebel has Naboth killed and tells Ahab to go and possess his vineyard.

God sends Elijah to meet him and pronounce judgment on Ahab, Jezebel and Ahab's posterity. Ahab repents. God relents and promises to bring the calamity during the lifetime of Ahab's son.

For three years there is no war between Syria and Israel. Jehoshaphat, king of Judah visits Ahab. He goes out to war with him against the advice of the prophet, Micaiah, the prophet. Jehoshaphat is almost killed in battle. Ahab is killed. Jehoshaphat follows his father, Asa, and does right in the sight of the Lord.

PRAYER
Dear Lord,
I thank You that You are God of the valleys and God of the mountains. I thank You for Your mercy and grace on the just as well as the unjust. I invite You, Lord, to be my wisdom, and lead me into victory. In the name of Jesus Christ. Amen.

TODAY'S CHALLENGE: To trust God for victory in the valley as well as on the mountain.

What else is God saying to me today?

What is my response?

DAY ONE HUNDRED AND SEVENTY-THREE: READ II Kings 1-3

After the death of Ahab, Moab rebels against Israel. Ahaziah falls in his house and is injured. He inquires of Baal-Zebub as to whether he will recover. God sends Elijah to intercept, asking. "Is there not a God in Israel?" He informs the messenger that Ahaziah will die of his injury. The king sends two companies of men to bring Elijah and kill him. They all die by fire from heaven. The leader of the third company, begs Elijah to spare his life and the life of his men. Elijah goes with the men and tells Ahaziah that he will die. Ahaziah dies according to the word of Elijah.

When the Lord is about to take Elijah to heaven by a whirlwind, Elisha will not leave his side. When asked what he wants, Elisha asks for a double portion of Elijah's spirit to be upon him. This request is granted when he sees Elijah taken into heaven and his mantle falls upon Elisha. He takes the mantle, divides the waters of the Jordan and begins to perform miracles also.

Jehoram, the son of Ahab becomes king over Israel in Samaria. He does evil in the sight of the Lord, but, not as wickedly as his parents, Ahab and Jezebel. He entreats Jehoshaphat, king of Judah, to fight with him against the Moabites. Because of Jehoshaphat, God helps them to defeat the Moabites.

PRAYER
Dear Heavenly Father,
Thank You that You remember and defend the righteous. Thank You that You are my God and King. I ask for Your spirit to rest upon me also, so that I will be able to perform every work that You have for me to do on the earth. In the name of Jesus Christ, I pray. Amen.

TODAY'S CHALLENGE: To earnestly desire God's anointing.

What else is God saying to me today?

What is my response?

DAY ONE HUNDRED AND SEVENTY-FOUR:
READ II Kings 4-6

A certain widow cries out to Elijah for help. Creditors are threatening to take her two sons as slaves. He tells her to take the only thing she has in her house; a jar of oil. She follows the directive of the prophet and is able to pay off her creditors, and she and her sons live on the rest.

One day Elisha goes to Shunem. A notable woman makes a special room for him. Elisha tells her that she will have a son. After the son grows, he becomes ill while in the field with his father. The child dies. The faith of the Shunamite woman echoes through history. "It shall be well," she confesses to everyone she meets. She finds Elisha who prays and God miraculously raises the child from the dead. On another occasion, as Elisha returns to Gilgal, a pot of stew that is being prepared is accidentally poisoned. Elisha puts flour in the pot and the poison dissipates. Other miracles that he performs include the healing of Naaman, who had leprosy, causing an ax head to float, and the blinding of Syrian invaders.

Ben-Hadad besieges Samaria and there is a famine so severe that a donkey's head and dove droppings are sold for silver, and certain people resort to cannibalism.

PRAYER
Dear Lord,
Thank You for such displays of Your miraculous power. I invite You, the Lord God, who works miracles to perform, into my life. The miracles that mere human endeavors could never orchestrate. I thank You, in the name of my Lord and Savior Jesus Christ. Amen.

TODAY'S CHALLENGE: To say in the face of great trials "It is well."

What else is God saying to me today?

What is my response?

DAY ONE HUNDRED AND SEVENTY-FIVE:
READ II Kings 7-10

In spite of the great famine, Elisha tells the Elders that the famine will be over within twenty-four hours.

There are four men with leprosy at the entrance of the gate of Samaria. They decide to surrender to the Syrians in hopes of saving their lives. When they arise at twilight to enter the camp of the Syrians, no one is there. The Lord had caused the Syrians to hear the noise of a great army and they had run away hastily in fear, leaving all of their animals, tents, food, clothing silver and gold behind. The four men report this to the king. After being convinced that it is not a trap, the people plunder the tents of the Syrians and Elisha's prophesy is fulfilled. The king also returns the Shunamite woman's land back to her.

Elisha foretells the death of Ben-Hadad, king of Syria. He weeps as God reveals to him the evil that Hazael will do to the children of Israel. Hazael suffocates Ben-Hadad and begins to reign in his place.

Meanwhile, Jehoram, the son of Jehoshaphat begins to reign in Judah. He does evil just as Ahab had done. He marries Athaliah, the daughter of Ahab and Jezebel. God tells Elisha to anoint Jehu, son of Jehoshaphat king of Israel. Jehu kills Jehoram and Ahaziah. He has the priests throw Jezebel down from a window and the dogs eat her flesh just as Elijah had foretold. Ahab's seventy sons and all that remain of his household are executed. Jehu also calls for a meeting of all Baal worshippers and has them killed. However, Jehu does not stop the worship of the golden calves.

PRAYER
Most Holy Awesome God,
There is nothing impossible for You. You can bring deliverance out of disaster and feast out of famine in the twinkling of an eye. When I am faced with situations that look hopeless, please help me to remember the story of the four lepers. You are a God who is forever faithful. In Jesus name, I pray. Amen.

TODAY'S CHALLENGE: To know that God never runs out of resources.

What else is God saying to me today?

What is my response?

DAY ONE HUNDRED AND SEVENTY-SIX: READ 11-14:20

In Judah, Athaliah, the mother of Ahaziah destroys all of the royal heirs after the death of her son. Only Joash is hidden from her wrath. He is hidden for six years in the house of the Lord and Athaliah reigns over the land. After six years Jehoiada the priest organizes the people and brings out the king's son. They kill Athaliah and at eight years old, Joash is crowned king of Judah. Under the guidance of Jehoiada the priest and his mother, Zibiah, Joash does what is right in the sight of the Lord. He repairs the temple. Later in order to appease Hazael, Joash gives him the temple treasures. After a forty-year reign, Joash's servants revolt and kill him in the house of Millo.

Jehoahaz, the son of Jehu becomes king over Israel and does evil. The Lord delivers them into the hands of Hazael, king of Syria. Jehoahaz pleads with the Lord and He sends a deliverer, but the people do not depart from their sins.

Elisha becomes ill. Before he dies he presents an illustrated prophesy to Jehoahaz who does not participate fully and cuts short his ability to defeat Syria. Elisha dies and is buried. Later that year a young man who died in battle is buried in Elisha's tomb. When his body touches the bones of Elisha, he revives and stands on his feet.

PRAYER
Dear Lord,
It is so apparent that positions of influence and authority come with great responsibility. I pray to walk humbly before You and those who I lead or influence. Help me not to do evil as so many of Israel and Judah's kings did. If I sin and You deliver me, please help me to be so grateful that I will completely forsake that sin and cling to You. In the name of Jesus Christ, I pray. Amen.

TODAY'S CHALLENGE: To let God put me in the position that He has for me and not to resort to manipulation and deceit in order to get promoted.

What else is God saying to me today?

What is my response?

DAY ONE HUNDRED AND SEVENTY-SEVEN: READ Joel 1-3

Joel's name means "Yahweh Is God." During his ministry, the land of Judah is wasted due to their idolatry. The prophet Joel calls the attention of the elders. He commands them to take note of this complete and unparalleled destruction and to understand that it is a judgment from God. He describes the nation that oppresses them as a "warlike nation with teeth of a lion."

The wine has been cut off from the mouth of the drunkard, the grain and drink offering has been cut off from the priests. Every living thing has withered or been devoured. He admonishes the priests to lament and lie all night in sack cloth, to consecrate a fast, a sacred assembly and cry out to the Lord.

He tells the people that the day of the Lord is at hand. He describes an ominous invasion and calls the people to repentance. He also commands a blowing of the trumpets to call the people to assemble and fast. He tells them that the land will eventually be refreshed. He speaks prophetically of a time when God will cause His people to rejoice. God will restore them with abundance, remove the shame and afterwards pour out His spirit on future generations. He will also judge the oppressing nation for their violence against Judah and He will bless His people again.

PRAYER
Dear Lord,
Please never let me be so blind or so deaf that I cannot see what You are doing or hear what You are saying to me. Help me to hear and obey Your call to seasons of fasting and prayer. Deliver me from all forms of idolatry so that Your judgment will not fall on me or my posterity. In the name of Jesus Christ. Amen.

TODAY'S CHALLENGE: To answer the trumpet's call to fast.

What else is God saying to me today?

What is my response?

DAY ONE HUNDRED AND SEVENTY-EIGHT:
READ II Kings 14:21-25/Jonah 1-4

Sixteen year old, Azariah is made king of Judah instead of his father. Jeroboam, son of Joash becomes king of Israel and Samaria. He does evil in the sight of God. He restores certain territory of Israel as God had spoken by the prophet Jonah.

God uses Jonah, the prophet, the son of Amittai during the time of Jeroboam II's reigned in Israel. He restores territory from Hamuth to the Sea of Arabah. He does evil in the sight of the Lord. Jonah is commissioned by God to go about 500 miles to Nineveh, a city of the Assyrians, who were long-standing enemies of Israel.

God tells Jonah to go to the great city of Nineveh and cry out against it because of their wickedness. In disobedience, Jonah boards a ship and flees to Tarshish to escape the presence of the Lord. The sea becomes tempestuous and Jonah tells the mariners his story and that they must throw him overboard in order to calm the sea. Reluctantly, they do so. Meanwhile, God had prepared a great fish which He commands to swallow Jonah. He was in the belly of the fish for three days and three nights. Jonah then calls out to the Lord from his Abyss. God speaks to the fish and it vomits Jonah onto dry ground.

Again God commands Jonah to go and preach to the Ninevites. The people of Nineveh heeds Jonah's warning and repent with fasting. Because they repent, God relents from the disaster that he said He would bring upon them. Jonah becomes angry because of God's mercy. Jonah tells God that this was the reason that he did not want to preach to the Ninevites. God chides Jonah for his selfishness.

PRAYER
Dear Heavenly Father,
Thank You for the mercy that You showed to both Jonah and the inhabitants of Nineveh. When I desire to see Your punishment on the wicked, help me to remember that in many ways I am too. I pray for Your grace and mercy for myself and for all people everywhere. In the name of Jesus Christ, I pray. Amen.

TODAY'S CHALLENGE: To realize that God loves everybody.

What else is God saying to me today?

What is my response?

DAY ONE HUNDRED AND SEVENTY-NINE:
READ II Kings 14:26-29/ Amos 1-3

Although God judges Israel, He does not say that He will blot out her name from under heaven, but He delivers them by the hand of Jeroboam.

Amos, the herdsman prophet, announces the demise of both Judah and Israel. Although they presently enjoy prosperity, he points out their various transgressions and declares judgment. He speaks judgment on Damascus, Gaza, Tyre, Edom, Ammon, Moab, as well as Judah and Israel. Although the foreign nations have no covenant with the God of Israel, judgment is pronounced upon them for their mistreatment of Israel and many other nations.

The children of Israel will be punished for all of their iniquities. Amos asks a series of rhetorical questions such as: "Can two walk together unless they are agreed?" He deduces that the Lord will do nothing unless He reveals it to His servants, the prophets.

PRAYER
Dear Lord,
In times of prosperity, help me to never forget the Lord, my Deliverer. Help me to remember that You will reward my faithfulness, but will punish my disobedience. In the name of Jesus Christ, I pray. Amen.

TODAY'S CHALLENGE: I have a covenant with Almighty God.

What else is God saying to me today?

What is my response?

DAY ONE HUNDRED AND EIGHTY: READ Amos 4-6

Amos, whose name means "Burden Bearer," addresses the women who are married to principal men, but, who oppress the poor as cows of Basham. He points out the hypocrisy of the people who offer public sacrifices, but whose deeds are wicked. He points out a series of natural disasters that have come upon them, yet they fail to repent. He instructs the house of Israel to seek the Lord and live. He warns that if they do not repent, God will cause there to be 'wailing in the streets and highways' because of their idolatry and they will be taken into captivity.

Amos speaks woe to those who are at ease in Zion and trust in Samaria. God will raise up a nation against them. He emphasizes the fact that God does not accept their offerings or songs, rather He says, "Let justice run down like water and righteousness like a mighty stream." He warns Zion and Samaria to not revel in their comfort and unjust practices because the Lord will afflict them.

PRAYER
Dear Lord,
Please give me the wisdom to enjoy Your blessings without becoming indifferent to the needs of others, to live in Your protection without becoming smug and to walk proudly as Your child without arrogance. In the name of Jesus Christ, I pray. Amen.

TODAY'S CHALLENGE: To take heed to true prophetic voices.

What else is God saying to me today?

What is my response?

DAY ONE HUNDRED AND EIGHTY-ONE: READ Amos 7-9

Amos describes a vision that God shows him. He sees a swarm of locusts eating the grass of the land. He intercedes and God relents. God then shows him conflict by fire. Again Amos intercedes and God relents. However, eventually God's judgment will be poured out. He describes signs in nature and a time of famine for the word of God.

Amos also speaks of a future restoration of Israel after God judges all of the sinners of His people. God will raise up the ruins. God will replant them in their land and they will no longer be pulled up.

PRAYER
Dear Merciful Lord,
I invite You to build up the waste places in my spirit, soul and body. Please repair the damaged areas of my life and replant them, according to Your wisdom and will. In the name of Jesus Christ, I pray. Amen.

TODAY'S CHALLENGE: To invite God to raise up the ruined places in my life.

What else is God saying to me today?

What is my response?

DAY ONE HUNDRED AND EIGHTY-TWO:
READ II Kings 15-17

Azariah, the son of Amaziah becomes king of Judah during the twenty-seventh year of the reign of Jeroboam, king of Israel. He is sixteen years old when he begins to reign and reigns for fifty-two years. He did what was right in the sight of the Lord. But he did not remove the high places from where the people burned incense. The Lord strikes the king and he is a leper until he dies. He dwells in isolation in his house and Jotham, his son, judges the people of the land.

Zechariah begins to reign over Israel during the thirty-eighth year of Azariah's reign. He does evil in the sight of the Lord. His son, Shallum kills him publicly and reigns in his stead. Israel has nineteen kings. All of them do wickedly in the sight of the Lord. Because of their persistent idolatry and disobedience to God, He allows the Assyrians to take them into captivity.

PRAYER
Dear Heavenly Father,
I pray that You may never need to allow my enemies to rule over me. I surrender all areas of my life to You, and ask You to keep my life pure and free from idolatry and disobedience. In the name of Jesus Christ, I pray. Amen.

TODAY'S CHALLENGE: To discern what is evil in the sight of the Lord and not do it.

What else is God saying to me today?

What is my response?

DAY ONE HUNDRED AND EIGHTY-THREE: READ Hosea 1-4

Hosea's name means "Salvation" or "Deliverance." The word of the Lord comes to Hosea as a final warning just before Israel is taken into captivity for her continued disobedience and idolatry.

God dramatizes His relationship with Israel through Hosea's relationship with his harlot-wife, Gomer. Gomer bears Hosea a son and God tells him to name him Jezreel, because he would soon avenge the bloodshed of the city of Jezreel. Gomer conceives again. This time she bears a daughter, Lo-Ruhamah, meaning "I will no longer have mercy on the house of Israel." After Lo-Rhumah is weaned, Gomer conceives and bears a son, Lo-Ammi; meaning, "you are not my people, and I will not be your God." Yet God says that He will eventually restore Israel.

Hosea describes the unfaithfulness of Israel and the mercies of God. The Lord then tells Hosea to go again and love his wife who is committing adultery just as Israel is doing. As Israel increases, their sins increase. However the prophet says that in the future Israel will fear the Lord.

PRAYER
Dear Lord,
I pray for the gift and blessing of being faithful to You and in all of my relationships. Thank You for Your great love that pursues me unconditionally. Let me never take Your love for granted, may You never call me Lo-Ruhamah or Lo-Ammi. In the name of Jesus Christ, I pray. Amen.

TODAY'S CHALLENGE: To not walk away from God's love.

What else is God saying to me today?

What is my response?

DAY ONE HUNDRED AND EIGHTY-FOUR: READ Hosea 5-7

Hosea tells Israel and Ephraim that their harlotry and defilement is not hidden from God. They as well as Judah stumble in their iniquity. They seek help from Assyria and king Jareb, but, he cannot cure or heal them. Hosea calls the people to return to the Lord. If they repent, he says that God will heal them and revive them. God tells the people that He requires them to show mercy to others, rather than sacrifices: which are an outward form of ritualistic worship.

Hosea laments, that God would have healed Israel, but, in their pride they refused to return to the Lord or to seek him. Ephraim is also captured as a 'silly dove without sense' who seeks help from Egypt and Assyria, but, refuses to cry out to the Lord with their heart.

PRAYER
Dear Lord,
It is so easy to go to church and do good deeds, but, You require a righteous heart. Please help me not to substitute good works for a holy life and a pure heart. I ask You to remove foolish pride from me so that I can be healed in my places of brokenness and seek salvation, in You alone. In the name of Jesus Christ, I pray. Amen.

TODAY'S CHALLENGE: To not offer God *ritual* when He requires righteousness.

What else is God saying to me today?

What is my response?

DAY ONE HUNDRED AND EIGHTY-FIVE: READ Hosea 8-10

Israel has fallen into complete apostasy. The Assyrian army will come upon them like an eagle. The Lord's anger is aroused against them and He will break the calf of Samaria into pieces. Ephraim has hired lovers and made altars for sin. They have continually played the harlot against God and made love for hire.

Hosea warns them: not to rejoice. They have despised the prophets and spiritual man and God will cast them away.

PRAYER
Dear Lord,
Please give me the wisdom to not trade what is good for what is defiled. Help me to remain faithful to You throughout my life so that You will never have to turn away from me. In the name of Jesus Christ, I pray. Amen.

TODAY'S CHALLENGE: To remain faithful to God always.

What else is God saying to me today?

What is my response?

DAY ONE HUNDRED AND EIGHTY-SIX: READ *Hosea 11-14*

God loves Israel in spite of the fact that they sacrificed to Baals and burned incense to carved images. Hosea describes the infinite love of God. His heart breaks as He recalls how He loved Israel as a child in Egypt, taught Ephraim to walk, drew them with bands of love, and stooped to feed them, yet they turned from Him.

Hosea prophesies that after God calls His people back from captivity, they will repent. Hosea reviews Israel's history: noting their tendency to turn from God and follow their own wicked minds.

God speaks through Hosea of how Ephraim made themselves idols of silver, but, God reminds them that He is their only Savior. He longs to be their king, but, they refuse Him and now must bear their sorrow. However, there is redemptive hope. Israel will be restored. In that day, says the Lord, "I will heal their backsliding. I will love them freely." Then they will say. "The ways of the Lord are right."

PRAYER
Dear Heavenly Father,
Help me to stay close to You. Help me to never tire of the sweet fragrance of Your presence. I acknowledge You as my only Savior, my only deliverer and the one who has drawn me with true love. I praise You, thank You, and worship You my Lord and King, in the name of Jesus Christ, I pray. Amen.

TODAY'S CHALLENGE: What good is there in my life that was not provided by the hand of God?

What else is God saying to me today?

What is my response?

DAY ONE HUNDRED AND EIGHTY-SEVEN:
READ II Kings 18, 19

Twenty-five year old Hezekiah, son of Ahaz and Abi, begins to reign in Judah. He does what is right in the sight of the Lord and trusts in Him. The Lord is with him and prospers him. He removes the high places and holds to the Lord's commandments. He rebels against the king of Assyria and does not serve him.

During the fourth year of his reign, the king of Assyria besieges Samaria and takes it. Because they transgressed the laws of God, Israel is taken captive. In the fourteenth year of King Hezekiah's reign, the king of Assyria comes against the fortified cities of Judah. Hezekiah repents to the king of Assyria and pays him silver and gold. He even strips the gold from the temple and gives it to him.

King Sennacherib's servants tell the people to surrender and not trust in Hezekiah or the Lord. Upon hearing this, Hezekiah goes into the house of the Lord. God tells Isaiah to tell Hezekiah not to be afraid. Hezekiah prays to God and in the end, the angel of the Lord kills one hundred and eighty-five thousand Assyrians and king Sennacherib's own sons kill him as he worships in the temple of Nisroch his god.

PRAYER
Dear God,
In the face of threatening circumstances, and when I am afraid, I turn to You and pray. I believe that You will hear me and deliver me as I walk upright before You as king Hezekiah did. Thank You for the angels that fight also for me. Grant me victory in every battle, I pray in the name of Jesus Christ. Amen.

TODAY'S CHALLENGE: To ignore the voice and threats of the enemy.

What else is God saying to me today?

What is my response?

DAY ONE HUNDRED AND EIGHTY-EIGHT: READ Isaiah 1-3

Isaiah, the prophet, whose name means "Yahweh Is Salvation," has visions concerning Judah and Jerusalem during the reigns of Uzziah, Jotham, Ahaz, and Hezekiah, kings of Judah.

He calls heaven and earth to witness against the wickedness and apostasy of Judah. He refers to the ox and the donkey, saying that even they know their owners, but, God's people have forsaken Him and provoked His anger. He says that their sinfulness warrants destruction as Sodom and Gomorrah, but, God has left a remnant.

He admonishes the people to wash themselves from their evil. He bemoans the degeneration of a city, once faithful, now a harlot. Israel will be judged and humbled because of her haughtiness, but, Isaiah also foresees that in the latter days the mountain of the Lord's house will be re-established.

PRAYER
O Dear God in Heaven,
Please help me to stay close to You, so that the sweet fragrance of Your presence and Your voice will continue to draw me closer to You. Help me to NEVER forget that You are my Lord and my Salvation. In the name of Jesus Christ, I pray. Amen.

TODAY'S CHALLENGE: To always stay so close to God that I can hear him even if he *whispers*.

What else is God saying to me today?

What is my response?

DAY ONE HUNDRED AND EIGHTY-NINE: READ Isaiah 4-6

Isaiah prophesies that in the day of God's judgment, there will be no more glorious covering for Israel. Only after God washes the filth of the daughters of Zion will there be a covering, a place of refuge and shelter for Israel.

The prophet uses allegory to describe the infidelity of Israel and the wild off-spring that she produces as a result. He speaks woe to those who indulge in excesses and practice wickedness. They shall be brought low.

In the year of king Uzziah's death, Isaiah sees a vision of God's throne. Seraphim cry, "Holy, holy, holy is the Lord of hosts; the whole earth is full of His glory." A vision of God's holiness causes Isaiah to realize the uncleanness of his own lips and those of the people around him. An angel takes a coal of fire from the altar and touches his lips and tells him that his iniquity is taken away. Isaiah answers God's call to go as a messenger to His people.

PRAYER
Dear Lord,
Help me to recognize and reject all things that beckon me from the protection of Your covering. Help me to not indulge in excesses or practice wickedness. Touch me and take away my iniquity so that I too can go as Your messenger to those to whom You desire to send me. In the name of Jesus Christ, I pray. Amen.

TODAY'S CHALLENGE: To be cleansed and prepared to answer God's call.

What else is God saying to me today?

What is my response?

DAY ONE HUNDRED AND NINETY: READ Isaiah 7-9

When the news of an eminent attack from the Syrians, reaches Ahaz, king of Judah, the people's hearts are moved as the trees of the woods are moved with the wind. God sends Isaiah to speak peace to him, telling him not to fear. God tells Ahaz to ask for a sign of their deliverance, but, Ahaz is afraid to tempt the Lord. God gives this sign, "Behold, the virgin shall conceive and bear a son, and shall call his name Emmanuel. He will learn to refuse the evil and choose the good."

God gives Isaiah a sign that Assyria will be permitted to invade the land. He was told to write the names of his future son, Maher-Shalal-Hash-Baz, on a scroll. Before the child is able to talk, the invasion will take place. He warns the people to fear God and heed His word. God tells the people that the gloom will not last forever. God will send a deliverer. "For unto us a Child is born, unto us a Son is given; and the government will be upon His shoulder, and His name will be called Wonderful, Counselor, Mighty God, Everlasting Father, Prince of Peace."

PRAYER
Dear Lord,
Thank You that in the face of eminent danger You have promised the Prince of Peace. I invite You into every area of my life as my counselor, God, Father and Prince of Peace. In the name of Jesus, I pray. Amen.

TODAY'S CHALLENGE: To learn to refuse the evil and choose the good.

What else is God saying to me today?

What is my response?

DAY ONE HUNDRED AND NINETY-ONE: READ Isaiah 10-12

Isaiah declares woe to those who decree unrighteous decrees that oppress people and take advantage of the weak and vulnerable. He declares that in the day that God metes out punishment, there will be no help for them. Although God allows them to take His people captive in order to chasten them, the Assyrians will also be judged for their arrogance.

Isaiah prophecies that there shall come forth a Rod from the stem of Jesse. He is described this way:

> "The Spirit of the Lord shall rest upon Him,
> The Spirit of wisdom and understanding,
> The Spirit of counsel and might,
> The Spirit of knowledge and of the fear of the Lord." (Isaiah 11:2)

In that day Israel will praise the Lord and claim Him as their Salvation.

PRAYER

Dear God, My Salvation,

Thank You for being a God who is ever watchful and faithful to both punish evil and reward good. You are a just God. If there are areas of my life that have become captive to sin or oppression, I call upon You to help me and deliver me. I also pray for the spirit of righteousness to be upon me so that your blessings can flow to me unhindered. In the name of Jesus Christ, I pray. Amen.

TODAY'S CHALLENGE: To repent so that I do not need to be taken captive.

What else is God saying to me today?

What is my response?

DAY ONE HUNDRED AND NINETY-TWO: READ Isaiah 13-15

Isaiah describes his words as a "burden" against Babylon. God will send His weapons of indignation to destroy the whole land because of its evil. Indeed in the day of God's wrath, judgment will be on the world because of its evil, arrogance, and iniquity.

The Lord will have mercy on Jacob and will still choose Israel and settle them in their own land. They will rule over their oppressors. After Israel's restoration they will sing a proverb against Babylon. Assyria, Phillista and Moab will be destroyed.

PRAYER
Dear Merciful God,
Thank You for not totally destroying the people who are called by Your name. Although we may suffer trials, even chastening, Your promise of restoration is ever our hope. In the name of Jesus Christ, I pray. Amen.

TODAY'S CHALLENGE: To not fall into the category of people who incur the wrath of God.

What else is God saying to me today?

What is my response?

DAY ONE HUNDRED AND NINETY-THREE:
READ Isaiah 16-18

Isaiah intimates that Moab will be destroyed because of its pride and haughtiness. All gladness and joy will be taken away. The Lord tells Isaiah: that within three years, the glory of Moab will cease and only a small, feeble remnant will remain.

Damascus will also cease from being a city, and will be a ruinous heap. There is also a proclamation against Ethiopia who sends ambassadors by sea as weapons against Syria and Israel.

PRAYER
Dear Lord, God,
I here and now reject and resist pride and haughtiness. I pray that I and my family and loved ones will remain steadfast in You and in a place of blessing and fulfillment. In the name of Jesus Christ, I pray. Amen.

TODAY'S CHALLENGE: To not have my joy and gladness removed.

What else is God saying to me today?

What is my response?

DAY ONE HUNDRED AND NINETY-FOUR: READ Isaiah 19-21

Isaiah declares that the idols of Egypt will totter in the presence of the Lord. God will cause internal strife in Egypt and even the rivers will turn foul. In that day, Egypt will be afraid because of what the Lord will do and they will know God. In the future Egypt, Israel and Assyria will *all* be God's people.

The Lord tells Isaiah to remove his sack cloth and sandals and walk around naked, his buttocks exposed. In like manner, the king of Assyria will lead the Ethiopians captive. Isaiah further describes a vision, which culminates with a proclamation that Babylon will be destroyed.

PRAYER
Dear Lord,
Rather than being destroyed along with my idols, I willingly cast them at Your feet. Please reveal to me any idols that are in my life of which I am unaware. I declare You alone as my God and the recipient of all of my worship. In the name of Jesus Christ, Amen.

TODAY'S CHALLENGE: To serve the Lord willingly.

What else is God saying to me today?

What is my response?

DAY ONE HUNDRED AND NINETY-FIVE: READ Isaiah 22-24

The prophet has a burden against the Valley of Vision, Jerusalem. The joyous city will be tread down by the Lord of hosts. On a day, when God called them to mourning, weeping and humility, they celebrated saying, "let us eat and drink for tomorrow we die." For that iniquity God provided no atonement.

The prophet also pronounces judgment on Tyre. Its great ships shall be laid waste because of its pride and idolatry.

Isaiah prophecies of a future time when God will judge all the inhabitants of the earth. It will be universal, no exemptions, no exceptions. He describes destruction by fire. All joy and mirth will be taken away. After the judgment is completed the Lord of hosts will reign on Mount Zion.

PRAYER
Dear Lord,
You are God of the nations. All Nations, cities and people will be judged by You. I pray that the nations especially the one in which I live, the cities, especially mine, and the people, especially I, will acknowledge You as God and live in peace with Your perfect plan. In the name of Jesus Christ, I pray. Amen.

TODAY'S CHALLENGE: To not trust in my accomplishments or abilities, but in my God.

What else is God saying to me today?

What is my response?

DAY ONE HUNDRED AND NINETY-SIX: READ Isaiah 25-27

Isaiah writes a prophetic song which the children of Israel will one day sing. "O Lord, You are my God. I will exalt You. I will praise Your name, for You have done wonderful things." He points out that God has faithfully subdued nations, been a stronghold for the poor and needy in their day of distress and a refuge from the storm.

In that day, a song of salvation will be sung in Judah, including the phrase. "You will keep him in perfect peace whose mind is stayed on You." God will cause His people to take refuge in Him. He will punish Israel's enemies who are as dreadful as Leviathan. God will cause Israel's enemies to perish, but, will cleanse Israel and restore her.

PRAYER
Dear God,
Even in Your chastening of Your people, Your great love is the motivation and restoration is Your goal. Thank You for being a loving Heavenly father who does everything for my good, even chastening me when necessary. In the name of Jesus Christ. Amen.

TODAY'S CHALLENGE: During the time of chastening, to expect and sing of God's restoration.

What else is God saying to me today?

What is my response?

DAY ONE HUNDRED AND NINETY-SEVEN:
READ Isaiah 28-30

Isaiah prophecies woe to Ephraim and Jerusalem to the crown of pride and the drunkenness of Ephraim. Their beauty and might are fading. They will be trampled under foot. The Lord sought to teach them "precept upon precept," but, they scorned knowledge and made a covenant with death.

God will lay siege to Jerusalem and the strength that she once knew will be like an altar of burnt offering in the day of God's judgment because of their disobedience. The people draw near to God with their mouth and honor him with their lips, but, have removed their hearts from him.

God chides them for their rebellion against God. They make plans to take counsel, but, not with the Lord. They reject His guidance and seek alliance with Egypt for their salvation.

PRAYER
Dear Lord,
I pray to cherish and hold dear all that You have given me and that it will not fade through neglect. Please teach me and cause me to understand. I choose to seek Your guidance and I declare my allegiance to You. In the name of Jesus Christ. Amen.

TODAY'S CHALLENGE: To never offer God full words from an empty heart.

What else is God saying to me today?

What is my response?

DAY ONE HUNDRED AND NINETY-EIGHT:
READ Isaiah 31-33

Isaiah reminds the people that the Egyptians are men and not God. Their horses are flesh, not spirit. He tells them that as a young lion roars over his prey, the Lord of hosts will come down to fight for mount Zion and defend Jerusalem. Isaiah speaks of a day when a king will reign in righteousness and princes will rule in justice. He commands the complacent women to rise up and gird themselves with sack cloth.

Because ultimately a remnant of Jerusalem trusts in the lord, those who plunder them and deal treacherously with them will be dealt with treacherously by God. Although Israel will be humbled, they will see the majestic king in His beauty because He will save them.

PRAYER
Dear Lord,
All the strength of men are as nothing before You. When in battle, I ask You to fight for me. In the name of Jesus Christ, I pray. Amen.

TODAY'S CHALLENGE: To rise out of complacency.

What else is God saying to me today?

What is my response?

DAY ONE HUNDRED AND NINETY-NINE: READ Isaiah 34-36

Isaiah continues to speak of God's judgment on those who are rebellious and will not heed the voice of God. God's sword shall be filled with blood; but he prophecies peace to those who are obedient. He assures the people of a time in the future when they shall see the glory of God, when sorrow and sighing shall flee away. Isaiah repeats the account of Sennacherib's boasting and demise as recorded in chapter eighteen.

PRAYER
Dear Lord,
Thank You that those who do wickedly will be punished by God. Help me to walk in obedience to You so that Your peace will dwell with me. Thank You that all of the boasting of the enemy has no power against the decrees of the Lord. In the name of Jesus Christ. Amen.

TODAY'S CHALLENGE: To be quiet when the enemy boasts.

What else is God saying to me today?

What is my response?

DAY TWO HUNDRED: READ Isaiah 37-39

Isaiah assures King Hezekiah that God has heard King Sennacherib's threats as well as Hezekiah's prayers. Sennacherib's army is destroyed and he is murdered by his own sons.

Hezekiah becomes ill and receives a death sentence from God. He turns to the wall and prays. God extends his life for fifteen additional years. He wrote his thoughts during his illness.

During this time, the king of Babylon, having heard that Hezekiah was healed sends letters and a present to him. Hezekiah entertains certain men from Babylon and shows them all of his treasures. Isaiah comes and tells him that some day all that he has shown of his father's possessions will be taken away by the Babylonians. Hezekiah comforts himself with the fact that it will not happen in his lifetime.

PRAYER
Dear Lord God,
You favor righteousness and despise wickedness. Thank You that you will answer prayer miraculously for those who trust in You. I pray for Your blessing of health and freedom from sickness so that I may live the number of years that You have appointed for me on the earth. In the name of Jesus Christ. Amen.

TODAY'S CHALLENGE: To be careful when people come to flatter me.

What else is God saying to me today?

What is my response?

DAY TWO HUNDRED AND ONE: READ Isaiah 40-42

Isaiah moves forward in history and speaks comfort to God's people. God has declared that her warfare is ended, her iniquity pardoned and she has received double for her sins.

The Lord promises restoration of His people. All flesh is as grass before God, and the nations as a drop in a bucket. The Lord comes with a strong hand and He shall feed His flock. The prophet proclaims that the Lord is not faint or weary. "He gives power to the weak. Those who wait on the Lord shall renew their strength." God tells His people to Fear not, the Lord will help and strengthen them and not forsake them.

The promise of God is captured in this favored passage, "Behold the former things have come to pass, and a new thing I declare, before they spring forth I tell you of them."

PRAYER

Dear Lord,

You rejoice when You can bless Your children. Thank You for the exuberance of the words of comfort that Isaiah speaks. I receive and partake of all the blessings, comfort and peace that are my inheritance as a child of God. Please help me to live in a state of perpetual eligibility for your blessings. In the name of Jesus Christ, I pray. Amen.

TODAY'S CHALLENGE: To prepare my heart for the new things that God will do.

What else is God saying to me today?

What is my response?

DAY TWO HUNDRED AND TWO: READ Isaiah 43-45

God calls Israel His redeemed, called by His name. He vows His faithfulness to her through the waters and the fire. He tells them again, "Do not remember the former things, nor consider the things of old. Behold I will do a new thing." God tells Israel that He will not deal with them as before. After their purging, He is ready to blot out their transgressions and bless them. Isaiah points out the folly of idolatry and declares that there is no God, except the Lord.

God sends words to Cyrus, who has not known Him, but who He has known. He promises hidden riches of secret places for the sake of His servant Jacob and Israel His elect.

PRAYER

Dear Lord God Almighty,
You alone are God and Creator of all the heavens and earth. All nations and kings are subject to You. Thank You that You will use circumstances in my life to bless other people. Help me to be a witness of Your sovereignty in all of my affairs of life, knowing that You will be with me through the fire and the waters. In the name of Jesus Christ, I pray Amen.

TODAY'S CHALLENGE: To not limit God in my thinking.

What else is God saying to me today?

What is my response?

DAY TWO HUNDRED AND THREE: READ Isaiah 46-48

God announces to the house of Jacob repeatedly that He alone is God. He will carry them. Idols have no life or power. Babylon, who has been Israel's dreadful oppressor, is called down from its lofty position of power to sit in the dust. Isaiah declares that God will take vengeance on her. God Himself is Israel's redeemer. Babylon is condemned for trusting in enchantments and wickedness, they have no savior.

God tells Israel that He has "refined" them, but, not as silver, He has tested them in the furnace of affliction because of their stubbornness. However, He consistently identifies Himself as Israel's only redeemer who will also teach them to profit and lead them.

PRAYER
Dear Lord,
Perhaps You repeatedly reminded the Israelites that only You can save and redeem them, because just like me, they were surrounded by idols, and tempted to trust in something or someone other than the living, invisible God. Please remind me as often as necessary that You alone are my God. Thank You Lord. In the name of Jesus Christ, I pray. Amen.

TODAY'S CHALLENGE: To avoid the temptation to need a god that I can see.

What else is God saying to me today?

What is my response?

DAY TWO HUNDRED AND FOUR: READ Isaiah 49-51

The nation of Israel shall speak to the Gentiles of their heritage in God and God will give them as a light to the Gentiles. Zion feels forsaken, but, God speaks comfort. A woman may forget her nursing child, but God says surely He will not forget Israel. "See" He says. "I have inscribed you on the palms of my hands, your walls are continually before me."

Isaiah reminds Israel that it was their sins and transgressions that caused them to be sold into slavery. Isaiah speaks of God's servant who God will help to restore Israel. God assures the righteous of His comfort and restoration. He tells them to be strengthened and trust in Him, not in man.

PRAYER
Dear Lord,
When my own transgressions cause me pain, help me to not accuse You. When You tell me that You are restoring and blessing me, help me to believe You. In the name of Jesus Christ, I pray, amen.

TODAY'S CHALLENGE: After a trial, to accept God's comfort.

What else is God saying to me today?

What is my response?

DAY TWO HUNDRED AND FIVE: READ Isaiah 52-54

Isaiah awakes Jerusalem heralding good news. Their bonds are loosed and they are redeemed without money. God declares that His people shall know when He speaks. The bearer of good news will proclaim to Jerusalem. "Your God reigns." The prophet announces that God has redeemed Jerusalem. The people are instructed to leave from where they are and not touch any unclean thing. The God of Israel will be their rear guard.

Isaiah speaks of God's servant who will be highly exalted, though his visage will be marred. Isaiah asks who will believe the report. He describes a man of sorrows, who has borne our grief, carried our sorrows, was bruised for our iniquities, chastened for our peace, and by whose stripes we are healed. This is all done for the transgression of God's people.

Isaiah encourages the barren to sing, the childless to expect children and the people to fear not, shame or disgrace. The Lord is their Redeemer. "No weapon formed against the servants of the Lord shall prosper."

PRAYER
Dear Lord,
Thank You for being my Redeemer, and for all of the many great benefits that I have as a servant of God. Help me to praise You often as I meditate on Your goodness to me. In the name of Jesus Christ, I pray. Amen.

TODAY'S CHALLENGE: To expect miracles.

What else is God saying to me today?

What is my response?

DAY TWO HUNDRED AND SIX: READ Isaiah 55-57

The prophets invites people to come and partake freely of the goodness of the Lord and in His abundance. Those who are inclined to wickedness are admonished to forsake his way and call upon the Lord. If they return to the Lord He will abundantly pardon. "For my thoughts are not your thoughts, nor your ways, my ways says the Lord." His word shall not return void. He admonishes the people to keep justice and do righteous for God salvation is approaching. Those who hold fast to the name of the Lord will be rewarded. Those who trust in idols will find no redemption, but, even the backslidden who fear God will be delivered.

PRAYER
Dear God,
I know that You understand my ways. Please help me to understand Your ways and to obey them even if I don't understand. Please help me not to allow my lack of understanding prevent me from freely receiving Your abundance. In the name of Jesus Christ, I pray. Amen.

TODAY'S CHALLENGE: To receive God's goodness that I have not earned or bought.

What else is God saying to me today?

What is my response?

DAY TWO HUNDRED AND SEVEN: READ Isaiah 58-60

God condemns outward displays of piety in fasting. He compares the fast that the people practice to the fast that He has chosen. He promises that when the people choose to fast in order to loose bands of wickedness, undo the heavy burdens and let the oppressed go free, they will see miraculous results.

The Lord's answer to unanswered prayer is not that His arms are short, but because of the iniquities and transgressions of the people. God looks for an intercessor for sinful man, and finds no one; therefore He promises to send a redeemer to Zion and those in Israel who turn from their transgressions.

God speaks a series of incredible blessings and promises to Zion. "Arise, shine, for your light has come! And the glory of the Lord is risen upon you;" captures the essence of this chapter which is replete with promise.

PRAYER

Dear Lord,

Help me to fast Your way. Surely I and those who I care about need the benefits that are derived from a God-directed fast. Please forgive my transgressions and cleanse me from my iniquities so that You can say to me also, "Arise, shine . . ." In the name of Jesus Christ, I pray. Amen.

TODAY'S CHALLENGE: Am I the reason for my unanswered prayer?

What else is God saying to me today?

What is my response?

DAY TWO HUNDRED AND EIGHT: READ Isaiah 61-63

God's anointed speaks of his mission to preach good tidings, heal the broken hearted, proclaim liberty to the captives and a great number of other things that he will do for the people because the Spirit of the Lord is upon him.

Just as God's people have been publicly humiliated, God is committed to bringing them public glory. He promises, "The Gentiles shall see your righteousness and all kings your glory."

Although God was once angry at them, the prophet recalls the loving kindnesses of the Lord. He remembers God's faithfulness in delivering them from Egyptian bondage through the Red Sea. He exclaims, "You, O Lord, are our Father; our Redeemer from Everlasting is Your name."

PRAYER
Dear Lord,
Thank You for being attentive to all of the needs of Your people on a personal and intimate level. I intercede now for those who are broken-hearted, those who are in various kinds of bondages, and those who need Your salvation. In the name of Jesus Christ, I pray. Amen.

TODAY'S CHALLENGE: To never forget the great things that God has already done for me.

What else is God saying to me today?

What is my response?

DAY TWO HUNDRED AND NINE: READ Isaiah 64-66

Isaiah continues to pray to God to tear the heavens and come down upon His adversaries, and to meet the righteous. He then concludes that "All our righteousness is like filthy rags, and we need to be saved."

God says, that He has stretched out His hand for a long time to a rebellious people who do not ask for Him. His remnant will be brought forth, but, others will have sorrow of heart.

God declares that He will create new heavens and a new earth and He will rejoice in Jerusalem, His people. He will answer before they call and long enjoy the works of their hands.

God promises to make His habitation with those who are poor in spirit rather than in a house that man can build. God promises new heavens and a new earth which will remain. All flesh shall come to worship Him. Those who transgress against God, their worm will not die nor their fire be quenched.

PRAYER
Dear God,
Thank You that You know how to vindicate Your people. I reach for Your hand which is outstretched to me. I thank You that in Your eternal heavens and earth, You have provided a permanent place for the righteous. In the name of Jesus Christ, I praise you. Amen.

TODAY'S CHALLENGE: To tell someone else about God's salvation.

What else is God saying to me today?

What is my response?

DAY TWO HUNDRED AND TEN: READ *Micah 1-4*

Micah, whose name means: "He Who Is Like Yahweh" and is a contemporary of Isaiah, prophesies to Samaria and Jerusalem. He warns of the impending judgment of Israel. He says that the Lord Himself is a witness against them and will come down to earth and tread down their high places. He describes an incredible display of God's destructive power.

Micah says that he will strip himself naked and mourn for Israel and Judah with wailing and howling because of the disaster that will come. He accuses the lying prophets of taking away the glory of God, and the rulers exploit the people.

However, God will restore and gather the remnant of Israel and the Lord will reign in Zion. The people will learn the ways of the Lord and walk in them. Wars will cease and the people will "beat their swords into plowshares and their spears into pruning hooks."

PRAYER
Dear Lord,
In spite of the destruction that comes to the wicked, You always make provisions for those who are faithful to You. I ask You for the strength that I need to trust You in the midst of a wicked generation who may be incurring God's wrath. I pray for the hastening of the day when wars will cease and God will reign in Zion. In the name of Jesus Christ, I pray. Amen.

TODAY'S CHALLENGE: To learn the ways of the Lord and walk in them.

What else is God saying to me today?

What is my response?

DAY TWO HUNDRED AND ELEVEN: READ Micah 5-7

Although Israel will be stricken, Micah prophesies the coming of a ruler in Israel, who is everlasting. He will feed His flock and be great to the ends of the earth. In that day, all of Israel's enemies shall be cut off and the sorcerers and soothsayers shall be no more.

The Lord tells Israel to arise and plead their case before the mountains. He asks them what has He done to them; to remember how He has delivered them. He has been good to them. He does not require thousands of offerings of rams or oil, but He does require them to do justly, to love mercy, and to walk humbly before their God.

The people will repent and God will forgive and restore them. Their enemies who rejoiced over them will be ashamed when God restores them. Israel will say. "When I fall, I will arise; when I sit in darkness, the Lord will be a light to me."

PRAYER
Dear Lord,
Thank You for giving ultimate victory to Your people. If I fall, help me to arise. If I experience darkness, be my light. In the name of Jesus Christ, I pray. Amen.

TODAY'S CHALLENGE: To do justly, love mercy and walk humbly before my God.

What else is God saying to me today?

What is my response?

DAY TWO HUNDRED AND TWELVE: READ *Nahum 1-3*

Nahum's name means "Comforter." He prophesies against Nineveh. He announces God's avenging wrath against Nineveh, the enemies of His people, Judah. Although God is slow to anger, He has great power and will not allow the wicked to go free. He describes God's power to control the wind, the clouds, the sea, the rivers and the mountains.

Though His enemies may be many, God will cut them down. He distinguishes between those who trust in Him and those who are evil. Nahum pronounces judgment on Nineveh. "Though Nineveh of old was like a pool of water, now they flee away." God's wrath is kindled against them and He will burn its chariots, devour its young lions, cut off its prey from the earth, and silence the voice of its messengers.

This devastation will come because of the innumerable sins that Nineveh has committed. Nahum calls it "the bloody city" full of lies, robbery, murder and sorcery. Its wickedness has continuously affected every nation. Those who have been long victimized by Nineveh's terror can take comfort in the fact that they will be vindicated.

PRAYER
Dear Lord,
In spite of the fact that You are long suffering, You will not continue to tolerate evil or allow the wicked to go unpunished. When I see people who appear to flourish in their wickedness, help me to be comforted by the truth that You will not allow the wicked to go free, and You will vindicate the righteous. In the name of Jesus Christ, I pray. Amen.

TODAY'S CHALLENGE: To not become bitter if the wicked seem to prosper.

What else is God saying to me today?

What is my response?

DAY TWO HUNDRED AND THIRTEEN: READ II Kings 20, 21

Hezekiah, king of Judah, become sick and near death. Isaiah tells him to set his house in order because he is going to die. Hezekiah turns his face to the wall and prays to God. He asks God to remember his faithfulness in walking upright before Him. He weeps bitterly. Immediately God sends Isaiah back to tell Hezekiah that his prayer has been heard, God has added fifteen years to his life, and that He will deliver the city from the hands of the Assyrians. They take a lump of figs and lay it on Hezekiah's boils and he recovers.

As a sign to Hezekiah. God causes the shadow of the sundial to go backward ten degrees. At that time, the king of Babylon's son sends letters and a present to Hezekiah having heard of his recovery. Hezekiah entertains them and shows them all of the treasures in his house and in his kingdom. Isaiah tells him that the Babylonians will one day take away everything that he showed them, and also his future sons.

After Hezekiah dies, his twelve year old son, Manasseh, begins his reign, and does evil in the sight of the Lord. He rebuilds the high places which his father had destroyed and zealously embraces various forms of idolatry and leads the nation into the same. As a result, the prophets prophesy calamity upon them that will tingle the ears of the hearers.

PRAYER
Dear Lord,
You are the author of life, and in charge of the death of Your saints. I ask You to take away our fear of death, and rather help us to be committed to doing Your will in our allotted years. In the name of Jesus Christ, I pray. Amen.

TODAY'S CHALLENGE: To trust the Lord with my life and my death.

What else is God saying to me today?

What is my response?

DAY TWO HUNDRED AND FOURTEEN: READ Zephaniah 1-3

Zephaniah, whose name means "The Lord Has Hidden," prophesies during the reign of Josiah, king of Judah. He announces the great day of the Lord, when He will utterly consume everything from the face of the earth. He will also stretch His hand against Judah and Jerusalem. God will destroy Baal, the idolaters, pagan priest, various idol gods and backsliders. That day is described as a day of wrath and great destruction.

Zephaniah urges the people to gather and repent before the decree is issued, before the Lord's fierce anger comes. He names all of the nations that will be forsaken and desolate, so there will not be places of refuge from this wrath.

He says that Jerusalem is a rebellious, disobedient city, which refuses to repent. But even so, there is hope. A remnant of Israel shall 'do no unrighteousness.' As a nation they will be preserved. In that day, God will take away judgments, gather the repentant, and give them praise and fame.

PRAYER
Dear Lord,
Thank You for Your love and patience. Your love for Your people and Your faithfulness to Your covenant are evidenced in Your dealings with the nation of Israel. Thank You so much for loving me and being patient with me. I ask You on this day to show me at least *one* thing that I can do to show You my gratitude. In the name of Jesus Christ, I pray. Amen.

TODAY'S CHALLENGE: To repent quickly when confronted with my sin.

What else is God saying to me today?

What is my response?

DAY TWO HUNDRED AND FIFTEEN: READ Habakkuk 1-3

Habakkuk's name means: "Embrace." Habakkuk is overwhelmed by the wickedness that is all around him. He wonders if God is concerned. He cries out, and asks God why will He not hear and save. The righteous find no relief. Judgment is perverse. There is strife and contention, the wicked surround the righteous. Habakkuk wonders what is God going to do?

God answers that He will bring a bitter and hasty nation, a terrible and dreadful nation the Chaldeans, with powerful, swift, horses. Habakkuk is further puzzled. How can a Righteous, Holy, God look on wickedness and treachery without punishing it. He asks God many questions and says, "I will stand my watch to see what He will say to me."

God tells him to "write the vision' and make it plain on tablets, that he may run who reads it . . . though it tarries wait for it." The proud will perish, but, "the just shall live by faith." Habakkuk speaks woes to the wicked and proud, to those who load themselves with many pledges and plunders many nations. He speaks woe to those who asks wood to save them and stones to teach them, even if it's overlaid with gold and silver, it has no life. "But the Lord is in His holy temple, let all the earth keep silence before Him."

Habakkuk prays to God after hearing His speech and asks God to revive him. He praises God and declares. "Though the fig tree may not blossom, nor fruit be on the vines, though the labor of the olive may fail . . . yet, I will rejoice in the Lord. I will joy in the God of my salvation."

PRAYER
Dear Heavenly Father,
Habakkuk's frustration is understandable. The pride and arrogance of the wicked sometimes seem undaunted. However, I am assured that You are at work in my world, my life, and my circumstances. Speak to each, O Lord, and let Your perfect will be done, in Your perfect time. In the name of Jesus Christ, I pray. Amen.

TODAY'S CHALLENGE: Wait.

What else is God saying to me today?

What is my response?

DAY TWO HUNDRED AND SIXTEEN: READ II Kings 22-25

At eight years old, Josiah begins to reign as king in Jerusalem. Under the guidance of his mother Jedidah, he reigns for thirty-one years. He does what is right in the sight of the Lord. He did not vary at all.

During the eighteenth year of his reign, he sends Shaphan the scribe to the house of the Lord to the high priest, Hilkiah to count the money. In so doing Hilkiah tells Shaphan that he has found the Book of the Law and gives it to him to read. Shaphan reads it to the king. Upon hearing the words, Josiah tears his clothes. He sends the priests to inquire of the Lord. They go to Huldah the prophetess and speak to her. Huldah tells them that surely because of all of the rebellion of the people, the Lord will bring calamity on Judah. Because Josiah's heart is tender toward God, Huldah tells them that this will not occur until after his death.

Josiah gathers the people and reads the words of the Book. The king stands by a pillar and makes a covenant to follow the Lord. He cleanses the land from idolatry and sorcery and institutes the Passover. However God still intends to judge Judah. Josiah is killed in battle by the king of Egypt.

PRAYER
Dear Lord,
Thank You for Your mercy. Thank You for revealing Yourself to those whose hearts are right before You. Please reveal to me any hidden areas of Your word, so that I may humble myself and implement it in my life. In the name of Jesus Christ, I pray. Amen.

TODAY'S CHALLENGE: To change.

What else is God saying to me today?

What is my response?

DAY TWO HUNDRED AND SEVENTEEN:
READ OBADIAH/*Jeremiah 1, 2*

Obadiah, "Servant of Yahweh," ministers a message of warning to the Edomites and an announcement of restoration to Israel. The Edomites are descendants of Esau and the Israelites are descendants of Jacob. These brothers were bitter rivals at one time; apparently a vestige of that bitterness still lingers in the Edomites. They are experiencing a false sense of security and pride. Obadiah tells them, "the pride of your heart has deceived you." God declares that He will bring them down to stubble because of their violence against his brother, Jacob.

God tells them that they should not have gazed at Jacob in the day of his captivity, nor rejoiced over Judah's destruction. God says to the Edomites, "As you have done, it shall be done to you." But on Mt. Zion there shall be deliverance, the house of Jacob shall possess their possessions.

The prophet Jeremiah is sent to Judah during the reigns of kings, Josiah, and his son, Jehoiakim. He acknowledges that God called him before he was born. God assures Jeremiah that He will speak through him.

God sends him to remind Jerusalem that He has loved them from their youth. He asks them what has He done to them to cause them to forsake him. They are so backslidden that they call a tree their father, and a stone their mother. Yet they maintain their innocence and will not repent. God is bringing charges against them.

PRAYER
Dear Lord,
Please forgive me for holding grudges. Please help me to truly forgive those who wronged me. Help me to not rejoice over the humiliation of my brothers and sisters in the Lord. Further, Dear Lord, help me to never forget Your goodness to me, and that You alone are my God. In the name of Jesus Christ, I pray. Amen.

TODAY'S CHALLENGE: To remember that God can read my heart.

What else is God saying to me today?

What is my response?

DAY TWO HUNDRED AND EIGHTEEN: READ Jeremiah 3-5

Jeremiah challenges the hypocrisy of the people. They say that if a divorced woman becomes involved with another man, she is polluted and her husband should not return to her again. Yet they have played the harlot with many lovers and returned to God.

God says that backsliding Israel has played the harlot under every green tree and every high mountain. Because of her adulteries, God has given her a certificate of divorce. Seeing all of this, her treacherous sister, Judah, does not fear God, but, plays the harlot also, while pretending to honor God.

God implores Israel to return to Him and put away her abominations and she will not be moved. God tells the men of Judah and Jerusalem that He will bring disaster and great destruction upon them from the north; but, if Jeremiah can find a just man among them who seeks truth He will pardon Israel. Instead the prophets prophesy falsely, the priests rule by their own power, and the people love it.

PRAYER
Dear God,
Help me not to break Your heart. In the name of Jesus Christ, I pray. Amen.

TODAY'S CHALLENGE: To heed the early warning signs from God.

What else is God saying to me today?

What is my response?

DAY TWO HUNDRED AND NINETEEN: READ Jeremiah 6-8

Jeremiah warns the descendants of Benjamin that disaster is coming from the north. Jerusalem is given to wickedness, everyone is given to covetousness and destruction is eminent. The great nation from the north that will come upon them is cruel and has no mercy. The people have trusted in lying prophets who say peace when there is no peace. The people have provoked God to wrath by their hypocrisy, oppression of the poor and fatherless, idolatry and rebellion. They even burn their sons and daughters on the high places of Tophet, yet, offer sacrifices and incense to the God of Israel and are not repentant or ashamed. Jeremiah mourns greatly for the people.

PRAYER
Dear Lord,
How easy it is for us to assimilate into the society around us, even when it stands in blatant opposition to what we know is right. I ask You for the strength and security of character to be the only one who stands for righteousness if necessary. In the name of Jesus Christ, I pray. Amen.

TODAY'S CHALLENGE: To not provoke God to wrath.

What else is God saying to me today?

What is my response?

DAY TWO HUNDRED AND TWENTY: READ *Jeremiah 9-12*

Jeremiah laments, "Oh that my head were waters, and my eyes a fountain of tears, that I might weep day and night for the slain of the daughters of my people!" He desires to leave his people because they are adulterous and treacherous men. God says that He will refine them and try them. At the word of the Lord, Jeremiah tells them to call for the mourning, wailing women because the devastation will be great. He tells them that it is foolish to follow the Gentiles. Their gods shall perish.

God sends Jeremiah to tell the men of Judah that all who transgress the covenant are cursed. He instructs Jeremiah not to pray for them for He will certainly bring calamity upon them. The men of Anathoth threaten to take Jeremiah's life if he continues to prophesy such in the name of the Lord. God promises to bring catastrophe upon them. However, at a future date, He will restore His people.

PRAYER
Dear God,
Thank You for the "mirror" that the nation of Israel provides for the world. We are like they were without Your grace. I ask for a daily abundance of Your grace for myself and Your people everywhere. In the name of Jesus Christ, I pray. Amen.

TODAY'S CHALLENGE: To see Israel's mistakes and avoid them.

What else is God saying to me today?

What is my response?

DAY TWO HUNDRED AND TWENTY-ONE:
READ Jeremiah 13-16

God instructs Jeremiah to bury a linen sash near the Euphrates. When He sends Jeremiah back to retrieve it, the sash is greatly marred and ruined. God tells Jeremiah that this sash illustrates how He will ruin the great pride of Jerusalem. God calls the people to humble themselves.

God describes the shame and punishment that shall come upon the people. He tells Jeremiah not to pray for them. He says. "Even if Moses and Samuel stood before Me, my hand would not be favorable toward this people. Cast them out of my sight and let them go forth." God says that He is weary of relenting.

God reassures Jeremiah that he will be delivered from those who fight against him. He tells Jeremiah not to take a wife in this place because the sons and daughters there will die and be as refuse on the earth. He is also instructed to not celebrate feasts of fellowship with them.

PRAYER
Dear Lord,
When I see the punishment of God on people, I am sure that it is only because they have continuously trampled upon His love, grace, and mercy. Dear God, please help me to be the kind of person who will make Your heart glad, not sad. In the name of Jesus Christ, I pray. Amen.

TODAY'S CHALLENGE: To take time to listen when God speaks.

What else is God saying to me today?

What is my response?

DAY TWO HUNDRED AND TWENTY-TWO:
READ Jeremiah 17-20

Jeremiah describes Judah's sins as "written with a pen of iron," indelibly engraved on their hearts. Therefore, they have kindled God's anger. Jeremiah prays for healing and salvation for himself.

God sends Jeremiah to the potter's house to see a demonstration of how He is re-making and re-shaping His people. He admonishes the people to repent, but, they refuse saying, "We will walk according to our own plans and the dictates our own hearts." They verbally persecute Jeremiah. God says that their destruction will be so great that they will eat the flesh of their own sons, daughters and friends out of desperation.

Pashur, the son of the priest, hears Jeremiah's prophesy of doom. He strikes him and puts him in stocks. Jeremiah tells him that he will be destroyed in Babylon. Jeremiah worships the Lord, but, despises his own life because he feels that his life is filled with labor and sorrow and his days are consumed with shame.

PRAYER
Dear Lord,
Sometimes being Your messenger is wearisome. Today I pray for protection, provision, strength, grace, and courage for all of Your servants in every place on the earth. In the name of Jesus Christ, I pray. Amen.

TODAY'S CHALLENGE: To remember to pray for God's ministers everyday.

What else is God saying to me today?

What is my response?

DAY TWO HUNDRED AND TWENTY-THREE:
READ Jeremiah 21-23

King Zedekiah sends Pashur and others to tell Jeremiah that Nebuchadnezzar, king of Babylon, is making war against them. He asks if perhaps the Lord will make him go away.

Jeremiah sends word to Zedekiah telling him that not only will God *not* send the Babylonians away, He will join them in fighting against Israel. He tells the people to surrender to the Babylonians and save their lives. Those who do not, will die by sword, famine and pestilence.

Jeremiah denounces Josiah's sons, Shallum and Jehoiakim. They did not follow the right ways of their father. God also speaks woe to the shepherds who destroy and scatter the sheep of the Lord's pasture. God Himself will gather the remnant of His flock and set up shepherds over them who will feed them. He will raise to David a Branch of Righteousness. He condemns the false prophets who He does not speak to, yet they prophesy.

PRAYER
Dear Lord,
How futile and superstitious to ask for Your help after constantly refusing to repent and exercise humility before You. Please help me to avoid the confusion that comes from acknowledging God only in crisis. In the name of Jesus Christ, I pray. Amen.

TODAY'S CHALLENGE: To repent before I pray.

What else is God saying to me today?

What is my response?

DAY TWO HUNDRED AND TWENTY-FOUR:
READ Jeremiah 24-26

God shows Jeremiah two baskets of figs; in one is good figs, in the other, very bad ones. God explains that these represent the two groups of people who will go into Babylon. He will favor the good ones and bring them back to possess their land. The bad ones will be consumed.

In the first year of Nebuchadnezzar, God tells Jeremiah that because the people have refused to hear the prophets, nor did they repent, the whole land will be desolate and the people will be in captivity for seventy years. After this, He will punish the king of Babylon for their iniquity and make a perpetual desolation. Likewise, God will judge all wicked nations.

God commissions Jeremiah to go to the house of the Lord and prophesy the doom of the city. The priests and prophets seize Jeremiah and tell the people that he deserves to die. Ahikam, the son of Shaphan is with Jeremiah so that he is not delivered into the hands of the people to be put to death.

PRAYER
Heavenly Father,
No one can withstand the fire of Your wrath. Today, I pray for my generation before they are sentenced to final destruction. I pray for the rebellious to repent, the priests and prophets to exercise righteousness and the righteous to pray. In the name of Jesus Christ, I pray. Amen.

TODAY'S CHALLENGE: To pray for those who are incurring God's wrath.

What else is God saying to me today?

What is my response?

DAY TWO HUNDRED AND TWENTY-FIVE:
READ Jeremiah 27-29

God tells Jeremiah to make bands and neck yokes and send them to the kings of Edom, Moab, the Ammonites, Tyre, and Sidon. They are warned to not listen to their lying prophets, but, to save themselves by surrendering to the king of Babylon or they will be destroyed.

Hananiah prophesies that the yoke of Babylon will be broken off of the necks of the captives in two years and they will be restored. God tells Jeremiah to confront Hananiah and pronounce his death.

Jeremiah sends a letter to the elders of Israel who are now in captivity in Babylon. He tells them to inhabit the land and pray for its peace. After seventy years, God will visit them and cause them to return to their own land. God says, "For I know the thoughts that I think toward you, says the Lord, thoughts of peace and not of evil, to give you a future and a hope."

PRAYER
Dear Lord,
Thank You for making provision and giving promise in the middle of captivity. Thank You that You are with me wherever I go. I delight in Your presence and invite You to lead my family and I all the days of our lives. In the name of Jesus Christ. Amen.

TODAY'S CHALLENGE: To believe that God is with me when I'm in trouble.

What else is God saying to me today?

What is my response?

DAY TWO HUNDRED AND TWENTY-SIX:
READ Jeremiah 30-32

God tells Jeremiah to write in a book that he will bring His people Israel and Judah back from captivity to possess their land after they are corrected. God will then be the God of all the families of Israel and they shall be His people. He will have mercy on Ephraim because he has heard their mourning. He promises also to make a new covenant with Judah and Israel. He will put His laws in their minds and hearts.

Jeremiah buys a field and instructs Baruch to bury the deed in a durable earthen vessel. God assures them that vineyards, houses and fields will be possessed again. Jeremiah cannot understand how all of these things will come to pass. God answers, "Behold, I Am the Lord, the God of all flesh. Is there anything too hard for me?"

PRAYER
Dear Heavenly Father,
When wounds have been afflicted due to disobedience, praise You for the healing that You extend. Help me to know that there is nothing too hard for You, You are the God of all flesh. I pause now and ask You to do that thing in my life that seems impossible. In the name of Jesus Christ, I pray. Amen.

TODAY'S CHALLENGE: To submit to the sovereignty of God.

What else is God saying to me today?

What is my response?

DAY TWO HUNDRED AND TWENTY-SEVEN:
READ Jeremiah 33-36

God promises that when His people call upon Him He will answer in extraordinary ways. He continues to affirm that He will bring restoration as He promised. He declares that He will not break His covenant with His servant, David.

God warns Zedekiah, king of Judah that he will deliver the city to the king of Babylon. The people are told to set all of their male and female slaves free. They do so, but, later change their minds and bring them back into captivity. God promises to liberate them to the sword, to famine and to pestilence for their treachery and disobedience. The Rechabites are obedient to their founder. Noting their loyalty and integrity, God says that Jonadab, the son of Nechab, of the Rechabites, shall not lack a man to stand before the Lord.

Jeremiah speaks the word of the Lord to Baruch and he writes it on a scroll. The words on the scroll foretells the Babylonian captivity and is given to king Johoiakim. He burns the scroll and refuses to repent. God directs Jeremiah to write another copy of the scroll and to add to its contents the destruction of the house of Jehoiakim.

PRAYER
Dear Lord,
As I see how You deal with the wicked I want to draw even closer to You. I pray for integrity of heart, and deliverance from all forms of hypocrisy. I realize that the contents of my heart are not hidden from You; please help me to make them pure. In the name of Jesus Christ, I pray. Amen.

TODAY'S CHALLENGE: To not be afraid to obey God.

What else is God saying to me today?

What is my response?

DAY TWO HUNDRED AND TWENTY-EIGHT: READ Jeremiah 37-39

God tells Jeremiah how to answer the princes so that he is not put to death. He remains in prison until the day that Jerusalem is taken captive by Babylon.

When Jerusalem is seized, Zedekiah, king of Judah tries to escape. He is captured. His sons are killed and the king of Babylon binds him in bronze fetters and carries him to Babylon along with others. The captain of the guard leaves all of the poor people and gives them vineyards.

King Nebuchadnezzar charges his servants to not harm Jeremiah. He is freed from prison and goes home with Ahikam, the son of Shaphan. While he was in prison, God told Jeremiah to tell the leaders of Ethiopia that they will not be taken captive because they put their trust in God.

PRAYER
Dear Lord,
Thank You for Your tender mercy and justice. Thank You for remembering Your servant Jeremiah and protecting him from harm. I pray for a heart as faithful as Jeremiah's, even when it causes me to be unpopular. In the name of Jesus Christ. Amen.

TODAY'S CHALLENGE: To suffer persecution and remain faithful to God.

What else is God saying to me today?

What is my response?

DAY TWO HUNDRED AND TWENTY-NINE:
READ Jeremiah 40-42

The captain of the guard sets Jeremiah free and tells him he can go and dwell wherever he desires among the remnant of Judah, or he can go to Babylon where he will be cared for. He then advises Jeremiah to go and dwell with Gedaliah whom the king of Babylon had made governor over the remnant of Judah. All the remnant who were in various places come to receive food from the governor. Johanan warns Gedaliah that the king of the Ammonites has sent Ishmael to murder him. Gedaliah does not believe him and is soon murdered by Ishmael and his men. They kill many other people, and they take all of the people of Mizpah captive. The people are rescued by Johanan.

All of the captains of the forces, including Johanan come to Jeremiah and ask him to ask God what they should do. They vow that they will do whatever God says, whether pleasing or displeasing to them. After ten days the Lord tells Jeremiah to strictly warn them to not flee to Egypt. If they do so, they will be overtaken by the famine, sword and pestilence. They are to stay in the land and not be afraid of the king of Babylon. Additionally, God tells them that He knows that they are hypocrites and have no intention of obeying the Lord. Therefore they will die by the sword, famine, and pestilence.

PRAYER
Dear Lord,
Please deliver me from all forms of hard-heartedness and hard-headedness. Help me to not be so deaf or so blind, that I cannot hear Your warnings or see Your signposts. Help me to have an honest heart before You, so that I can live under Your mercy and protection. In the name of Jesus Christ, I pray. Amen.

TODAY'S CHALLENGE: To avoid the sin of arrogance.

What else is God saying to me today?

What is my response?

DAY TWO HUNDRED AND THIRTY: READ Jeremiah 43-46

The proud men accuse Jeremiah of speaking falsely to them. They are determined to flee to Egypt and so they do. The word of the Lord comes to Jeremiah, warning them that they will perish in Egypt. Still the people decide that they will follow their own minds. The women say that it was well with them when they offered incense to the queen of heaven.

God tells Baruch, Jeremiah's scribe that He will spare his life. Jeremiah prophesies against Egypt, warning them that the great nation of Babylon will take them captive. He assures the Israelites who are captive in Babylon, that He is with them and will eventually restore them.

PRAYER
Dear Lord,
May I never have the audacity to blatantly disobey You. In the name of Jesus Christ, I pray. Amen.

TODAY'S CHALLENGE: To continually reach out to rebellious people.

What else is God saying to me today?

What is my response?

DAY TWO HUNDRED AND THIRTY-ONE:
READ Jeremiah 47-49

The prophet Jeremiah pronounces judgment on the Philistines. He describes the attack as "waters rising from the north." The men shall cry and fathers will forsake their children because the Lord will plunder them.

Moab, who has been at ease and who is exceedingly proud, will also be plundered. God will also judge the Ammonites with their many gods. They will be driven out headlong. God says that He will bring calamity on the Edomites and make there dwelling places desolate. These judgments He also declares on Damascus, Kedar and Hazor and on Elam. In the latter days, however, He will bring back the captives of Elam.

PRAYER
Dear Lord,
No one will escape Your sight. When the rolls are called, may I be among those who You call "faithful." In the name of Jesus Christ, I pray. Amen.

TODAY'S CHALLENGE: To realize that God personally knows each inhabitant of every city, everywhere.

What else is God saying to me today?

What is my response?

DAY TWO HUNDRED AND THIRTY-TWO:
READ Jeremiah 50-52

God speaks judgment against Babylon. Her cities shall be shamed, her idols humiliated, her images broken in pieces. In those days the children of Israel will come weeping, seeking the Lord, and asking the way to Zion. God says, He will destroy Babylon and punish its king. He will bring His people home. He elaborates extensively on the woes of the Babylonians and the restoration of Israel. Jeremiah also reviews the fall and captivity of Jerusalem.

PRAYER

Dear Lord,

If we look carefully we see that You are consistent. You fulfill Your word always. Today I ask for a greater revelation and understanding of how to live in harmony with Your holy word and will. In the name of Jesus Christ, I pray, Amen.

TODAY'S CHALLENGE: To submit to every word of God.

What else is God saying to me today?

What is my response?

DAY TWO HUNDRED THIRTY-THREE:
READ Lamentations 1-5

The author of Lamentations pens a dirge-like poem describing the ruin and desolation of a once majestic city. "The princess has become a slave." Judah has gone into captivity, Zion mourns. The multitude of her transgressions has brought on this great calamity.

Jerusalem, once pleasant, has become vile with grievous sins. Jerusalem, the beauty of Israel has been thrown down to the ground. Her enemies hiss at her and gnash their teeth. In God's fierce anger He has allowed the people to be slain and great famine to come upon them because of their disobedience.

The writer describes his personal anguish in the midst of this devastation as so great that his flesh and skin have aged. He laments that he is a ridicule and taunting to his people. He feels hopeless until he remembers something that gives him hope. "It is of the Lord's mercies that we are not consumed, because His compassions fail not. They are new every morning, great is Thy faithfulness."

He realizes that the way out of trouble is to return to the Lord and call on Him. It is Israel who turned from the Lord, but, the Lord remains forever.

PRAYER
Dear Lord,
The blight of sin spreads like cancer and devastates everything that it touches. Seeing the ruin of a once majestic city causes me to mourn over the vileness of my own society. I pray for our nation to return to God and its people to abandon the vile things that may arouse God's fierce anger against us. I pray this for my nation, my city, my church, my family, and myself. In the name of Jesus Christ. Amen.

TODAY'S CHALLENGE: To realize that when I point my finger to accuse God, three fingers point back to me.

What else is God saying to me today?

What is my response?

DAY TWO HUNDRED AND THRITY-FOUR:
READ I Chronicles 1-3

After the Babylonia exile, the nation of Israel needed a re-education and reminder of its history and its' God.

*The writer traces Israel's ancestry back to Adam, noting all the sons of Abraham, Ishmael and his family; the sons of Abraham and Keturah and the family of Isaac, the family of Seir and the kings of Edom. The family of Israel which are the twelve tribes of Israel include the tribe of Judah from which king David descended. God's covenant with David was a key to Judah's preservation. All of the sons of David are named, as are the sons of Solomon, and Jeconiah.

PRAYER
Dear Lord,
Thank You that from the time of Adam's sin and the birth of Seth, You have been faithful to preserve some one to call upon Your name and carry the message of redemption to the human race. I pray that I and my family will build on any Godly foundations that were laid by our fore parents and pass them on to future generations. In the name of Jesus Christ, I pray. Amen.

TODAY'S CHALLENGE: To make my memory an honor to God and my family.

What else is God saying to me today?

What is my response?

*The synopses and prayers in first and Second Chronicles are written in the past tense to note that the author is speaking of what happened in the past.

DAY TWO HUNDRED AND THIRTY-FIVE:
READ I Chronicles 4-6

The family of Judah is listed, and the writer takes note of Jabez. He was described as more honorable than his brothers. Jabez called on the God of Israel saying, "O that You would bless me indeed, and enlarge my territory, that Your hand would be with me and that You would keep me from evil, that I may not cause pain."

The family of Simeon was noted for defeating the Amalekites. Rueben, the first born of Israel defiled his father's bed and his birthright was taken and given to the sons of Joseph. Judah prevailed over his brothers and a ruler came from his family. The sons of Gad and Manasseh are listed, as are the family of Levi. Aaron, Moses and Miriam came from this tribe. They were all children of Amram. From this tribe came musicians and the family of Aaron was a family of priests.

PRAYER
Dear Lord,
As the writer lists the many descendants of Judah, Jabez stands out in his recollection. I pray in the same spirit as did Jabez. O Lord, that You would bless me indeed and enlarge my territory, that Your hand would be with me and that You would keep me from evil, that I may not cause pain. In the name of Jesus Christ, I pray. Amen.

TODAY'S CHALLENGE: To avoid the sin of Rueben.

What else is God saying to me today?

What is my response?

DAY TWO HUNDRED AND THIRTY-SIX:
READ I Chronicles 7-9

The descendants of Issachar had brave soldiers and family leaders in their clan. There were 22,600 people in Tola's family by the time David became king. The descendants of Benjamin and Dan, Naphtali, Manasseh and of Ephraim. Ephraim's two sons are killed while trying to steal livestock. His daughter, Sheerah built towns of Lower Beth-Horon, Upper Beth-Horon, and Uzzen-Sheerah.

The descendants of Asher were also brave soldiers and respected family leaders. They had a total of 26,000 soldiers. Benjamin's many descendants are also listed. King Saul was of the tribe of Benjamin. He had four sons. All of the people of Israel were listed in the book of Israel's kings. Judah was carried away to Babylon because of her unfaithfulness.

The first people to return to their towns were the priests, then the Levites, temple workers, and other Israelites. The Levites were assigned to attend to all the duties of the temple, day and night.

PRAYER
Dear Lord,
Every member of Your family is important and has a purpose. I pray that parents will set a Godly example, and propagate a Godly message throughout our future generations. Please raise up strong warriors of the word and of prayer in my family so that we can establish Your kingdom on earth. In the name of Jesus Christ, I pray. Amen.

TODAY'S CHALLENGE: To be a strong, brave soldier in God's army.

What else is God saying to me today?

What is my response?

DAY TWO HUNDRED AND THIRTY-SEVEN:
READ I Chronicles 10-13

The Philistines fought against Israel and many Israelites were killed. Among them were Saul's three sons, and Saul himself was badly wounded. He commanded a soldier to kill him, but, he would not, so Saul fell upon his own sword and died.

As prophesied by Samuel, the elders anointed David and he became king over Israel. David became a mighty ruler because the Lord of hosts was with him. He captures Jerusalem and establishes Mount Zion. God had anointed David as king years early so the people supported him. He had three mighty warriors who defeated many men in battle. Several warriors from Saul's' tribe served David, warriors also came from the tribes of Gad, and Judah. Many mighty solders came to Hebron to declare their allegiance to King David. All of the people were pleased that he was king. David arranged to have the Ark of the Lord returned to the city. Uzza dies when he tried to keep the Ark from falling. This happened because only the priest could carry the Ark. David becomes angry at God's action and refused to move the Ark any further. The Ark was taken to the house of a man named, Obed-Edom.

PRAYER
Dear God,
How sad to recall Saul's death which serves as a reminder of his life. His disobedience cost him everything. I pray for the tender, yet, firm voice of the Holy Spirit to forever unction and guide me. Like David, I pray that Your hand would be upon me. In the name of Jesus Christ, I pray. Amen.

TODAY'S CHALLENGE: To respect God's way of doing things.

What else is God saying to me today?

What is my response?

DAY TWO HUNDRED AND THIRTY-EIGHT:
READ I Chronicles 14-16

King Hiram of Tyre sent carpenters, stone workers and materials to build David a house. He married additional women and had more children. When the Philistines heard that David was king, they prepared to make war with him. God told David that He would give him the victory. He defeated the Philistines and the fear of David was upon all the nations.

David pitched a tent for the Ark. He told the people that only the Levites may carry the Ark because God had chosen them to do so. All Israel accompanied the Ark into the city with singing and music. David openly danced and praised God. His wife Michal, Saul's daughter, despised him.

David appointed Asaph and his relatives to sing a song of praise to the Lord, thanking and praising Him for His miracles.

PRAYER
Dear Lord,
I too rejoice at Your presence. Thank You for the honor of being able to praise You with all of my heart. I offer praise and thanksgiving to You with all of my heart. In the name of Jesus Christ, I pray. Amen.

TODAY'S CHALLENGE: To praise God when its unpopular.

What else is God saying to me today?

What is my response?

DAY TWO HUNDRED AND THIRTY-NINE:
READ I Chronicles 17-19

After David moved into his palace, he desired to build a house for God. Nathan the prophet told David that God would cause one of his sons to build him a house and that there would be kings among his descendants forever. David offers a humble prayer of thanksgiving. He recalled before God how good God had been to his family.

David later defeated the Philistines and captured the town of Gath and other villages. Everywhere David went, God gave him victory. When David offered condolences to the son of Nahash, king of Ammon, the Ammonite officials humiliated David's officials and they returned home after some time. David made war with them, and they ran and soon surrendered to him.

PRAYER
Dear Lord,
As David did, I thank You for choosing me to be in Your family and making me special. I ask You to help me to live in that truth so that I need never feel rejected, unwanted or unloved. God will also fight my battles and give me victory. I am special to You, therefore, I command all feelings of inferiority and unworthiness to flee from me in the name of Jesus Christ, I pray. Amen.

TODAY'S CHALLENGE: To know that I am special to God.

What else is God saying to me today?

What is my response?

DAY TWO HUNDRED AND FORTY: READ I Chronicles 20-23

In the spring of the year, during the times that kings go to war, Joab defeated the cities of Amnon, including their capital city. David took the gold crown of their king. He took the precious jewels from it and put it in his crown. They also defeat three men of Gath who were giants.

Satan stood up against Israel and moved David to number the people. Against Joab's warning, David would not change his mind. This made God angry and He punished Israel. David repented and asked God to forgive him. David was terribly grieved when he saw the consequences of his sin upon the people. He bought a threshing place from Araunah and built an altar in to the Lord. There he offered sacrifices and the destruction stopped.

David felt that the temple of the Lord should be built there. He sent for his son Solomon and told him to build a temple for the Lord. He provided all of the supplies which Solomon needed. When David was old, he chose Solomon to be king. He also appointed certain Levites to the various duties of the temple.

PRAYER
Dear Lord,
Please help me not to commit sins that will harm other people. I ask Your forgiveness and strength for the times of my weaknesses and vulnerability to Satan. I also thank You for accepting my prayer of forgiveness and bringing me to a place of restoration. As David did for Solomon, help me to lay a solid and abundant foundation for my future generations, both spiritually and naturally. In the name of Jesus Christ, I pray. Amen.

TODAY'S CHALLENGE: To realize that what I do affects others.

What else is God saying to me today?

What is my response?

DAY TWO HUNDRED AND FORTY-ONE:
READ I Chronicles 24-26

King David assigned Aaron's descendants into work groups and the rest of the Levites were also assigned to various duties. The descendants of Asaph, Heman and Jeduthun were in charge of the music. They skillfully played various instruments and sang praises to God.

Temple guards were also appointed according to their families. Guards were also assigned to the treasury and other positions.

PRAYER
Dear Father in Heaven,
Thank You that You have a special place in Your family for me and for each one of Your children. I submit myself to You today, and ask You to show me clearly what my various gifts are and place me in the best position to use them for Your honor and glory. In the name of Jesus Christ, I pray. Amen.

TODAY'S CHALLENGE: To allow God to position me in life and in ministry.

What else is God saying to me today?

What is my response?

DAY TWO HUNDRED AND FORTY-TWO:
READ I Chronicles 27-29

King David assigned and arranged army commanders by the month. A leader was also assigned from each tribe. These included officials who were in charge of the king's treasures.

David called all of the elders and leaders together for a meeting in Jerusalem. David spoke to them. He told them that he wanted to build the Lord a house, but, that God would not allow him to because he had killed too many people in battle.

He told them that God had promised to let Solomon build the temple. He charged the people to worship and obey God. Afterwards he gave Solomon the plans for building the temple. David gave part of his own gold and silver with which to build the house of God. The tribal leaders also gave gold, silver, bronze, and other materials that were needed. David praised the Lord in front of everyone. After David died, God made his son, Solomon, the greatest king that ever lived.

PRAYER
Dear Lord.
I praise You for the humble spirit that You gave to King David. Thank You for his desire to always honor You first. I humbly submit myself to You. I ask You to do whatever You will in my life and cause me to assist and help to train those who are assigned to follow me and build on the foundation that that You have allowed me to lay. I ask this in the name of Jesus Christ. Amen.

TODAY'S CHALLENGE: To give generously to the building of God's kingdom.

What else is God saying to me today?

What is my response?

DAY TWO HUNDRED AND FORTY-THREE:
READ II Chronicles 1-3

God made Solomon a powerful king. On an occasion, Solomon sacrificed a thousand animals to please the Lord. God appeared to him and told him that He would give him anything he asked for. Solomon praised and thanked God and asked God for wisdom and knowledge. God was pleased with his answer, and told Solomon that He would make him more rich and famous than any king before or after him.

Solomon sent for skilled workers from Tyre to help him build the temple. He also assigned the foreigners among them and the Israelites to a work force. Solomon began building the temple to its specifications.

PRAYER
Dear Heavenly Father,
I too ask You for wisdom and knowledge above all things. Please allow me to see Your wisdom at work in me in all of my life endeavors and all of my relationships. I thank You as I receive this great gift from You, Almighty God. In the name of Jesus Christ, I pray. Amen.

TODAY'S CHALLENGE: To complete my assigned tasks.

What else is God saying to me today?

What is my response?

DAY TWO HUNDRED AND FORTY-FOUR:
READ II Chronicles 4-6

Solomon made all of the elaborate and costly furnishings for the temple. After the temple was finished, Solomon put all of the things that David had dedicated into the house of the Lord.

He assembled all of the elders and the heads of tribes so that they could make a covenant with God. The priests brought in the Ark of the Covenant and placed it in the most holy place. One hundred and twenty priests were praising the Lord and singing when suddenly a cloud filled the temple. The priest could not continue ministering because the glory of the Lord filled the house of God.

King Solomon spoke to the people and blessed them. He then prayed a prayer of dedication.

PRAYER
Dear Lord,
Both in private and in the congregation, I pray that the worship will be so pure in the places where I assemble that Your presence will fill them. In the name of Jesus Christ, I pray. Amen.

TODAY'S CHALLENGE: To offer pure worship.

What else is God saying to me today?

What is my response?

DAY TWO HUNDRED AND FORTY-FIVE:
READ II Chronicles 7-9

After Solomon's prayer, fire came down and consumed the offerings and God's glory filled the temple. The people knelt and worshiped the Lord saying. "For He is good, for His mercy endures forever." Solomon and the people dedicated the Temple to the Lord.

After both the temple and Solomon's house were completed, the Lord appeared to Solomon again in a dream. He told Solomon that if ever He withholds His blessings because the people sin, there is a remedy. "If my people who are called by name will humble themselves and pray and seek my face, and turn from their wicked ways, then I will hear from Heaven and will forgive their sin and heal their land."

Solomon completed both his palace and the temple. He conquered cities, built fleets of ships and became even greater and acquired more gold and abundant wealth. When the Queen of Sheba visited Solomon she nearly fainted as she beheld his splendor and blessings and heard his wise sayings. Solomon reigned for forty years and died. His son, Rehoboam became king after him.

PRAYER
Dear God,
You are good, Your mercy endures forever. Thank You for the abundance of blessings that You have bestowed upon me. I dedicate my temple, my body to You, and I open my life to receive even greater blessings from Your generous bounty. In the name of Jesus Christ, I pray. Amen.

TODAY'S CHALLENGE: To expand my expectation of how abundantly God will bless me.

What else is God saying to me today?

What is my response?

DAY TWO HUNDRED AND FORTY-SIX:
READ II Chronicles 10-13

Rehoboam, Solomon's son, went to Shechem to be crowned king. The people of the northern kingdom sent for Jeroboam, Solomon's former servant who was in hiding in Egypt. The people, with Jeroboam asked Rehoboam if he would make their work easier. Rehoboam refused the wise advice of the elders, and took the advice of his peers, who told him to speak harshly to the people and make their work even harder. The people from the Northern tribe did not accept Rehoboam as their leader. They chose Jeroboam to rule over them; leaving only the tribe of Judah for Rehoboam to rule over.

Rehoboam prepared to attack Israel, but, heeded God's warning not to do so. Rehoboam fortified certain cities in Judah and the priests and Levites of the northern tribe also supported King Rehoboam.

Soon after he was established in his kingdom, Rehoboam and all the people of Judah began disobeying God. God allowed them to be captured by Shishak of Egypt; however when the king and the people repented, God prospered them again. Rehoboam died after ruling for seventeen years in Jerusalem. Abijah became king of Judah after his death. Abijah challenged Jeroboam, king of Israel and took some of his cities.

PRAYER
Dear Lord,
Rehoboam failed to rule with the same heart as his father Solomon and did not adequately build on the foundations of David and Solomon. Lord, I ask You earnestly to help me to have the wisdom and discernment to follow wise and Godly examples in leadership and continue the things that please You and the things that bless me and others around me. In the name of Jesus Christ, I pray. Amen.

TODAY'S CHALLENGE: To seek and heed wise counsel.

What else is God saying to me today?

What is my response?

DAY TWO HUNDRED AND FORTY-SEVEN:
READ II Chronicles 14-16

After Abijah died, his son Asa ruled as king over Judah. He obeyed God and told everyone to worship the Lord God and to stop worshipping idols. He had a large army of valiant men. Zerah of Ethiopia attacked Judah with over a million soldiers. Asa prayed to the Lord and the Lord caused them to defeat Zerah's great army.

God spoke to Azariah. He warned King Asa and the people to not disobey God or He would desert them. Asa ordered the destruction of all idols and he repaired the Lord's altar. The people promised to follow the Lord.

King Baasha of Israel invaded Judah and captured the city of Ramah. King Asa sought to sign a peace treaty with the king of Syria and asked him to make king Baasha leave his country. Hanani, the prophet, rebukes king Asa for seeking help from Syria instead of from the Lord. He told him that his kingdom would never be at peace because of his actions. The king became furious and put Hanani into prison. He was also oppressed some of the people. Later Asa became severely ill in his feet. He did not seek the Lord, but, sought physicians, so he died.

PRAYER
Dear Lord,
Help me not to begin trusting You, then becoming deceived, thinking that I can trust in other things instead of You. Forever You are my security and my provider. In the name of Jesus Christ. Amen.

TODAY'S CHALLENGE: To remain humble and seek the Lord, especially when it looks like I can handle things on my own.

What else is God saying to me today?

What is my response?

DAY TWO HUNDRED AND FORTY-EIGHT:
READ II Chronicles 17-19

Jehoshaphat became king of Judah after his father Asa died. He strengthened his defense against Israel. He followed the Lord and the Lord blessed him. He became very powerful and the nations around feared him because the Lord was with him. He became very rich and famous. He signed a treaty with Ahab, king of Israel and his son married Ahab's daughter.

King Jehoshaphat joined with king Ahab in battle and was almost killed, but, he cried out to the Lord. Ahab died in battle after ignoring the words of God's prophet, Micaiah. The prophet Hanani met Jehoshaphat after the battle and rebuked him for making friends with the wicked king Ahab.

Jehoshaphat appointed judges to settle disputes. He told the judge to be fair in their decisions. He often traveled through his kingdom and urged the people to turn to God and worship Him.

PRAYER
Dear Lord,
Help me to have a pure heart and seek peace, but, give me the wisdom to not make a contract with, or friends with, people who are Your enemies. I ask this in the name of Jesus Christ. Amen.

TODAY'S CHALLENGE: To use my position of influence to encourage people to follow the Lord.

What else is God saying to me today?

What is my response?

DAY TWO HUNDRED AND FORTY-NINE:
READ II Chronicles 20-22

The armies of Moab, Ammon and others joined together to make war against King Jehoshaphat. The king was afraid so he prayed and proclaimed a fast throughout the land and asked the Lord what he should do. All of the people came to seek the Lord.

The Lord spoke through Jahaziel and told them to not be afraid because this would be *His* battle. He said. "You will not need to fight in this battle. Position yourselves, stand still and see the salvation of the Lord." The king appointed singers to go out before the Lord. They praised God and sang. "Praise the Lord, for His mercy endures forever." As soon as they began singing, the Lord confused the enemy's camp and they completely destroyed each other.

After Jehoshaphat's death, his son, Jehoram reigned as king. After Jehoram became king, he had his brothers killed. He married Ahab's daughter and followed the sinful practices of that family. He caused confusion among the people. The prophet Elijah sent him a letter telling him that God would punish him and the people who followed him. He told him that he would die from a terrible stomach disease. He suffered greatly for two years from the stomach disease and died.

Ahaziah became king after Jehoram's death. His mother, Athaliah, encouraged her son to sin against God. God instructed Jehu to kill him. Upon hearing that her son was dead, Athaliah destroyed all of the royal heirs. However, Jehosheba was able to save one son, Joash. She hid him in the temple for six years while Athaliah ruled as queen of Judah.

PRAYER
Dear Lord,
Thank You for reminding me that my biggest battle is no match for my great God. Help me to remember that praise is a weapon that causes confusion in the enemy's camp. "Thanks be to God for His mercy endures forever." In Jesus name. Amen.

TODAY'S CHALLENGE: To praise God when I'm overwhelmed.

What else is God saying to me today?

What is my response?

DAY TWO HUNDRED AND FIFTY: READ II Chronicles 23-25

After six years, Jehoiada the priest enlisted the support of key leaders and reminded them of God's promise to David. He encouraged them to crown Joash king. The Levites and the people of Judah heeded his words. Jehoiada had the commander of the army to execute Athaliah.

Joash thrived as a seven year old king, under the guidance of his mother and the priest, Jehoiada. Joash repaired the temple and did good deeds for the people.

After the death of Jehoiada the priest, the leaders of Judah influenced Joash. They immediately stopped worshipping in the temple and began worshipping idols. This aroused God's anger. Zechariah warned them that God would punish them. The people, along with Joash, stoned him to death. As he died he prayed that God would punish them all. The following year all of the leaders were killed by the Syrian army who invaded them. Joash was wounded in the battle. While he was in bed recovering, two of his officials killed him.

His son, Amaziah became king after. Amaziah obeyed the Lord by doing right, but, he refused to be completely faithful. As soon as he began disobeying the Lord, people from Jerusalem plotted against him and killed him.

PRAYER
Dear Lord,
If by providence or fate, I am called to a position of power and influence, please help me to continue worshipping and loving You completely. In the name of Jesus Christ, I pray. Amen.

TODAY'S CHALLENGE: To not try to manipulate myself into position.

What else is God saying to me today?

What is my response?

DAY TWO HUNDRED AND FIFTY-ONE:
READ II Chronicles 26-29

After King Amaziah's death, the people crowned his son, sixteen year old, Uzziah, king of Judah. He did what was right in the sight of the Lord. Zechariah was an advisor to him. As long as He sought the Lord, he prospered.

During his reign, Uzziah warred against the Philistines. He created a powerful army with very sophisticated weapons. God helped him and he became powerful and his fame spread throughout the world. He soon became proud and presumptuous. One day he disobeyed God by going into the temple to burn incense, a duty that only the Levitical priests were authorized by God to do. Azariah, the priests warned him not to do it. The king became very angry and God immediately struck him with leprosy. He had leprosy for the rest of his life. He was not allowed in the temple or in his own palace. His son, Jotham ruled in his stead.

Jotham obeyed the Lord and did what was right, but, the people of Judah continued sinning against the Lord. After his death, Ahaz, his son, became king. Ahaz disobeyed God like the kings of Israel. He made idols and sacrificed his own sons. God punished them by allowing them to be defeated by their enemies. In desperation Ahaz destroyed the temple furnishings and erected shrines to the gods of the Syrians. This caused the final destruction of Ahaz as well as Judah. After his death, Hezekiah, his son, became king. He obeyed the Lord and did what was right.

PRAYER
O Merciful Lord,
Thank You for Your love and patience with Your people. Help me to obey You and do what is right in Your sight. Please keep me from pride and presumption. In the name of Jesus Christ, I pray. Amen.

TODAY'S CHALLENGE: To choose to do what is right.

What else is God saying to me today?

What is my response?

DAY TWO HUNDRED AND FIFTY-TWO:
READ II Chronicles 30-32

Hezekiah celebrated the Passover with the largest crowd that ever attended. He invited all of Israel with a letter that reminded them of God's goodness. They celebrated for seven days. The people were so excited that they extended the celebration for seven more days. The priests and Levites asked God to bless the people, and He did.

After the celebration, the people went throughout Judah and smashed all of the images of foreign gods and destroyed all of the various shrines. The people brought an offering for the Levites, a tenth of everything they owned. The king cared for his people and he did what was right and good. He was successful because he obeyed the Lord with all of his heart.

King Sennacherib of Assyria attacked Judah. The prophet Isaiah and King Hezekiah asked the Lord for help. God sent an angel that killed all of the soldiers and commanders in the Assyrian camp.

Hezekiah became very ill. He prayed and God extended his life for fifteen years. God made Hezekiah extremely rich. After he died he was buried in a site that was reserved for only the most respected kings. His son, Manasseh, became king after him.

PRAYER
Dear Lord,
Thank You for the faithful life of king Hezekiah. May my worship to You move me to smash every idol in my life, and extol You as Lord of all. In the name of Jesus Christ, I pray. Amen.

TODAY'S CHALLENGE: To continue the celebrations that bring me closer to God.

What else is God saying to me today?

What is my response?

DAY TWO HUNDRED AND FIFTY-THREE:
READ II Chronicles 33-36

Manasseh was only twelve years old when he became king of Judah. He disobeyed the Lord. He rebuilt the shrines that his father had destroyed, and even practiced witchcraft and magic. God allowed him to have a ring put in his nose and taken captive to Babylon. There he repented and prayed to the Lord. The Lord restored him as king and he feared the Lord and tore down the shrines and idols. He ordered everyone in Judah to worship the Lord.

After his death, his son, Amon ruled over Judah. He disobeyed the Lord and restored idol worship. He was assassinated in his palace. His son Josiah became king in his place. Josiah was only eight years old when he became king. He obeyed the Lord and followed the example of David. He abolished idol worship in Judah. Through Hilkiah and Shaphan, The Book Of God's Law was found and read to the king. They were sent to inquire of Huldah, the prophetess, who received the word of the Lord for the king. The king assembled the people and read from the book. He destroyed all of the idols and commanded that the people celebrate Passover.

After the death of Josiah, his son, Jehoahaz was crowned king. The king of Egypt took him captive after three months and appointed his brother, Jehoiakim king of Judah. This king disobeyed the Lord and did evil. He was captured by the king of Babylon and taken away as a prisoner. After him was, King Jehoiachin. He did evil in the sight of the Lord. He too was taken captive to Babylon and the King of Babylon appointed Zedekiah king of Judah. He disobeyed God and God punished him and Judah. God allowed the King of Babylon to destroy Jerusalem. It remained that way for seventy years, just as the prophet Jeremiah prophesied. At the end of seventy years, God moved on Cyrus of Persia and he allowed anyone who wanted to, to return to Judah and begin rebuilding the temple.

PRAYER
Dear Lord,
You are consistent. Evil brings destruction and righteousness brings blessings. Help me to daily read Your word so that I will remember Your commandments and consistently obey them. In the name of Jesus Christ, I pray. Amen.

TODAY'S CHALLENGE: To quickly repent if I sin.

What else is God saying to me today?

What is my response?

DAY TWO HUNDRED AND FIFTY-FOUR: READ Ezekiel 1-3

Ezekiel's name means "God Strengthens." Ezekiel is by the river Chebar, among the captives that were taken into Babylon when he has what is called an "open" vision. He is not asleep. He describes a whirlwind emerging from the north. It has an amber color that radiates. Out of the midst of it he sees living creatures that look like men; only they have four faces, each is different. He also sees a man seated above a throne. He has the appearance of the glory of God. Upon seeing this awesome sight, Ezekiel falls to his face. A voice tells him to stand up and the Spirit enters him. The voice tells him that he is being sent to the rebellious, impudent, stubborn nation of Israel.

He encourages Ezekiel to not be afraid, assuring him that He will be with him and will put His word in his mouth. Ezekiel is instructed to eat a scroll. He is then taken by the Spirit to the captives at Tel Abib. For seven days he sits among them, so astonished that he cannot speak. After seven days God tells him that he is being sent as a watchman to warn the wicked.

PRAYER
Dear God,
Wherever we go, Your love follows. I pray for Your Spirit to visit me in my areas of captivity and set me free. Please help me to respond to Your call and not be stubborn and rebellious. In the name of Jesus Christ, I pray. Amen.

TODAY'S CHALLENGE: To allow God to put His word in my mouth.

What else is God saying to me today?

What is my response?

DAY TWO HUNDRED AND FIFTY-FIVE: READ Ezekiel 4-7

God tells Ezekiel to draw a picture of Jerusalem on a clay tablet and lay siege against it. He is then commanded to lie on his left side for 390 days for the house of Israel, and forty days for Judah. God says that he will restrain him so that he cannot move until the days are ended.

Ezekiel is instructed to take wheat, barley, beans, lintels, millet and spelt to make bread for himself. This will be his only diet during this time. He is to eat and drink only certain amounts at a time. This is to demonstrate that Israel's supply will be cut off and they will lack bread and water.

God will execute judgment against Jerusalem in the sight of the nations. He will bring great calamity because of their multiplied disobedience, more than any nation around them. God promises to leave a remnant; however the end has come and their disaster has dawned.

PRAYER
Dear Lord,
Please break any vestige of pride and rebellion that may be lurking within me. Help me to be pliable so that You can easily mold me to fit into Your perfect will. In the name of Jesus Christ, I pray, amen.

TODAY'S CHALLENGE: To honor God among non-believers.

What else is God saying to me today?

What is my response?

DAY TWO HUNDRED AND FIFTY-SIX: READ *Ezekiel 8-11*

The hand of the Lord falls upon Ezekiel as he is sitting in his house with the elders of Judah. The Lord lifts him up and suspends him by his hair and gives him visions of the inner court and the idols there. He shows him increasingly greater images of the elders of Israel who secretly worship every abominable creature imaginable; and they think that God does not see.

God calls for angels and tells them to mark the foreheads of the men who sigh and cry because of these abominations. He commands another angel to kill, to spare not, and have no pity. These are commanded to slay old and young, male and female who do not have the mark on their foreheads, beginning with the elders.

Ezekiel is commanded to prophesy against the wicked counselors of the city. One of them falls dead immediately. Ezekiel cries out to God. God promises Ezekiel that He will be with the people in captivity and after they have repented, He will put a new heart and a new spirit within them.

PRAYER
Dear Lord,
Wickedness spreads like cancer and You will not tolerate it. Please help me to not give in to any temptation to participate in the wickedness in my environment. May I bear the mark of God so that I may be spared from His wrath. In the name of Jesus, I pray. Amen.

TODAY'S CHALLENGE: To know that all walls are made of glass to God's eyes.

What else is God saying to me today?

What is my response?

DAY TWO HUNDRED AND FIFTY-SEVEN: READ Ezekiel 12-14

God tells Ezekiel to demonstrate to the people their doom by taking his belongings, digging through a wall and walking into captivity blindly. He warns them that this is not a false vision and it will not be postponed.

Ezekiel is also told to prophesy against false prophets of Israel who prophesy out of their own hearts for gain, perverting judgment. God will remove them from their places. He tells Ezekiel that Israel's sin is great. He says that if a land is persistently unfaithful and He decides to destroy it; even if Noah, Daniel and Job were in it, they could only save themselves.

PRAYER
Dear Lord,
You give Your people every opportunity to repent. Help me not to question You when judgment falls on the persistently disobedient. In the name of Jesus Christ, I pray. Amen.

TODAY'S CHALLENGE: To be sure that in the midst of wickedness, I remain righteous.

What else is God saying to me today?

What is my response?

DAY TWO HUNDRED AND FIFTY-EIGHT: READ Ezekiel 15-18

God promises to burn Israel like the wood of a vine from the forest. He depicts Israel as an abandoned child who was struggling in her own blood when he found her and caused her to live. He then covered her nakedness, beautified her and adorned her with silk and fine jewelry. God helped her to become a lovely woman. When she learned that she was attractive enough to have any man she wanted she played the harlot. Her rebellion will result in her lovers abusing her. God will however, remember His covenant with her. She will remember and be ashamed.

Ezekiel is told that Israel will no longer use the excuse of their forefather's sins. Each person will carry his own iniquity. If a wicked man repents, he shall live. If a righteous man commits iniquity he shall die. The soul who sins will die.

PRAYER
Dear Faithful and Just God,
Thank You that You are righteous and fair. Thank You for rescuing and delivering me. Thank You that each person will bear their own iniquity. In the name of Jesus Christ, I thank you. Amen.

TODAY'S CHALLENGE: To not live so that people will use me as an excuse for their sin.

What else is God saying to me today?

What is my response?

DAY TWO HUNDRED AND FIFTY-NINE: READ Ezekiel 19-21

Ezekiel writes a funeral dirge for Israel's leaders. When the people come to Ezekiel to inquire of the Lord for them, the Lord says he will not give them an answer. Instead He tells Ezekiel to remind them of the awful sins of their forefathers and how they have continued in their rebellion.

God promises to soon draw out His sword against Jerusalem. He tells Ezekiel to groan in sorrow and despair. The Lord will allow the king of Babylon to take them away as prisoners. He also announces to Ammon that their days of oppressing others are over. God's furious anger is also kindled against them. They will be punished in the land of their birth.

PRAYER
Dear God,
I pray for the spiritual leaders who influence the people. Help them to take their positions seriously and not cause the people to sin against God. I pray this in the name of Jesus Christ. Amen.

TODAY'S CHALLENGE: To not repeat the sins of my foreparents.

What else is God saying to me today?

What is my response?

DAY TWO HUNDRED AND SIXTY: READ Ezekiel 22-24

Israel's idols and murders have made them guilty and they will soon be punished. Sexual sins, bloodshed, oppression of strangers and mistreatment of the fatherless and widow are among Israel's many sins.

God depicts Samaria and Jerusalem as two sinful sisters. Samaria (Ohola), was his wife, but, continued to be a prostitute. (Oholibah), Jerusalem was even more sinful. God condemns the two sisters and they will be punished.

Ezekiel's wife dies and God tells him not to mourn her or show grief. This was to demonstrate something to Israel.

PRAYER
Dear Lord,
I pray for mercy for the strangers, the fatherless and the widows. Please remember them and in all places that they are and please send help to them in various ways, even through me. In the name of Jesus Christ, I pray. Amen.

TODAY'S CHALLENGE: To constrain my emotions when necessary.

What else is God saying to me today?

What is my response?

DAY TWO HUNDRED AND SIXTY-ONE: READ Ezekiel 25-27

The children of Amnon celebrated when God's people were destroyed. God tells Ezekiel to condemn them. They will be conquered by tribes from the east. Their capital city will be plundered and they will not be a nation again. He also pronounces judgment on Moab, Edom, Phillistia and Tyre.

God tells Ezekiel to sing a funeral song for Tyre. The songs tell of the prosperity and pride that characterizes the sea coast city of Tyre. They will die a gruesome death.

PRAYER
Dear Lord,
When all is well with me, please help me to reach back and provide comfort or whatever I can to others who may not be as comfortable as I am. Please direct me and grant me discernment so that I may know exactly what to do. In the name of Jesus Christ. Amen.

TODAY'S CHALLENGE: To avoid prosperity's deadly sin, pride.

What else is God saying to me today?

What is my response?

DAY TWO HUNDRED AND SIXTY-TWO: READ Ezekiel 28-30

God pronounces judgment on the king of Tyre who thinks he is a god and that Tyre is his throne. He is a clever businessman, but, his wealth has made him arrogant. God will show him that he is only a man. God tells Ezekiel to sing a funeral song for the king of Tyre. He is also told to condemn the city of Sidon and to tell them that God is their enemy. God promises to gather the people of Israel who are scattered and restore them to their land.

Ten years after their Babylonian captivity, the Lord speaks to Ezekiel of his plans to overthrow Egypt. They refused to help the people of Israel, but, broke the arms of those who reached out for help. Egypt will lie in utter ruins for forty years. God says He will hand over the nation of Egypt to the king of Babylon and Egypt will be barren and all of its idols smashed.

PRAYER
Dear Lord,
Though You are long suffering, Your judgment against the arrogant and proud is sure. I pray for mercy and the spirit of repentance on those who I know are arrogant and proud. In the name of Jesus Christ, I pray. Amen.

TODAY'S CHALLENGE: Rebellion and its consequences are a choice.

What else is God saying to me today?

What is my response?

DAY TWO HUNDRED AND SIXTY-THREE:
READ Ezekiel 31-33

God describes Egypt as a great cedar tree which He will now chop down. They are more powerful than any nation on earth, but, He will chop them down and they will join the godless and other victims of violent death. Ezekiel writes a funeral song for the king of Egypt. God will devise unusual ways to bring destruction upon him. God says to Egypt. "You may be more beautiful than the people of other nations, but you will also die and join the godless in the world below."

God informs Ezekiel that he is chosen to be a watchman for Israel. He is to warn them so that they can choose to repent. If not they have chosen judgment. The Lord is just. If a sinner repents, his past sins are forgiven; likewise if a righteous person chooses to become a sinner, his past good is not remembered. The people of Israel hear Ezekiel's words, but, they have no change of heart.

PRAYER
Dear Lord,
I thank You that You are just. I ask You to please help me to be diligent, and give me wisdom in warning sinners to repent and encouraging those who are righteous to continue obeying and honoring You. In the name of Jesus Christ, I pray. Amen.

TODAY'S CHALLENGE: To not be too proud to change.

What else is God saying to me today?

What is my response?

DAY TWO HUNDRED AND SIXTY-FOUR: READ *Ezekiel 34-36*

The leaders of Israel are like shepherds who take care of themselves and ignore the sheep. God tells Ezekiel to tell them that they are doomed. God will seek out His sheep and take care of them Himself. The strong people have oppressed the weaker ones, like strong sheep who use their horns to oppress the weaker. God's judgment is pronounced upon them. God promises Israel that they will eventually live in peace.

God says, He is Edom's enemy and will turn their nation into an empty wasteland.

He assures Ezekiel that Israel's mountains which their enemies thought they owned will once again house the people and trees of Israel. God will answer Israel's prayers and cause them to flourish again.

PRAYER
Dear God,
Thank You for caring so lovingly for those who are weak and oppressed. Help me to faithfully care for them also. In the name of Jesus Christ, I pray. Amen.

TODAY'S CHALLENGE: To discern what is dear to God's heart and make it dear to mine.

What else is God saying to me today?

What is my response?

DAY TWO HUNDRED AND SIXTY-FIVE: READ Ezekiel 37-39

The Spirit of God takes Ezekiel to a valley full of dry bones. God asks Ezekiel if the bones can live. He tells God that only He knows. God tells Ezekiel to prophesy to the bones. The bones began to rattle and come together. Muscle and skin come on them. Then God commands Ezekiel to blow breath upon them and they come alive. God tells Ezekiel that the people of Israel are like these bones, but, God's spirit will give them breath and bring them home again.

God tells Ezekiel that he will bring Israel and Judah together. God tells Ezekiel to condemn the wicked ruler Gog in the land of Magog. God tells them that He knows of their evil plan to attack Israel, but, they themselves will be defeated. He will attack them with diseases and punish them with death. When God punishes the wicked, Israel will know that He is God who sent them away, but, who is bringing them back.

PRAYER
Dear God,
The vision of the dry bones gives me hope also. I pray that every plan that You have for my life, every dream, every vision that seems to have dried up, will come together and live. I ask You, the author of life to speak life to them and they will flourish. In the name of Jesus Christ, I pray. Amen.

TODAY'S CHALLENGE: To believe that all of the pieces of God's plan for my life will come together.

What else is God saying to me today?

What is my response?

DAY TWO HUNDRED AND SIXTY-SIX: READ Ezekiel 40-42

Ezekiel is taken by the Spirit and shown in visions a high mountain in Jerusalem. He sees buildings and a man with a measuring tape in one hand and a measuring stick in another.

He shows Ezekiel the east gate, the outer court, the north gate, the south gate, the gates leading to the inner courtyards, the rooms for sacrificing animals, the rooms belonging to the priests, the inner courtyard and the temple, the storage room of the temple, and the temple inside and out. A wall separates what is sacred from what is ordinary.

PRAYER
Dear Lord,
You have a specific purpose for everything that You create. Just as the specifications of the measurements and designation of the temple areas were important, so I invite You to perfect Your purpose for every area of my life for Your glory. In the name of Jesus Christ, I pray. Amen.

TODAY'S CHALLENGE: To realize that God has a purpose in everything that He does.

What else is God saying to me today?

What is my response?

DAY TWO HUNDRED AND SIXTY-SEVEN: READ Ezekiel 43-45

Ezekiel is taken back to the east gate of the temple where he sees again the vision like he had seen before. He bows his face to the ground and the Lord's glory comes through the east gate into the temple. He is carried into the inner court by the Spirit and God speaks to him there, telling him that this temple is His throne on earth. He tells Ezekiel how the altar must be dedicated.

He tells Ezekiel that since He came through the east gate, no one must use it, it must remain closed. No godless foreigners are allowed to come into the temple when sacrifices are being offered. Some of the Levites have begun serving idols. They will be punished. The Zadok priest remained faithful so they are allowed to continue serving God.

God tells Israel to set aside an area of land that will be sacred to Him. Certain areas of land will also be set aside for Israel's rulers and certain festivals will be celebrated.

PRAYER
Dear God,
Thank You for bringing order out of chaos. I invite You, Lord of Lords, to bring Your divine order into every area of my work, family and life, so that we can function in the harmony that reflects Your purpose. In the name of Jesus Christ, I pray. Amen.

TODAY'S CHALLENGE: To incorporate those things in my life and family that help us to live in harmony with God and each other.

What else is God saying to me today?

What is my response?

DAY TWO HUNDRED AND SIXTY-EIGHT: READ Ezekiel 46-48

God gives various instructions for the observation of the Sabbath and the offering of sacrifices and order in worship. He gives laws about the ruler's land and the sacred kitchens.

Ezekiel sees a stream flowing from under the entrance of the temple. This water flows eastward to the Jordan River valley and empties into the Dead Sea. Fruit trees grow all along this river and produce fresh fruit every month. God tells them how to divide the land by tribe. A special section of land will be set aside for God and the rest divided among the other tribes. God gives dimensions of the New Jerusalem. The new name of the city will be "The-Lord-Is-Here!"

PRAYER
Dear God,
Thank You for Your enthusiastic restoration of Israel. You alone can make all things new. Please search through the ruined areas of my soul, allow the stream of your Holy Spirit to produce good fruit within me, restore me and establish a new image within me. I pray this in the name of Jesus Christ. Amen.

TODAY'S CHALLENGE: To realize that God knows exactly how to repair every broken area of my life.

What else is God saying to me today?

What is my response?

DAY TWO HUNDRED AND SIXTY-NINE: READ Daniel 1-3

Daniel's name means "God is My Judge". He was taken captive into Babylon as a teenager. Daniel and three of his friends are chosen by the king's officials to be trained for three years to become officials to the royal palace. Daniel has the gift of interpreting dreams. One night King Nebuchadnezzar has a very disturbing dream. He insists that his wise men tell him both the dream and its interpretation or they will be killed. They tell the king that his is impossible. The king becomes angry and gives orders for every wise man in Babylon, including Daniel and his three friends to be put to death.

Upon discovering this, Daniel asks the king to give him some time and he will give the king the interpretation. He tells his friends to pray with him. God reveals the dream to Daniel in a night vision. Daniel praises Lord. He tells the king that his soothsayers and magicians cannot interpret the dream, but, there is a God in heaven who is a revealer of secrets. He then proceeds to tell the king his dream and the interpretation thereof. The king bows before Daniel and declares that his God is the God of gods, the Lord of kings, and the revealer of secrets.

King Nebuchadnezzar makes a golden image which is to be worshiped by everyone at the sound of music. Violators will be thrown into a fiery furnace. The king becomes furious when Shadrach, Meshach and Abed-Nego refuse, saying, "The God that we worship can save us, but even if He doesn't, we won't worship your god." The king orders the furnace to be heated seven times hotter than usual and has strong men bind the three and throw them inside. The flames are so hot that they leap out and kill the soldiers. The king jumps up and says that he sees not three, but *four* men in the furnace, and the fourth looks like a god. The king goes to the furnace and calls out; "Servants of the Most High God come out!" The three come out unharmed without even the smell of smoke on their clothes. The king blesses the Lord of Heaven.

PRAYER,

Praise God! Praise God! Praise God! Although in captivity, You anointed Daniel and promoted him; and these three young men trusted God and took a position of faith even when their lives were in jeopardy. Lord, You are great and greatly to be praised! In the name of the Lord Jesus Christ, amen.

TODAY'S CHALLENGE: To trust God for miracles in the face of death.

What else is God saying to me today?

What is my response?

Day TWO HUNDRED AND SEVENTY: READ Daniel 4-6

King Nebuchadnezzar sends a letter throughout the earth to all nations and races of people. In it he praises the God of heaven and tells people about his dream and Daniel's gift of interpretation. The king relates a second dream which Daniel was asked to interpret. Daniel became terribly confused and told the king that he wishes that this dream pertained to his enemies because it was not good news. He tells the king that the dream is about him and that he will be forced to live with wild animals and eat grass like a wild animals for seven years until he learns that the Most High God rules over all kingdoms of the earth. He implores the king to turn from his sins and have mercy on those whom he has mistreated and the Lord will bless him.

About twelve months later, while on his roof, the king began admiring his palace and the city of Babylon. He was proud saying, "Look at the wonderful city that I have built by my own power and for my own glory!" Before he could finish speaking, a voice from heaven spoke and told him that for seven years he would eat grass as though he were an ox. The king reports that as time passed his hair grew long like eagle's feathers and his finger nails like the claws of a bird. Finally, he prayed to the God of heaven and his mind was healed. Only then was the king restored. For this reason he says. "Praise and honor the King who rules heaven!" Everything he does is honest and fair and he can shatter the power of those who are proud." Daniel is able to interpret the writing on the wall for King Belshazzar and receives a promotion. Daniel is thrown into a den of lions because he refuses to worship the king, but, continues praying to God three times a day as usual. God sends an angel to protect Daniel all night and he is not harmed. King Darius orders everyone to worship Daniel's God.

PRAYER
O Dear Lord,
King Nebuchadnezzar personifies the foolish pride that is a universal human trait. Right now I confess pride as an abominable sin. I ask You to please extricate it from me. I join the king in declaring to the world that God is God of the heavens and earth and He rules in the kingdoms of men. Amen.

TODAY'S CHALLENGE: To honor God and give Him glory.

What else is God saying to me today?

What is my response?

DAY TWO HUNDRED AND SEVENTY-ONE: READ Daniel 7-9

Daniel has dreams and visions which are very terrifying to him. It is explained to him that the four beasts that he saw represents four earthly kingdoms, "But God Most High will give his kingdom to His chosen ones, and it will be theirs forever and ever." Daniel both sees and hears these great things. He turns pale with fear and keeps these things to himself.

Daniel has a vision of a powerful ram with two horns, then a goat comes and breaks the horns of the ram, leaving him powerless. He also sees and hears angels. While he is pondering on what he is experiencing, a voice tells Gabriel to help him understand. The angel comes over to Daniel and he falls on his face in fear. He tells Daniel that the vision is concerning the end of time. Daniel becomes weak for several days because of these powerful visions.

Daniel discovers the writing of Jeremiah the prophet and discovers that the Lord decreed that Jerusalem would lie in ruins for seventy years. Daniel confesses his sins and prays to the Lord. While still confessing his sins, the angel Gabriel appears to Daniel again and tells him that God thinks highly of him. He tells Daniel that his people must suffer for seventy weeks. He explains several things to Daniel.

PRAYER
Dear Lord,
Thank You for being God of the past, present, and future. When You reveal Your plans move me to pray as the Holy Spirit leads. I confess my sins and the sins of my society and I look forward to the time when You will be Lord of all nations. I pray for Your mercy, grace and restoration in the name of Jesus Christ. Amen.

TODAY'S CHALLENGE: To prepare my heart for what God has in store for the future.

What else is God saying to me today?

What is my response?

DAY TWO HUNDRED AND SEVENTY-TWO:
READ Daniel 10-12

A message comes to Daniel from God about a horrible war. For three weeks Daniel is in sorrow. He eats no meat and drinks no wine, nor does he oil his face. While standing by the Tigres River, he sees someone dressed in linen and wearing a gold belt. The vision frightens Daniel and everyone around. Daniel falls down, but, the man helps him up and tells him not to be afraid. He tells Daniel that he has come to tell him about things that will happen to his people in the future. He explains the reign of the four kings and their exploits.

He tells Daniel that Michael, the chief of angels, protects the Israelites and will come during a time of great tribulation. Those who have their names written in The Book will be protected. Many dead will be raised; some to eternal life some to eternal shame. "Everyone who has been wise will shine as bright as the sky above, and everyone who has led others to please God will shine like stars. "He commands Daniel to keep this message secret until the end times. The angel's last words to Daniel are, "Be faithful until the end! You will rest and at the end of time, you will rise from death to receive your reward."

PRAYER
Dear Lord,
During the times of great tribulation, You promise to faithfully watch over Your people. I thank You. Help me to lead others to please You and to be faithful to the end. In the name of Jesus Christ, I pray. Amen.

TODAY'S CHALLENGE: To be sure that my name is written in "The Book."

What else is God saying to me today?

What is my response?

DAY TWO HUNDRED AND SEVENTY-THREE:
READ Esther 1-3

King Xerxes of Persia gives a royal party that lasts for many days. During this time he shows off all of his wealth and generously entertains everyone. While intoxicated, he sends for his beautiful wife, Vashti. He wants her to put on her crown and let his guests see how beautiful she is. Queen Vashti refuses and the king becomes angry. One of his officials urges the king to put her away and seek another queen.

A search is made throughout all of the provinces for a new queen. Esther, a beautiful Jewess, who was raised by her cousin Mordecai, is taken to the palace. Mordecai warns Esther not to divulge that she is Jewish. The young women all receive beauty treatments for one year and are presented to the king. Esther finds favor with everyone. The king falls in love with Esther immediately and makes her his queen. The king makes a great feast in her honor. Mordicai overhears a plot to harm the king. He tells Esther. She informs the king of Mordecai's deed. This is recorded in the king's chronicles in his presence.

A man named Haman is promoted above all of the king's princes. All of the king's servants bow and pay homage to Haman, but, Mordacai will not do so. Because Haman is furious at Mordecai, he devises a scheme to kill all of the Jews in Persia. Haman tricks the king into signing a decree to have all the Jews destroyed. Everyone is confused.

PRAYER
Dear God,
Sometimes the most unusual situations work out to place Your servants in strategic positions. I pray for favor also and ask that You strategically position me in life so that You can get the maximum glory. In the name of Jesus Christ. Amen.

TODAY'S CHALLENGE: To submit to God's preparation process.

What else is God saying to me today?

What is my response?

DAY TWO HUNDRED AND SEVENTY-FOUR: READ Esther 4-7

Mordecai tears his clothes and weeps and mourns through out the city and at the palace gate. Esther sends her servant to find out what is wrong with Mordecai. He sends a copy of the murder decree to her. He tells the servant that Esther should go to the king and beg him to have pity on the Jews. Esther is distraught. She sends word to Mordacai that anyone who approaches the king unsummoned will be put to death. Mordecai sends Esther a reply telling her that she will not escape just because she lives in the king's palace. "Who knows whether you have come to the kingdom for such a time as this." Esther tells Mordecai to tell all the Jews to fast with her and her handmaidens for three days, afterwards she will go to see the king although it is against the law "and if I perish, I perish!"

Three days later Esther dresses in her royal robes and approaches the king's throne. The king is happy to see her and holds out his golden scepter to her. He tells Esther that whatever she wants she may have, up to half his kingdom. She invites the king and Haman to dinner twice. Haman brags about his wealth and the fact that he received a dinner invitation from the queen. Haman's wife and friends suggest that Haman builds gallows seventy-five feet high and have Mordecai hanged the next day.

That night the king cannot sleep. He has a servant read him the records of events since he became king. When the servant reads the account of Mordecai, saving the king's life, he asks if he has been rewarded. The servant said that he has not. Haman comes in and the king asks him what should be done for a man that he wants to honor. Thinking the honor was to go to him, Haman gives his reply. The king sends Haman to do this honor for Mordecai.

That night at dinner Esther tells the king that her people are scheduled to be killed at the instigation of Haman. Right away Haman is hanged on the gallows that he had built for Mordecai.

PRAYER
Heavenly Father,
Please give me the courage to make the right decisions, especially when a lot is at stake. Give me the boldness to remain steadfast, knowing that You will take care of those who plot against me. I pray this in the name of Jesus Christ, my Lord, Amen.

TODAY'S CHALLENGE: To seek God on how to use my positions of influence.

What else is God saying to me today?

What is my response?

DAY TWO HUNDRED AND SEVENTY-FIVE: READ Esther 8-10

Before the day ended, the king gives Esther everything that belonged to Haman. Esther tells the king that Mordecai is her cousin. The king makes Mordecai one of his highest ranking officials. He also gives him the royal ring that Haman had worn. Esther weeps before the king and asks him to spare the lives of her people. Unable to change the law, the king gives Mordecai and Esther permission to write another law that will save them. These laws are quickly distributed throughout all of the cities. The Jews rejoice greatly. Many people accept the Jewish religion because they are now afraid of them.

The Jews fight and destroy their enemies, including Haman's ten sons. Mordacai institutes the Feast of Purim to celebrate what happened to them. King Xerxes does many great and famous things. Mordecai is also a popular leader and highest ranking official in the kingdom. He helps the Jews in many ways.

PRAYER
Dear Lord,
Your principles are consistent. Those who sin will be punished. Those who are righteous will enjoy the rewards of blessing and promotion. Thank You, Lord. Amen.

What else is God saying to me today?

What is my response?

DAY TWO HUNDRED AND SEVENTY-SIX: READ Ezra 1-4

In the first year of his reign King Cyrus of Persia announces that the Lord God of heaven and Israel's God has chosen him to build a temple in Jerusalem, which is in Judah. He encourages all who want to return to do so. The others help by giving silver and other necessities. King Cyrus returns everything that King Nebuchadnezzar had taken from the temple.

Ezra lists the names of all of the people who return. There are approximately fifty thousand people who return back to the various towns from which their families have come. The people along with the priests build an altar where it was before and begin offering sacrifices to the Lord. During the second year of the second month of their return, they begin building the temple. Everyone begins shouting and praising God because the work has begun. The foreign enemies of Judah and Benjamin ask if they can help rebuild the temple. They are refused so they begin harassing the Jews with official letters and aggravations that result in the work being stopped.

PRAYER
Heavenly Father,
Thank You for always fulfilling Your word. You can use whomever You choose to do Your service. Today I tilt my ear toward Your throne in worship, alert to hear Your word and direction to me. In the name of Jesus Christ. Amen.

TODAY'S CHALLENGE: To rejoice when I can participate in God's work through physical labor as well as with money.

What else is God saying to me today?

What is my response?

DAY TWO HUNDRED AND SEVENTY-SEVEN:
READ *Haggai 1, 2; Zechariah 1, 2*

The Lord sends the prophet Haggai to speak to the governor, the high priest, and the people of Judah who have returned to their land. The people had begun to rebuild the temple and stopped. The Lord's message to them is that it is time to arise and build His house. The prophet chides the people for building their own expensive houses and continuing with their lives, yet neglecting to rebuild the Lord's house. The people heed the voice of the prophet and resume the work of building the temple. God says to the people. "I am with You."

God stirs up the spirit of Zerubbabel and Joshua and the remnant of the people. They come and work diligently to restore God's temple. The people compare their efforts to the former one and feel that their temple is inferior to the first one. The Lord encourages them and tells them that He will fill this house with His glory and this temple will be more glorious than the first. God promises to richly bless the people in days ahead, and tells them to offer acceptable sacrifices. God speaks to Haggai and tells him to convey to Governor Zerubbabel that he will shake heaven and earth and wipe out kings and kingdoms, but, that he has been chosen to rule in the Lord's name.

Through the prophet Zechariah, God warns the people to not be stubborn like their ancestors, but, to turn to Him and He will help them. God says. "I am very protective of Jerusalem." Through a series of visions, God shows Zechariah that He will restore the people and the land, and Jerusalem will again be His chosen city.

PRAYER
Dear Heavenly Father,
Thank You for restoration and healing. Thank You for truly being a leader, teacher, provider, and protector, Father, to Your people. I welcome You into my life in a very personal way as my Father. Thank You, Lord. In the name of Jesus Christ, I pray. Amen.

TODAY'S CHALLENGE: To consciously and meditatively receive God as my father.

What else is God saying to me today?

What is my response?

DAY TWO HUNDRED AND SEVENTY-EIGHT:
READ *Zechariah 3-6*

Zechariah has a vision of Joshua the high priest. He is standing in front of the Lord's angel and Satan stands beside him ready to accuse him. The Lord intervenes and tells Satan that he is wrong. He tells him that Jerusalem is His chosen city and He has rescued Joshua from the fire. An Angel removes Joshua's clothes which are filthy, and adorns him in priestly garments. This signified that his sins are forgiven. The angel of the Lord tells Joshua that if he will obey God, he will put him in charge of the temple.

In another vision, Zechariah sees a lamp stand and Olive trees. God explains to him that it is a message to Zerubbabel: "I am the Lord All-powerful. So don't depend on your own power or strength, but on my Spirit."

Zechariah sees a vision of a flying scroll. The angel tells him that this scroll puts a curse on everyone who steals or lies. He is then shown a vision of a big basket. The angel tells him that this represents everything that the people have in mind. The vision of the four chariots represents the four winds of heaven which cover all four corners of the earth. God is Sovereign and rules over all the earth. God speaks of a crown that will be worn by His chosen leader.

PRAYER
Dear Heavenly Father,
I see that I and all people were created with an area of our lives that requires us to be connected to You in order to operate properly and to our maximum capacity. Unless we are connected to You, we will malfunction. I welcome and accept that connection and ask for Your wisdom in how to rely on the power and strength that only You can give me. In the name of Jesus Christ, I pray. Amen.

TODAY'S CHALLENGE: To know that I was never designed to live without being in total partnership with God.

What else is God saying to me today?

What is my response?

DAY TWO HUNDRED AND SEVENTY-NINE:
READ Zechariah 7-10

The people ask whether they should continue their custom of fasting. God's message to them is that He is not very concerned or impressed with their fasts. He wants them to observe His commandments which are these: "See that justice is done and be kind and merciful to one another! Don't mistreat widows or orphans or foreigners or anyone who is poor, and stop making plans to hurt each other." The Lord warns them that disobedience to this commandment is what caused their forefathers to be scattered among foreign nations and their beautiful land to be left desolate.

God is zealous for Zion and promises to bring it restoration. He promises them peace and blessings. God speaks against Israel's enemies, but, encourages Jerusalem to rejoice greatly and shout because their king is coming to save them. He will send showers of rain, punish unfaithful shepherds and will strengthen the house of Judah and have mercy on them.

PRAYER
Dear Lord,
It is so easy to observe religious rituals, and ignore Your will. Please give me the resources and strength to consistently help others who are in need. Please help me to not be so concerned with religious activities, but, to love and care for people. In the name of Jesus Christ, I pray. Amen.

TODAY'S CHALLENGE: To not try to please God with my ideas, but to obey His commandments.

What else is God saying to me today?

What is my response?

DAY TWO HUNDRED AND EIGHTY: READ Zechariah 11-14

The prophet announces destruction to Lebanon. The shepherds have no pity on the sheep, so God will become their shepherd. He gives names to the two sticks that He will use to tend the sheep: "Mercy and Unity." God will cripple the arms and blind the right eyes of the worthless shepherds who desert the sheep. God promises to give victory to both Jerusalem and Judah. However, He says they will both mourn when they see "the one they pierced with a spear."

Zechariah speaks prophetically of a time to come when there will be "a fountain in which David's descendants can wash away their guilt and shame." God will rid the people of all idols and controlling spirits and bad prophets. On the day of the Lord, Jerusalem will be restored. First it will be attacked and ravished, and the people scattered. Afterwards the Lord will appear with His angels, it will be a time of unending day.

PRAYER
Dear Holy Lord,
I see that You are a God of order. I welcome Your divine order in my life and all of my life affairs. Thank You for the glorious future that You have planned for Your people. In the name of Jesus Christ. Amen.

TODAY'S CHALLENGE: When I work for God, to do it God's way.

What else is God saying to me today?

What is my response?

DAY TWO HUNDRED AND EIGHTY-ONE: READ Ezra 5-7

The prophets Haggai and Zechariah encourage the people to resume their work of building the temple and they do so. Joshua the priest also encourages them. Governor Tattenai and some of his officials question the people, asking them who gave them permission to build the temple. God is with them so the governor does not stop the work. The governor and his officials write a letter to King Darius telling him what is going on, and asking if the Jews were authorized by Cyrus to rebuild the temple. King Darius orders someone to search through the records. Finally a scroll is found that confirms the Jews claim.

King Darius sends a letter to the Governor of Tattenai and his advisors warning them to stay away from the temple and to leave the people alone. He further orders the governor to pay the expenses for the project from the tax money and to give the priests whatever they need for sacrifices. He says, "If any of you don't obey this order, a wooden beam will be taken from your houses sharpened on one end and driven through your body." The governor and his advisor obey. The temple is completed with great success and the people celebrate the Passover.

Sometime later, Ezra, a scribe and expert in the Law of Moses arrives to Jerusalem from Babylonia. Other Jews, including priests, Levites and musicians arrive with him. Ezra had spent his entire life studying and obeying the Law of the Lord. He also taught it to others.

King Artaxerxes gives Ezra an incredible letter, lauding him as an expert in teaching the Laws of God. He gives him his blessings and encourages him to return to Jerusalem and attend to the things of the Lord. Furthermore the king provides Ezra with staff, silver, gold and great wealth with which to perform the duties of the Lord. Ezra praises God for allowing the king to honor the temple of the Lord and for helping him to bring back many people to Jerusalem.

PRAYER
Dear Lord,
Thank You for blessing Your people who do Your work. I ask You to raise up supporters and give abundant provisions to me and especially to those who are in full time ministry for You. In the name of Jesus Christ, I pray. Amen.

TODAY'S CHALLENGE: To expect blessings from unexpected places.

What else is God saying to me today?

What is my response?

DAY TWO HUNDRED AND EIGHTY-TWO: READ Ezra 8-10

Ezra leads a great number of people out of Babylon. The people fast and pray for God's protection from ambushes by the enemy and no harm comes to them. He finds Levites to serve in the temple and gives the gifts of gold and silver and other articles to the twelve priests to oversee.

Upon discovering that the people, including the priests and their sons, had married foreign wives, Ezra rips his clothes, his hair and his beard and sits in shock for hours. He prays to God, telling Him how ashamed he feels because of the disobedience of the people. The people listen to Ezra speak although it is raining very hard. All of the priests agreed to divorce their foreign wives and to sacrifice a ram as a sin offering. The priests and all of the men divorce their foreign wives and send them away with their children.

PRAYER
Dear Lord,
Please help me to remember that Your laws are there to protect me. Help me not to cause pain to myself and others because of disobedience. In the name of Jesus Christ, I pray. Amen.

TODAY'S CHALLENGE: To think about whom I may be hurting when I make decisions.

What else is God saying to me today?

What is my response?

DAY TWO HUNDRED AND EIGHTY-THREE:
READ Nehemiah 1-3

Nehemiah lived in the city of Susa under the rule of King Artaxerxes. He is told by his brother, Hanani who came form Judah, that the walls of Jerusalem are still broken down, and the gates burned. Nehemiah becomes very sorrowful. The king notices and asks him what is wrong. Nehemiah answers that he is sad because the city of his ancestors lie in ruins. The king asks what he can do. Nehemiah asks for permission to return to Jerusalem and repair the walls. The king grants him permission and complies with Ezra's request for a letter for the officials with whom he would come in contact. The king agrees and also sends a calvary troop and officers to accompany him. When Sanballot from Horon and Tobiah, the Ammonite hear about this, they become very angry. They do not want to see the Israelites succeed.

Three days after his arrival in Jerusalem, Nehemiah inspects the walls at night, telling no one what he has in mind. When he tells the Jewish officials, they are agreeable and ready to work. Sanballat and Tobiah began to harass them as soon as they hear about the plans. Nehemiah tells them that they have no possession or history in Israel and that God will cause their work to succeed. Ezra lists the names of the many people who worked on the wall.

PRAYER
Dear Lord,
Not everyone is happy about Your plans, but I am. Please list me among those who volunteer to work in the building of Your kingdom. Please provide me all of the workers and equipment that I need in order to complete the job successfully. I pray this in the name of Jesus Christ. Amen.

TODAY'S CHALLENGE: To be ready to do a job that might bring me criticism.

What else is God saying to me today?

What is my response?

DAY TWO HUNDRED AND EIGHTY-FOUR:
READ Nehemiah 4-6

Sanballot begins insulting the Jews in front of his friends and the Samaritan army. He taunts them and ridicules their work, saying, "Even a fox could knock over this pile of stones." Nehemiah prays to God that their enemies' insults will fall back on them. The people work hard and the wall is soon half finished. Sanballot and others see the wall going up and begin stirring up trouble and fighting with the people of Jerusalem. Meanwhile they continued building. They station guards around the area, day and night. Some of the people complain to Nehemiah. He intercedes for the poor and restitution is made.

Sanballot and his friends learn that Nehemiah and the Jews have completed the wall. Only the doors in the gates have not been hung. Sanbalot and Geshem send Nehemiah a message asking him to meet with them. He knows that they are planning to harm him, but four times he refuses. Sanballot sends an official letter falsely accusing Nehemiah. He realizes that their enemies are trying to frighten them to prevent them from completing the work. He prays for God to punish them. After fifty-two days, the work is completed. Their surrounding enemies become frightened because they realize that God has helped the Israelites.

PRAYER
Dear God,
In spite of opposition, please give me the power, strength and boldness to persevere until I complete each task that You have assigned me to do. In the name of Jesus Christ, I pray. Amen.

TODAY'S CHALLENGE: To not be frightened by the enemy's threats.

What else is God saying to me today?

What is my response?

DAY TWO HUNDRED AND EIGHTY-FIVE:
READ Nehemiah 7-9

After the wall is completed and the gates and doors are hung, the temple guards, singers and other Levites are assigned their work. Nehemiah assigns his brother, Hanani along with Hananiah, to be in charge. Ezra looks at the list of exiles who had returned and where they had settled.

On the first day of the seventh month, the people of all ages gather to hear Ezra read from the Law of Moses. Ezra, the priest, stands before the people and reads from early morning until noon and the people listened carefully. Ezra stands on a high platform where everyone can see him. When he opens the book, he and all the people praise and worship God. After this, the Levites go among the people and explain the meaning of Ezra's words to the people.

On the twenty-fourth day, the people fast and confess their sins and the sins of their ancestors. They listen to the Law for three hours and the next three hours they confess their sins and worship God.

PRAYER
Dear Lord,
I praise You for Your precious word and Your power to forgive sins. I confess my sins and the sins of my people before You. I ask for Your forgiveness of our ingratitude among other things. I offer this time to You in praise and worship. In the name of Jesus Christ. Amen.

TODAY'S CHALLENGE: To spend some time confessing my sins, and worshipping God today.

What else is God saying to me today?

What is my response?

DAY TWO HUNDRED AND EIGHTY-SIX:
READ Nehemiah 10-13

All of the people: the governor, the priests, the Levites, the leaders and all of the people make a firm agreement that they will obey the Laws of Moses which includes not marrying foreigners, bringing offering to the temple, not working on the Sabbath or other holy days and bringing their first-born sons to the priests who serve in the Lord's house.

Various tribes settled in certain areas of Jerusalem including the tribes of Judah, Benjamin, The Levites, and also temple guards and others.

Nehemiah dedicates the wall of Jerusalem and the priests and the Levites performed all of their duties well. The people send away anyone who has foreign ancestors. Nehemiah reminds some of the disobedient priests that as wise and great a king as Solomon was, his heart was turned to idolatry when he married foreign wives who did not serve the God of Israel. He sets many affairs of the people in order and prays that his service is acceptable to God and that God will bless him.

PRAYER
Dear Lord,
Help me to obey all of Your word, being aware that even wise men fall if they disobey Your laws. In the name of Jesus Christ. Amen.

TODAY'S CHALLENGE: To be wise enough to be obedient to God.

What else is God saying to me today?

What is my response?

DAY TWO HUNDRED AND EIGHTY-SEVEN:
READ Malachi 1-4

The book of Malachi opens with God telling the people that He loves them and rebuking them for their hypocrisy and gross disrespect for Him. They bring inferior offerings and service, yet, expect God's favor. God despises their behavior and reminds them that He deserves more than their rejects. "For I am a great king," says the Lord of Hosts, "and my name is to be feared among the nations."

The priests who will not hear and give glory to God's name will be cursed and their descendants rebuked. He rebukes them for corrupting the covenant of Levi. He also rebukes them for their treachery and infidelity. They embrace idols and profane their offerings. They deal treacherously with the wives of their youth, causing divorce, which God hates. They call evil good.

He tells them that the messenger of the Covenant will come to purge and purify. God calls the people to return to Him and not rob Him in tithes and offerings; He promises the blessings of the windows of heaven opened and the rebuking of the devourer for faithful tithers.

God is aware of their complaints against Him. God has a "Book of Remembrance" and He makes a distinction between those who serve Him and those who do not. Malachi describes the great Day of the Lord, the Day of Judgment.

PRAYER
Dear Lord,
You absolutely deserve all respect, glory, and honor. Please forgive me for dishonoring You at any time and in any manner. Flood my heart continually with the spirit of humility, so that I may live in awareness of Your great majesty. In the name of Jesus Christ. Amen.

TODAY'S CHALLENGE: To always give the Lord service and honor worthy of a king.

What else is God saying to me today?

What is my response?

DAY TWO HUNDRED AND EIGHTY-EIGHT:
READ Matthew 1-4

The book of Matthew traces the genealogy of Jesus Christ through the royal lineage of Joseph, Mary's husband. This is the account of Jesus' birth. A young woman named Mary is engaged to be married to Joseph. Before they get married she announces to him that she is going to have a child by the Holy Spirit. Joseph, a good man, does not want to embarrass her, so he decides to privately call off the wedding. While he is contemplating this, an angel of the Lord comes to him in a dream and tells him that the child that Mary is carrying is indeed from the Holy Spirit and not to be afraid to marry her. The angel tells him to name the child "Jesus," for He will save His people from their sins. What the prophets spoke is fulfilled. Soon after this, Joseph marries Mary, but does not sleep with her until after the baby is born. Joseph names the baby, "Jesus."

King Herod hears that a king is born and becomes troubled. Wise men from the east are following a star that will lead them to the Messiah. That night, in a dream, an angel of the Lord tells Joseph to immediately take Mary and Jesus to Egypt because Herod is seeking to kill him. Mary and Joseph do not return to Israel with Jesus until after Herod dies.

Years later, John the Baptist, begins baptizing and preaching to the people to "Repent, turn back to God." Crowds of people come to hear him. He tells them that one more powerful than he is coming and will baptize them with the Holy Spirit and fire. One day Jesus goes to the Jordan River to be baptized by John. John is astonished when he sees him. When Jesus comes up out of the water a voice from heaven says. "This is my beloved Son, in whom I am well pleased." The Holy Spirit leads Jesus into the wilderness where He fasts for forty days and nights. There He resists all of the temptations of the Devil who appears to him there. After the Devil leaves, angels attend to Jesus. Jesus then begins His ministry and chooses four fisherman as disciples. He preaches everywhere in Galilee and heals all manner of diseases. Large crowds begin to follow Him.

PRAYER
Dear God,
Thank You for Your great display of love in sending Your Son, Jesus, to take away my sins and the sins of the whole world. I welcome Jesus Christ personally into my life to take away all of my sins, and to heal all of my spiritual, mental, emotional and physical sicknesses. In the name of Jesus Christ. Amen.

TODAY'S CHALLENGE: To accept Jesus Christ as my Savior, forgiver of my sins, and healer of all my diseases.

What else is God saying to me today?

What is my response?

DAY TWO HUNDRED AND EIGHTY-NINE: READ Matthew 5-7

Jesus goes up on the side of a mountain and speaks to the crowd. His disciples gather and he teaches them how to determine the kind of people who please God and receive His blessings. He tells them that when people mistreat them because of Him, to rejoice. He tells the disciples that they should function as salt and light in the earth, and like a city on a hill. He tells them that He came to fulfill the Law of Moses, not to abolish it. He promises that not one minute' part of His word will be unfulfilled.

He teaches them that anger is dangerous and to seek reconciliation. He commands them to be faithful in marriage, stating that even looking at another woman and lusting for her means that you have committed adultery in your mind. "If your right eye causes you to sin, pluck it out." Don't divorce your wife unless she has committed some terrible sexual sin. He tells them to not swear and don't take revenge when they are wronged. Jesus tells them to love their enemies and give to the poor without bragging about it. He also teaches them how to pray; not by making vain repetitions like the hypocrites who like to show-off. He also tells them to fast privately. He warns against storing up treasures on earth and not in heaven. "Your heart will always be where your treasure is." He warns them to not be a slave to money or worry. He elaborates on the futility of worry and the wisdom in seeking God's kingdom and His righteousness as a priority and God will add all of the other things. He also teaching on judging, asking, seeking and knocking, the narrow gate, false prophets, a warning against presumption, and the parable of the foolish and wise builders.

PRAYER
Dear God,
I accept Jesus' words as Your words. I fully submit to His words because they produce goodness and life. Please help me to obey the words of Jesus in my daily life, although sometimes it's very hard. Please reveal to me what it means to seek Your kingdom first, and then give me the wisdom to do it. In the name of Jesus Christ, I pray. Amen.

TODAY'S CHALLENGE: To not panic when I see the commandments of Jesus, but realize that He is willing to help me obey them.

What else is God saying to me today?

What is my response?

DAY TWO HUNDRED AND NINETY: READ Matthew 8-11

As Jesus comes down from the mountain, he is approached by a leper who worships Him and asks for healing. Jesus heals him. He also heals a centurion's servant. He marvels at the man's faith, noting that it excelled that of the Israelites. Jesus heals many people, including Peter's mother-in law. During the evening, the people bring Him many people who are demon-possessed. He casts out the demons with a word and heals all of the sick.

Jesus and the disciples get into a boat. Jesus falls asleep and a terrible storm arises. The disciples are afraid and wake Jesus up. He arises and rebukes the waves and the sea and they calm down. After crossing the lake, Jesus encounters two demon-possessed men near the town of Gadara. Knowing that Jesus is about to cast them out, the demons beg to go into pigs that are nearby. Jesus complied and the pigs ran into the sea and drowned. Upon returning to His home town, He heals a crippled man, and tells him that his sins are forgiven. He is criticized for telling the man that his sins are forgiven. As Jesus is leaving, He sees a tax collector named Matthew. Jesus tells him to come with Him.

One day Jesus answers questions on fasting. While He is speaking, a man beseeches Him to come and heal his daughter. As they are on their way, a woman with an incurable blood disease touches His clothes. Jesus stops the procession to take note of her faith and to heal her. Meanwhile, they are told that the man's daughter is dead and that Jesus need not bother coming. Jesus tells the girl's father not to worry. Jesus proceeds to the house and raises the girl from the dead. He also heals two blind men and a man who is mute. Jesus notes that the fields are ripe, but, there are too few workers. He calls His twelve apostles and gives them power to cast out demons and to heal every kind of disease. He gives them instructions and sends them out. John, who is in prison, hears about what Jesus is doing. He asks for confirmation that He is the Messiah. Jesus sends him a reply. Jesus invites all who are tired of carrying their heavy burdens to come unto Him and rest.

PRAYER
Dear God,
Thank You that in Jesus is the fulfillment of every promise of God. I pray for workers in His kingdom and that His works and words will be carried throughout the earth to all people everywhere. I pray for the wisdom, the opportunity and the boldness to do my part. In the name of Jesus Christ, I pray. Amen.

TODAY'S CHALLENGE: To be both a partaker and a messenger of the ministry of the Lord, Jesus Christ.

What else is God saying to me today?

What is my response?

DAY TWO HUNDRED AND NINETY-ONE:
READ Matthew 12-15

Jesus answers questions about the Sabbath and establishes Himself as "Lord over the Sabbath." He enters a synagogue and heals a man who has a crippled hand. The Pharisees leave and begin plotting to kill Jesus. When Jesus realizes what is happening, He leaves that area and continues healing people, but warns them to not tell anyone. This fulfills a prophecy that Isaiah made years before.

On another occasion, Jesus cast demons out of a man who is blind and mute, and also heals him. The crowd is so amazed, they ask, "Can Jesus be the Son of David?" The Pharisees accuse Jesus of casting out demons by the power of Beelzebul, the ruler of the demons. Jesus knows their thoughts. He begins speaking on knowing a tree by its fruit, and the significance of the prophet Jonah's story. He tells them that when an evil spirit is cast out, if the former house remains empty, it will re-enter with seven other demons.

Jesus says that his family is made up of those who do the will of His Father in heaven. He teaches them through many parables. He explains that He uses parables or stories to explain the secrets of the kingdom and they are not for everyone to understand.

Herod hears about Jesus and fears that He is John the Baptist who has come back from the dead. He had earlier arrested John and had him beheaded. After Jesus hears about John, He goes across the Lake of Galilee to be alone, but, the crowd follows. His compassion moves him to heal them all. By evening they are all hungry. Jesus miraculously multiplies five loaves of bread and two fish and feeds over five thousand people. Jesus walks on water and heals many people in Gennesaret. A Canaanite woman asks Jesus to heal her daughter, after Jesus challenges her, she still has faith and receives her miracle.

PRAYER
Dear Lord,
Thank You for the compassion of Jesus Christ who is consumed with bringing salvation, healing and deliverance to the human race, all races of mankind. He is indeed the "Savior of the World." I thank You, Lord, for providing this for me and I humbly and gratefully ask for Your salvation, healing and deliverance to be fully activated in my life, and in the life of each of my family members and loved ones. In the name of Jesus Christ, I pray. Amen.

TODAY'S CHALLENGE: To accept Jesus as Savior, Healer, and Deliverer.

What else is God saying to me today?

What is my response?

DAY TWO HUNDRED AND NINETY-TWO:
READ Matthew 16-19

The Pharisees and Sadducees try to test Jesus by asking for a sign from heaven. He reiterates that the only sign will be that which was already given; the sign of Jonah. He warns His disciples against the "leaven" of the Pharisees and Sadducees, which refers to their teachings. Jesus queries His disciples asking them who they think He is. Peter answers. "You are the Messiah, the Son of the living God." Jesus tells him that only His Father in heaven could have revealed that to him. It is upon this revelation that He will build His church. He tells Peter that he will call him, "Rock." He tells them that He is giving them keys to the kingdom of Heaven, with the power to bind and loose.

From this time on, Jesus begins to speak of His suffering and death. About a week later Jesus takes Peter, James and John upon a very high mountain. He is transfigured, completely changed before their very eyes. At once, He is there talking with Moses and Elijah. God speaks from heaven and tells them to listen to His beloved Son, Jesus. Jesus gives them instructions as they descend the mountain. When they return to the crowd, Jesus commands a demon to leave a young boy. He tells His disciples that with a little faith they can do the same things; although some feats are accomplished with fasting and prayer.

Jesus teaches them that the greatest person in the kingdom is one who comes as a little child. He warns of the terrible penalty that awaits anyone who causes a little one to sin. He warns them to not be cruel to any child. He teaches on forgiveness and gives an illustration of an official who refused to forgive and the consequences that he suffered. He teaches on divorce, and how the love of riches can prevent one from entering the kingdom of heaven.

PRAYER
Dear God In Heaven,
I also believe that Jesus is the Messiah, the Son of God. Through faith in Him, and as His disciple, too, I now receive the keys to the kingdom; the power to bind and loose. I bind myself and my family and loved ones to the will and purposes of God and loose from us, all that is evil, detrimental, harmful and depraved. I choose to forgive everyone who has ever mistreated me, and I ask for forgiveness for all of my sins. I thank You and in the name of Jesus Christ, I submit my prayers to You Heavenly Father. Amen.

TODAY'S CHALLENGE: To continually allow the heavenly Father to reveal Jesus to me.

What else is God saying to me today?

What is my response?

DAY TWO HUNDRED AND NINETY-THREE:
READ Matthew 20-22

Jesus tells several parables that illustrate what the kingdom of heaven will be like. In the parable of the vineyard workers, He stresses the love of God and the truth that the first shall be last and the last first. He tells His disciples again about His death. The mother of James and John asks Jesus for special seats for her sons in His kingdom. Jesus explains that this is the Father's privilege to select and that the greatest among them is the slave, the one who serves. Jesus heals two blind men who cry out to him saying, "Lord, Son of David, have mercy on us."

Jesus sends his disciples to bring a donkey upon which He rides into Jerusalem. There many people spread their clothes on the ground and others take branches from the trees. The multitude follows Him and cries out, "Hosanna to the Son of David! Blessed is He who comes in the name of the Lord! Hosanna in the highest!" The crowd says. "This is Jesus, the prophet from Nazareth of Galilee."

Jesus curses a fig tree and it withers away. He tells His disciples, "If you have faith, when you pray, you will be given whatever you ask for." Jesus gives additional parables which are intended to show the Pharisees how they are rejecting Him as the Messiah and blindly refusing to believe that He is the Son of God. He tells the parable of the great banquet to illustrate the point that many are called, but, few are chosen. Concerning the paying of taxes, he tells His disciples to give God what belongs to Him, and give the Emperor what belongs to him. He explains that in the world to come, people won't marry, but, will be like the angels. When asked what is the greatest commandment, Jesus answers that the first and most important commandment is: "To love the Lord your God with all your heart, soul and mind and the second is to love others as much as you love yourself."

PRAYER
Dear Heavenly Father,
It is evident in the scriptures that the kingdom of heaven operates very differently from the world in which I live. I really need Your Wisdom, Strength and Faith, as I choose to live as a person who belongs to Your kingdom. Help me to *give, forgive, serve and love* in a manner that demonstrates that I belong to Your Kingdom. Please help me to have a greater revelation of what faith *really is* and how to employ it. In the name of Jesus Christ, I pray. Amen.

TODAY'S CHALLENGE: To love the lord my God with all of my heart, soul and mind; and to love others as much as I love myself.

What else is God saying to me today?

What is my response?

DAY TWO HUNDRED AND NINETY-FOUR:
READ Matthew 23-25

Jesus tells the crowd that the Pharisees are expert teachers of the law and to obey their teachings, but, do not follow their personal hypocritical way of living. He tells them that the Pharisees say one thing and do another. They burden the people and won't help. He tells them that the Messiah is their only leader and they should not call anyone else Rabbi or Father. He tells them that the greatest people among them are the ones who are servants. Those who exalt themselves shall be humbled. He condemns the Pharisees for their hypocrisy. Jesus laments over Jerusalem whom He wants to embrace and protect, but they reject Him.

While sitting on the Mount of Olives, Jesus tells His disciples that in the latter days, many people will come pretending to be Him, the Messiah, and will fool many people. He gives them many signs to indicate the time of His return. He describes the great tribulation of which the prophet, Daniel spoke and He tells them about the coming of the Son of Man. He gives the parable of the fig tree, but, tells them that no one knows the day or hour of his return except the Father in heaven.

He tells them to be watchful. To illustrate His point, He tells two parables; one of the wise and foolish virgins, and another about the three stewards and the talents. He concludes by telling them about the judgment day when every one will give an account to God for how they have lived. Jesus stresses that when we mistreat some one because we think they're unimportant, we mistreat Jesus. Some people will go into eternal life and some into everlasting punishment.

PRAYER
Dear Father In Heaven,
Please help me to not be a hypocrite. Everyone's heart is an open book to You, and You can see intents and motives. Please help me with my life-plan. Help me to consistently do Your will, so that I can eagerly anticipate Your return. On the final day of judgment, it is my complete desire to enter into eternal life with You. In the name of Jesus Christ, I pray. Amen.

TODAY'S CHALLENGE: To not be a hypocrite.

What else is God saying to me today?

What is my response?

DAY TWO HUNDRED AND NINETY-FIVE:
READ Matthew 26-28

Jesus tells His disciples that on Passover, He will be handed over to His enemies. Meanwhile the chief priests and leaders are meeting at the home of Caiaphas, the high priest, planning how they can have Jesus arrested. Judas Iscariot goes to the chief priests and asks how much they will give him, if he will help them arrest Jesus. They offer him thirty silver coins.

On the first day of the Feast of Unleavened Bread, during the Passover meal Jesus tells them that Judas will betray him to his enemies. As they are eating Jesus takes bread and wine and blesses it. He tells them concerning the bread, "Take, eat, this is my body." Of the wine he says, "Drink from it all of you, for this is My blood of the New Covenant, which is shed for many for the remission of sins." Jesus predicts Peter's denial and goes to the garden of Gethsemane to pray. He agonizes in prayer saying, "O Father, if this cup cannot pass away from me unless I drink it, Your will be done." While He is speaking with the disciples Judas comes with a great multitude carrying swords and clubs. Judas kisses Jesus to indicate Him to the mob. Jesus is arrested and taken to court. All of the disciples flee and Peter later denies Jesus.

The next morning, all of the chief priests and leaders plot to put Jesus to death. He faces Pilate, the Governor. Pilate washes his hands of the matter saying He finds no fault in Jesus, and hands Him over to the Jews. The soldiers strip Jesus of His clothes and places a crown of thorns on His head. They mock Him saying, "Hail king of the Jews." They spit on Him and strike Him on the head, and lead Him away to be crucified. From the sixth to the ninth hour there is darkness all over the land. About the ninth hour, Jesus cries with a loud voice, "Eli, Eli lama sabachtani?" meaning, "My God, my God why have You forsake me?"

Immediately, the veil in the temple rips from top to bottom, the earth quakes, graves split open, and many saints are resurrected. The people fear greatly and say, "Surely this was the Son of God!" Jesus is buried. After the Sabbath, on the first day of the week, Mary Magdalene and the other Mary find that Jesus' tomb is empty! An angel tells them that Jesus is risen from the dead. As they run to tell the disciples, Jesus meets them. They worship Him and He tells them to tell His disciples to come to Galilee to see Him. When the disciples see Jesus they worship, but, some people doubt. Jesus speaks to them saying, "All authority has been given to me in heaven and on earth, Go therefore . . . and lo, I Am with you always even to the end of the age."

PRAYER

Dear Lord, thank You for suffering the shame, pain, agony and humiliation of the betrayal, the trial and crucifixion. Thank You for yielding to the will of the Father, thank You for dying for my sins, thank You for arising from the grave.

TODAY'S CHALLENGE: To be forever grateful for Jesus.

What else is God saying to me today?

What is my response?

DAY TWO HUNDRED AND NINETY-SIX: READ *Mark 1-3*

The gospel of Mark begins with a confirmation that the account of Jesus Christ, the Son of God began just as God said it would through the prophet Isaiah. Some one is shouting "Prepare the way of the Lord, make a straight path for him!" John the Baptist showed up in the desert preaching, "Repent and be baptized, so that your sins will be forgiven!"

People from everywhere come to John and are baptized. During this time, Jesus also comes to John to be baptized. As Jesus comes out of the water, The Holy Spirit descends upon Him like a dove and a voice from heaven says, "This is my beloved Son, in whom I am well pleased." Immediately the Spirit leads Jesus into the wilderness for forty days. There He is tested by Satan. Meanwhile, John the Baptist is arrested.

After leaving the wilderness, Jesus chooses four fishermen as disciples. Jesus begins His ministry. He casts an evil spirit out of a man and heals many people; including a man with leprosy, and a crippled man. He sees Levi, a tax collector, and chooses him as His disciple. Jesus heals a man with a crippled hand while in a synagogue. The Pharisees leave and begin plotting to kill Jesus. He chooses twelve apostles so that He could train them. Jesus casts a demon out and tells the crowd that His true family is those who obey God.

PRAYER
Dear God,
Thank You that Your word and Your promises are true. Thank You for Jesus Christ, the promised Messiah. Thank You for Jesus who came to make disciples of men and to bring healing from all types of diseases and deliverance from evil spirits. I invite the total ministry of Jesus Christ into my life, my circumstances, and my family. In the name of Jesus Christ. Amen.

TODAY'S CHALLENGE: To repent and be baptized.

What else is God saying to me today?

What is my response?

DAY TWO HUNDRED AND NINETY-SEVEN: READ Mark 4-6

Jesus begins to teach in parables. He tells a story about a farmer who sows seeds in a field. He speaks to them in parables because he is revealing secrets of the kingdom that are not for everyone around to hear at this time. He tells them that the kingdom of heaven is like a mustard seed. That evening as Jesus and the disciples are crossing the lake. Jesus is asleep when a violent storm arises. The disciples arouse Jesus. Jesus orders the wind and the waves to be quiet. He questions the disciples' faith.

When they approach the city of Gadara, Jesus casts legions of demons out of a man. They beg to go into the pigs. The pigs run into the sea and drown. When He returns to the other side of the lake, Jesus raises a young girl from the dead and heals a woman with a blood disease who touches the hem of His garment. When He returns to His hometown and begins to teach, the people are amazed and wonder from where did He acquire such wisdom.

Herod has John the Baptist beheaded. Jesus continues His ministry. He performs a miracle and feeds over five thousand people with only two fish and five loaves of bread. Jesus walks on the water and heals many people in Gennesaret.

PRAYER
Dear God,
Thank You that Jesus has All Power over nature, demons, and diseases, even death. Please teach me how to live in faith, and trust in Jesus Christ as I face life's difficulties. This I pray in the name of Jesus Christ. Amen.

TODAY'S CHALLENGE: To have faith in Jesus Christ.

What else is God saying to me today?

What is my response?

DAY TWO HUNDRED AND NINETY-EIGHT: READ Mark 7-10

Some of the Pharisees and teachers question Jesus because His disciples do not follow the ritualistic practice of hand washing as taught by their ancestors. Jesus chides their hypocrisy and teaches that what really makes people unclean is what comes out of their hearts.

Jesus goes to a region where a woman asks Him to heal her daughter. The woman is Greek. Jesus challenges her, but, she humbles herself, worships Him, and receives a miracle. He also heals a man who is deaf and mute. He feeds four thousand people with seven loaves of bread and a few fish. He heals a blind man at Bethsaida. When asked who Jesus is, Peter answers. "You are the Messiah!" Jesus warns them to not tell anyone about him. Jesus begins telling his disciples what will happen to Him. He tells them that the elders and chief priests will cause Him great suffering. Six days later Jesus takes Peter, James and John up on a high mountain. There He is transfigured before them and they see him talking with Moses and Elijah. God speaks from heaven saying, "This is my beloved Son, hear Him!"

The father of a young boy, asks Jesus to increase his faith. Jesus casts out a demon and heals the boy. Jesus teaches that the greatest people in the kingdom of heaven are those who become a slave and serve others. Jesus describes how terrible it is for anyone to cause even one of His little followers to sin. He teaches about divorce, blesses the children and points out how hard it is for some who loves riches to enter the kingdom of God. Jesus heals blind Bartimaeus who cries out to Him, despite the criticism of the crowd.

PRAYER
Dear God,
It is so apparent that Jesus loves people and that He came to earth to help us who were suffering and dying and could not help ourselves. We please Him when we also care for suffering people. I ask for Jesus to empower me so that I can faithfully help those who He sends me to. In the name of Jesus Christ. Amen.

TODAY'S CHALLENGE: To allow Jesus Christ to equip me to share in His ministry of helping suffering people.

What else is God saying to me today?

What is my response?

DAY TWO HUNDRED AND NINETY-NINE: READ Mark 11-13

When Jesus and His disciples enter Bethpage and Bethany. He sends them to get a donkey on which he rides into the city. As He approaches people lay their clothes and branches from trees on the ground in front of Him. People shout, "Hosanna, blessed is He who comes in the name of the Lord!" Jesus curses an unproductive fig tree and teaches His disciples more about faith. Jesus goes into the temple and turns over the tables of the moneychangers. He teaches the people that the house of God is a place of worship for all nations.

When they see the fig tree withered the next day, Jesus says to His disciples, "Have faith in God and don't doubt, you can tell this mountain to get up and jump into the sea and it will. Everything you ask for in prayer will be yours, if you only have faith." He warns them, however, that when you pray you must forgive others.

Jesus tells a parable of a vineyard to condemn the leaders who had rejected Him as the Messiah. He tells the people that the most important commandment is this. "You have only one Lord and God. You must love Him with all of your heart, soul, and mind and strength and love others as much as you love yourself."

In reference to Jesus being the Son of David, He quotes a scripture in which David calls the Messiah His Lord, proving that the Messiah was not his son. While sitting in the temple one day, Jesus notices rich people giving a lot of money. He points to a widow who only put in two coins. Because it is all that she has, Jesus tells them that her offering is worth more. As they leave the temple, Jesus warns them that many will come pretending to be Him and deceive many people. He gives them signs of the end times, and tells them that times will be hard, but, if they remain faithful to the end, they will be saved. No one knows the day or time when the end will come except the Father. They are told to be watchful and ready at all times.

PRAYER
Dear God,
Please help me to occupy my life on earth with Your will as my priority. Please attune my heart to the sound of Your voice, so that I may live in harmony with Your directives. In the name of Jesus Christ, I pray. Amen.

TODAY'S CHALLENGE: To daily cleanse my heart of all unforgiveness.

What else is God saying to me today?

What is my response?

DAY THREE HUNDRED: READ Mark 14-16

Two days before Passover the chief priests and leaders are planning how to arrest Jesus and put Him to death. In Bethany, while eating at the home of Simon, who once had leprosy, a woman pours expensive perfume on Jesus' head. Some people complain. Jesus tells them to leave her alone. He explains that she is preparing His body for burial. Judas goes to the chief and asks how much they would pay Him to help them arrest Jesus. While eating the Passover meal with His disciples, Jesus tells them that one of them will betray Him. During this meal, Jesus blesses bread and wine and directs them to eat and drink saying, "This is my body and my blood which is poured out for many people." Jesus prophesies that all of the disciples will reject Him, including Peter.

He goes to a place called, Gethsemane to pray. There Judas betrays Him to His enemies with a kiss. Jesus is arrested, taken before the council and questioned. They all agree to put Him to death. The next day the soldiers take Jesus to a place called Golgotha. The soldiers beat and mock Jesus and spit on Him. They nail Him to a cross and gamble for His clothes. About noon the sky turns dark, Jesus shouts, "Eloi, Eloi, lema sabachthani?" meaning, My God, my God why have You deserted me?" Jesus is buried in the tomb of Joseph of Arimathea.

After the Sabbath, Mary Magdalene, Salome, and Mary, the mother of James, approach the tomb with spices to anoint Jesus' body. They find that the stone had been rolled away from the tomb's entrance. An angel is inside. He tells them that Jesus is not there, and to go and tell His disciples to meet Him in Galilee. Jesus appears to many people and to the eleven disciples. He tells His disciples to go and preach the good news to everyone in the world. He describes the miraculous power that His followers will have by using His name. After this, Jesus is taken back to heaven where He sits on the right side of God.

PRAYER
Dear God,
Help me to never forget the awesome price that Jesus paid in being obedient to His Father, suffering pain and humiliation and dying on the cross for my sins and the sins of the whole world. Praise You God for raising Jesus from the dead and receiving Him back to His place at Your right side. I receive all of the power and benefits that I have been given as one of His followers. In the name of Jesus Christ. Amen.

TODAY'S CHALLENGE: To do all that Jesus said that I can do.

What else is God saying to me today?

What is my response?

DAY THREE HUNDRED AND ONE: READ Luke 1-3

Luke writes to Theophilis to clarify the things that he has heard, and to tell him the truth: During the time that Herod is king of Judea a priest named Zechariah is performing his priestly duties. An angel of the Lord appears to him and announces that he and his wife, Elizabeth, will have a son although they are old. The angel instructs him to name the child John and tells him of John's ministry. Because Zechariah asks for a sign, the angel identifies himself as Gabriel, and tells John that because of his unbelief he will not be able to speak for a while.

A month later, the angel appears to the virgin Mary and tells her that God is pleased with her and that she will conceive a son of the Holy Ghost. Mary answers. "I am the Lord's servant! Be it unto me according to your word." The angel also tells her about Elizabeth's miracle. Mary soon goes to visit Elizabeth. When Elizabeth hears Mary's voice, her baby leaps within her womb. After John is born, Zechariah confirms his name and immediately his speech is restored and he praises God.

Angels tell shepherds, who go and find Mary, Joseph and the baby Jesus. When Mary and Joseph go to the temple and present Jesus to the Lord, Simeon, a Godly man, takes the baby Jesus in his arms and praises God. The prophetess Anna is also in the temple. She tells everyone in Jerusalem who is looking for redemption, about Jesus.

Joseph and Mary return home to Nazareth, with Jesus. He grows in wisdom and God blesses him. He confounds the teachers in the temple because of His wisdom. During this time, God speaks to John, Zechariah's son. He goes along the Jordan valley calling to people to repent, to turn back to God. Many people come to see John. He tells them about Jesus. One day Jesus comes to be baptized by John. As He is being baptized, the sky opens, and God speaks from heaven. Luke's record is that Jesus was about thirty years old when he begins to preach.

PRAYER

O Dear God,

Thank You for sending Your son Jesus, to take away the sins of the world. I ask You for faith to believe the impossible as Mary did. I pray that You take away doubt and unbelief, which rendered John mute, and bless me with a spirit and heart that says, "Although it looks impossible, be it unto me according to Your word." In the name of Jesus Christ I pray, Amen.

TODAY'S CHALLENGE: To believe in God's miracles.

What else is God saying to me today?

What is my response?

DAY THREE HUNDRED AND TWO: READ Luke 4-6

After being baptized in the Jordan, Jesus is led into the wilderness. He fasts for forty days and nights, and the Devil comes to tempt Him. Jesus quotes the scriptures in the face of every test and the Devil leaves Him for a while. He returns to Galilee in the power of the Spirit. He teaches and preaches everywhere and news about Him spreads rapidly.

The people of Nazareth reject Jesus and try to throw Him off of a cliff, but, He escapes. In the town of Capernaum, He casts a demon out of a man. He heals many people and chooses His first disciples. He heals a man with leprosy and a crippled man who is brought to Him through the roof of the house.

He chooses Levi, a tax collector as one of His disciples, and eats with him and some of his friends. The Jewish leaders criticize Him. He heals a man with a crippled hand on the Sabbath Day and teaches the true meaning of the Sabbath. Afterwards, Jesus goes to a mountain where He prays all night. The next morning, He chooses twelve apostles from among His disciples. He continues teaching, healing and preaching. He teaches His disciples to love their enemies and not to judge others. He gives the parable of two builders to illustrate the importance of building one's life upon the solid rock of His word.

PRAYER

Dear Lord,
I thank You for the things that You suffered and conquered, proving that You are the Son of God. I invite Your power into my life, to cast out all evil spirits, to heal and restore every area of my life that has been crippled, and to use me as Your disciple and apostle according to Your will. Help me to follow Your example and Your teachings, and to build my life on the solid rock of Your eternal word. In the name of Jesus Christ, I pray. Amen.

TODAY'S CHALLENGE: To not be surprised when God chooses people that I would reject.

What else is God saying to me today?

What is my response?

DAY THREE HUNDRED AND THREE: READ Luke 7-9

After teaching the people, Jesus goes to Capernaum. There He heals the servant of an army officer who is not Jewish. Jesus marvels at the man's faith. In the town of Nain, Jesus has compassion on a widow who is about to bury her son. He raises the son from the dead. News about Him spread throughout the country. John the Baptist asks for conformation that Jesus is the Christ and Jesus responds. While visiting the home of Simon, a Pharisee, a woman who had committed sin, pours expensive perfume on Jesus. She washes His feet with her tears, and dries them with her hair. When she is criticized, Jesus defends her, and tells them that she has been more kind to Him than even His host. Many women help Jesus as He goes throughout towns and villages telling the good news. Jesus tells a parable about a farmer and explains why He uses parables.

He tells His disciples that light is to be put on a lamp stand and that hidden things will be revealed. Jesus tells the crowd that His family are those who hear and obey God's word. He calms a storm, drives demons out of a man and into a herd of swine, raises a dead girl, and heals a woman who has a blood disease.

Jesus instructs His apostles and performs a miracle of feeding five thousand with two fish and five loaves of bread. He asks His apostles if they know who He is. When Peters says He is the Messiah sent from God, He instructs them to not tell this to anyone. He tells them that He will soon suffer and die. A few days later He takes Peter, James and John to a high mountain, and is transfigured before them. They see Him talking to Moses and Elijah. The next day Jesus heals a boy and casts out a demon. He continues teaching His disciples. He tells them that the greatest person among them is the one who is most humble.

PRAYER
Dear Lord,
Thank You for the great love and gratitude that the woman showed to You. I humble myself also at Your feet. I abhor my sins, and thank You for cleansing me. Help me to be forever grateful to You. I welcome You as the forgiver of my sins, my Healer and Teacher. In the name of Jesus Christ, Amen.

TODAY'S CHALLENGE: To be great.

What else is God saying to me today?

What is my response?

DAY THREE HUNDRED AND FOUR: READ Luke 10-13

Jesus commissions seventy disciples and sends them out two-by-two. Upon their return, they are excited that demons obey them in the name of Jesus. Jesus tells them that He has given them power to trample on snakes and serpents; but to rejoice that their names are written in heaven. Jesus praises His Father in Heaven for revealing His truth and power to ordinary people. He tells them the parable of the good Samaritan.

While visiting Martha and Mary, He settles a dispute between them, concluding that is better to listen to His teachings than to be busy. After hearing Jesus pray, His disciples ask Him to teach them how to pray. He illustrates his teaching with the story of the friend who calls at midnight. He tells them that His Father will give the Holy Spirit to anyone who asks.

Jesus casts a demon out of a mute man and explains why they return. He condemns the Pharisees and teachers of the law. He tells the parable of the rich fool and admonishes His disciples to not worry about their necessities, but to seek first the kingdom of God, and these things will be added. He tells them to store treasure in heaven. He tells them to be faithful servants.

He heals a woman who has a spirit of infirmity on the Sabbath Day. The leader becomes angry. Jesus teaches that compassion is better than ritual. He compares the kingdom to a mustard seed and explains that the way into the kingdom is a narrow door. At that time, someone warns Him that Herod wants to kill Him. Jesus laments over Jerusalem.

PRAYER
Dear Lord,
Thank You for the power that You have given me over evil spirits, but, most of all I thank You that my name is written in heaven. Help me to sit at Your feet and absorb Your word, as Mary did. Please help me to seek Your kingdom as my daily priority and not worry, knowing that You will meet all of my physical and material needs. In the name of Jesus Christ, I pray. Amen.

TODAY'S CHALLENGE: To not worry.

What else is God saying to me today?

What is my response?

DAY THREE HUNDRED AND FIVE: READ Luke 14-17

While at the home of an important Pharisee, Jesus heals a man on the Sabbath and explains why it is proper to do so. Jesus teaches His disciples how to humble themselves and they will be exalted. He gives the parable of the great supper and the price of being a disciple. He gives the parable of the lost sheep and the lost coin. He also tells them the story of the prodigal son, the unjust steward and Lazarus and the rich man. Jesus warns against causing others to sin and the importance of forgiveness. He explains the power of faith that is the size of a grain of mustard seed.

While on His way to Jerusalem, He heals ten men with leprosy. Only one returns to say "Thank You." He explains to some Pharisees that God's kingdom is here with them, not something that they can see. "The kingdom of God is within you."

PRAYER
Dear Lord,
Please help me to have an understanding of life based on Your perspective. Please help me to realize and treasure the things of the kingdom of God above anything else, even my own life. Please help me to not cause others to sin and to be willing to forgive repeatedly. Help me to embrace the lessons on humility and how to be a servant. I thank You that Your kingdom is within me and pray that it will be expressed through me. In the name of Jesus Christ. Amen.

TODAY'S CHALLENGE: To not cause anyone else to sin.

What else is God saying to me today?

What is my response?

DAY THREE HUNDRED AND SIX: READ *Luke 18-21*

Jesus tells the story of a woman who persistently petitions an unjust judge. He teaches His disciples to keep on praying and never give up. He condemns hypocrisy and lauds humility. Jesus blesses little children and teaches that the only way to enter the kingdom of God is as a little child. He tells a story of a rich man and how hard it is for someone who thinks like he does to enter the kingdom of heaven, but, God can do anything. Jesus takes His apostles aside and tells them that He will be beaten and killed, but, will rise again on the third day. As Jesus approaches Jericho, He heals a blind man who cries out to Him.

Jesus sees a man named Zacchaues observing Him from a tree. He calls him down and brings salvation to him and his family. As Jesus is walking to Jerusalem He tells the people the parable of the ten servants and how they used their talents or money. As He enters Jerusalem, He sends the disciples to find a donkey upon which He rides into Jerusalem. A large crowd welcomes Him. They put their clothes on the road in front of Him and shout. "Blessed is the King who comes in the name of the Lord, peace in heaven and glory to God."

While teaching in the temple, Jesus tells the parable of the renters of a vineyard. He addresses questions on paying taxes and explains that in the world to come, people will not get married. He tells His disciples to guard themselves against the hypocritical teachers of the Law. He points out a widow who's offering, though small, is more valuable because it is all that she had.

Jesus tells them the signs of the end times, and foretells the destruction of Jerusalem and the coming of the Son of man. He gives the illustration of the fig tree. He warns the people to not weigh their hearts down with carousing, drunkenness, and cares of this life and the Day of the Lord comes upon them unexpectedly.

PRAYER,
Thank You for encouraging me to pray. Thank You for making Your kingdom available for anyone if they will follow You. Lord, please help me to use the gifts and talents and resources that You have given me to bless Your kingdom. I pray for strength and protection for Your church and for Israel as we face the end times. In the name of Jesus Christ, I pray. Amen.

TODAY'S CHALLENGE: To know that Jesus notices when I give all that I have.

What else is God saying to me today?

What is my response?

DAY THREE HUNDRED AND SEVEN: READ Luke 22-24

Near the time of the feast of Passover, Jesus sends Peter and John to prepare the meal. During the meal He expresses how reverently He has desired to eat this meal with them before He suffers. He breaks bread and tells them: that this is His body, broken for them and to do this in remembrance of Him. He tells them that the cup is the new covenant in His blood, shed for them. He reveals to them that the one who will betray Him is at the table with Him.

He teaches them that the greatest among them is the one who is a servant to all. He encourages Peter, but, tells him that he will deny Him. Jesus goes out to the Mount of Olives to pray. Afterwards while He is speaking to His disciples Judas kisses him on the cheek, betraying Him. Jesus is arrested, mocked and tortured all night. The next morning the Sanhedrin council hand Him over to Pontius Pilate, but, Pilate finds no fault in Him. Herod also questions and mocks Jesus. He puts a robe on Him and sends Him back to Pilate. The crowd demands His crucifixion.

As they take Him away, they lay His cross on the shoulder of Simon, a man from Cyrene for him to carry. While on the cross Jesus promises one of the thieves that He would be with Him in Paradise that same day. Around noon, the sky turns black, the sun stops shining and Jesus shouts, "Father, into your hands, I commit my Spirit." Then He dies. His body is buried in the tomb of Joseph of Arimathea.

Early the next morning, certain women go to the tomb carrying spices with which to anoint Jesus' body. They find that Jesus is not there. Two angels announce that He has risen from the dead. The women rush to tell the eleven apostles. Peter runs to the tomb and finds it empty. Jesus appears to two disciples from Emmaus; then He appears to the others. He commissions them to tell everyone what has happened and that He will send the Promise of the Father. He tells them to first wait in Jerusalem until they are endued with power from on high. He leads them to Bethany, lifts His hands and blesses them. As He does, He is lifted up into heaven out of their sight. They worship Him and return to the temple in Jerusalem praising God.

PRAYER
Heavenly Father,
Thank You for raising Jesus from the dead. Jesus, I Praise You for giving Your life and sending the Holy Spirit, as You promised. I pray to be continually endued with power from on high so that I can effectively fulfill the great commission of telling others about Jesus. In the name of Jesus Christ, I pray. Amen.

TODAY'S CHALLENGE: To tell as many people as possible about Jesus.

What else is God saying to me today?

What is my response?

DAY THREE HUNDRED AND EIGHT: READ John 1-3

John writes that in the beginning there was one called "The Word." The word was with God and with God created all things. He gave His light to everyone and the light shines in darkness, and darkness cannot put it out. God sent a man named John to tell about the light. The Word came to His own nation, but, they did not welcome Him, but, some people accepted Him. These received power to become children of God. The Word became a human being and lived among us.

When the Jewish leaders ask John who he is, he answers. "I am the voice of one crying in the wilderness: make straight the way of the Lord." He tells them that he baptizes in water, but one will come after him. John says he is unworthy to untie His sandals. The next day John sees Jesus approaching. He proclaims. "Here is the Lamb of God who takes away the sin of the world!" John baptizes Jesus and the Holy Spirit descends upon Him like a dove and remains.

Jesus chooses His first disciples and performs His first miracle at a wedding in Cana. Just before the Passover festival Jesus goes into the temple and chases out the moneychangers. He tells them not to make His Father's house a marketplace. During this time Jesus works many miracles and people put their faith in Him. A Pharisee and Jewish leader, named Nicodemus, comes to Jesus one night and asks Him questions. Jesus tells Him: that if anyone is to see the kingdom of God they must be born again. He explains to Nicodemus that only God's Spirit can change you into a child of God. "For God so loved the world that He gave His only begotten Son that whoever believes in Him should not perish but have everlasting life."

PRAYER
Dear God In Heaven,
I pray that Your Holy Spirit will be upon me and enable me to perform my God assigned tasks upon the earth as John and Jesus did. I thank You that I accept Your Son, Jesus Christ and believe in Him as my Savior and Lord. In the name of Jesus Christ. Amen.

TODAY'S CHALLENGE: To know and fulfill my purpose.

What else is God saying to me today?

What is my response?

DAY THREE HUNDRED AND NINE: READ John 4-6

While on His way to Galilee Jesus goes through Samaria and stops in a town called Sychar. At the well of Jacob, He talks to a woman who perceives by the things that He tells her, that He is a prophet. Jesus tells her that true worshippers are those who worship "in spirit and in truth." He reveals that He is the Messiah. A great number of Samaritans put their faith in Jesus because of this woman's testimony.

When Jesus returns to Galilee, an official begs Jesus to heal his dying son. Jesus tells him to go home, his son will live. Later Jesus goes to Jerusalem. He heals a man who has been crippled for thirty-eight years. Jesus heals people on the Sabbath. The leaders want to kill Jesus because of this, and because He called God His Father. Jesus tells the people about His authority as the Son of God.

Jesus crosses Lake Galilee and speaks to a large crowd who follow Him because of the miracles He performs. Later He feeds the crowd of over five thousand people with five small loaves of barley bread and two fish. That evening Jesus walks on the water to meet His disciples. Jesus teaches the people about bread from heaven. He tells them that the bread which God gives is the one who came down from heaven to give life to the world. Jesus says. "I am the bread of life."

PRAYER
Dear God Almighty,
Thank You so much for the love that You displayed in sending Jesus. I accept Him as the bread of life, and submit to His authority as the Son of God. I pray that You take and bless the little that I have and feed the multitudes with it. Please heal me in the areas of my life where I have been crippled by such things as doubt, unbelief, hatred, unforgiveness, hurt and rejection. Help me to worship You in spirit and in truth. In the name of Jesus Christ, I pray. Amen.

TODAY'S CHALLENGE: To ask Jesus to take away everything that cripples me.

What else is God saying to me today?

What is my response?

DAY THREE HUNDRED AND TEN: READ *John 7-10*

Jesus leaves Judea because the Jews seek to kill Him, so He walks through Galilee. It is almost time for the Feast of Tabernacles. Jesus goes to the feast secretly, not openly, as His brothers had suggested. The Jewish leaders look for Him there. The crowd argues about Jesus there. He goes into the temple and begins teaching. The leaders are amazed. When the Jewish leaders come to arrest Jesus, He foretells His death, resurrection and ascension. On the final day of the festival Jesus stands up and shouts. "If anyone thirsts let him come to me and drink. He who believes in me as the scripture has said, out of his heart will flow rivers of living water." The Pharisees reject Jesus.

The next day, while Jesus is teaching, they bring in a woman who has been caught in adultery. They want to test Jesus. Finally, Jesus stands up and challenges them saying. "He who is without sin among you, let him throw the first stone." Jesus tells the crowd that He is the light of the world and that the truth will make them free.

After Jesus leaves the temple, He sees a man who has been blind from birth and heals him on the Sabbath. The Jewish leaders insult the man, who was healed, and banned him from the temple. When Jesus tells Him who He is, the man says, "Lord, I put my faith in You! He worships Jesus. Jesus tells the people that He is the door of the sheep and that He came to give abundant life. The Jews seek to stone Him, but, He escapes and goes to a place beyond the Jordan where many people there believe in Him.

PRAYER
Dear God,
I thank You that Jesus is the light of the world. I worship You Jesus and invite You to heal me in all the areas in which I have been blind since birth. Help me to see and to convey to others that You are indeed the Good Shepherd who has come to give us abundant life. Lord, I embrace that life, and choose to live in its blessings and protection. I thank You and receive from You everlasting life. In the name of Jesus Christ. Amen.

TODAY'S CHALLENGE: To know and follow only the Good Shepherd's voice.

What else is God saying to me today?

What is my response?

DAY THREE HUNDRED AND ELEVEN: READ John 11-13

Lazarus, the brother of Martha and Mary of Bethany, is sick. Jesus loves them, but, after He hears the news, He remains in the place where He is for two more days. When He arrives at Bethany, He finds that Lazarus has died and has already been in the tomb for four days. Jesus tells Martha that her brother will live again. He further says, "I am the resurrection and the life. He who believes in Me, though he may die, he shall live." Jesus is taken to Lazarus' tomb. After praying to His Father, Jesus shouts, "Lazarus, come out!" The man who had been dead came out!

After this, the Jewish leaders assembled and decide that Jesus must be put to death. Jesus goes back to the home of Martha, Mary, and Lazarus to have dinner with them. While there, Mary pours expensive perfume on Jesus' feet and wipes them with her hair. Judas Iscariot protests.

The next day, as Jesus enters Jerusalem, the people take palm branches and greet Him. They shout, "Hosanna! Blessed is He who comes in the name of the Lord! The King of Israel!" Jesus tells the crowd that He must die on the cross. God speaks to Him from heaven in a voice that sounds like thunder to the people. Some still refuse to have faith in Jesus, but, many believe. Just before the Passover meal, Jesus tells His disciples that He loves them and washes their feet. Meanwhile the devil has made Judas decide to betray Jesus. During the meal Jesus tells them that one of them will betray Him. After Judas leaves, Jesus tells His disciples that they can not go where He is going, but, the new command that He gives them is: to love each other.

PRAYER
Dear Father In Heaven,
I love You and my heart rejoices as the account of Lazarus' resurrection renews my faith and trust in You. I see through this that there are no obstacles that are impossible for You to remove. Deadlines, even death cannot stop Your will. At this moment, I place every care, worry, concern, and situation into Your hands. I ask You, Mighty God to help me. Please speak to each circumstance and I know that they will change for Your glory. I worship You and receive Your miracles into my life. I thank You and have faith in You, through my Lord and Savior Jesus Christ. Amen.

TODAY'S CHALLENGE: To have faith in the Lord Jesus Christ to work miracles in my impossible circumstances.

What else is God saying to me today?

What is my response?

DAY THREE HUNDRED AND TWELVE: READ John 14-17

Jesus tells His disciples not to worry, but, to have faith in God. "In my Father's house are many mansions." He promises that He is going to prepare a place for them and will come back for them. Jesus identifies Himself as The Way, The Truth and The Life. He encourages the disciples to have faith in Him and they will do even greater works, because He is going to the Father. He will send the Holy Spirit to help them and whatever they ask the Father, in His name, He will do it. He speaks Peace to them and tells them not to allow their hearts to be troubled or afraid.

Jesus tells His disciples that He is the True Vine, and they must abide in Him. He tells them that a time will come when they will be put out of the synagogue and people will think, that by killing them, they are doing God a favor. Although the disciples are sad because He is leaving, Jesus tells them that it is better for Him to go back to the Father so that He can send the Holy Spirit to help them. He tells them that in this world: they will have tribulation, but, to be of good cheer, because He has overcome the world. After speaking to His disciples, Jesus looks up to heaven and prays for His disciples and for all who will become His disciples.

PRAYER
Dear Father in Heaven,
What rich and precious promises we have through Your Son Jesus Christ. I bow in honor and praise and worship to You and to Your Son. I ask You for and welcome His truth, His glory, His power, His peace, The Holy Spirit, and my place in Heaven. I also ask You, Father, for Jesus' prayer in John seventeen to be answered in my life, the life of my loved ones, and for all who love and follow the Lord Jesus Christ. I ask these things in the name of Jesus Christ. Amen.

TODAY'S CHALLENGE: To meditate on God's love and promises to me and to be grateful.

What else is God saying to me today?

What is my response?

DAY THREE HUNDRED AND THIRTEEN: READ *John 18-21*

After Jesus finishes praying, He and His disciples cross the Kidron Valley and go into a garden. Judas, who has promised to betray Jesus, is there with Roman soldiers and temple police. They carry lanterns, torches and weapons. They arrest Jesus and take Him to Annas and Caiaphas, then to Pilate. Simon Peter denies that he knows Jesus. After questioning Jesus, and finding Him innocent, Pilate releases Him to the people. They demand that Jesus be crucified. Jesus is taken to a place called Golgotha and nailed to a cross. While on the cross, Jesus says that He is thirsty. They give Him sour wine with hyssop. Jesus says, "It is finished!" He then bows His head and dies.

Joseph of Arimathea, a secret disciple of Jesus, is given permission to take Jesus' body down. He, along with Nicodemus, wrapped the body in a linen cloth and placed it in Joseph's new tomb, that is nearby. On Sunday morning, while it is still dark, Mary Magdalene and other women go to the tomb and find that the stone is rolled away and the Lord is not there. Peter and John run to the tomb and find it empty. Mary stands outside of the tomb weeping. When she looks inside, she sees two angels who ask her why she is weeping. She turns around and sees Jesus standing there. Thinking that He is the gardener she questions Him, until He calls her by her name. He talks with Mary. He suddenly appears to His disciples as they sit in a locked room. Jesus appears to other disciples also. He questions Peter's love for Him and commands him to take care of His sheep. Jesus did many things to numerous to be written in books. John says. "I don't suppose there would be room enough in the whole world for all the books that could be written."

PRAYER
Dear God in Heaven,
Hallowed be thy name. Thy kingdom come, Thy will be done on earth and in my life. Thank You, that Jesus proved that He is the Son of God. He told Peter to prove that He loves Him by feeding His sheep. Please show me how I can prove or show my love to You by the way I live and talk. I ask You for this power and blessing, so that my reunion with You will be glorious. In the name of Jesus Christ, I pray. Amen.

TODAY'S CHALLENGE: To be able to recognize Jesus through my tears.

What else is God saying to me today?

What is my response?

DAY THREE HUNDRED AND FOURTEEN: READ Acts 1, 2

Jesus stays with His apostles for forty days after He has been raised from the dead. He speaks to them about things pertaining to the kingdom. He commands them not to leave Jerusalem until they have received the promise of the Father, which is The Holy Spirit. He tells them that John baptized them with water, but, soon they will be baptized with the Holy Spirit. He tells them, "you will receive power when the Holy Spirit has come upon you; and you shall be witnesses to Me in Jerusalem, and in all Judea and Samaria, and to the end of the earth." When He had spoken these things, the apostles watched as a cloud took Him out of their sight. They keep looking up. Two men in white apparel appear and tell them; that the same Jesus will come again in like manner.

The apostles return to the city and go to the upper room where they are staying. They along with Mary the mother of Jesus and others continued in prayer and supplication with one accord. There is a total of about one hundred and twenty disciples of Jesus. They pray and choose Matthias to replace Judas Iscariot.

On the day of Pentecost, as they continue there, suddenly there is a noise from heaven like the sound of a rushing mighty wind. It fills the house. Then there appear tongues of fire and sit upon each of them. They are all filled with the Holy Spirit and begin to speak with other tongues as the Holy Spirit gives them utterance. Many Jewish religious leaders from every country in the world are there in Jerusalem. A crowd gathers and everyone is surprised and amazed, because they are hearing everything in their own languages. Peter stands up with the eleven apostles and speaks in a clear voice. He tells the crowd that they are not drunk, but, that what the prophet Joel said, has come true. Peter admonishes the people to turn back to God. He tells them that the Holy Spirit is for everyone, who the Lord chooses, no matter where they live.

PRAYER
Dear Lord,
Thank You for fulfilling Your promise to send The Holy Spirit to baptize everyone who believes. Thank You that according to the scriptures this promise is for all people throughout the generations. Lord, I believe. Please baptize me with the Holy Spirit, so that I may have the necessary power to fulfill Your ministry call on my life. I thank You, and I accept this promise. In the name of Jesus Christ. Amen

TODAY'S CHALLENGE: To be baptized with the Holy Spirit.

What else is God saying to me today?

What is my response?

DAY THREE HUNDRED AND FIFTEEN: READ Acts 3-5

One afternoon as Peter and John were going into the temple, a lame man, who is a beggar, asks them for money. Peter tells the man that they do not have money, but, rather commands him, "In the name of Jesus Christ of Nazareth, to rise up and walk!" The man is healed and enters the temple walking, leaping and praising God. As the people come to see the miracle, Peter tells them: that it is by the power and the name of Jesus Christ whom they denied, that this man is able to walk. The priests, the captain of the temple and the Sadducees are greatly disturbed by this preaching, so they put the apostles in custody until the next day. However, about five-thousand people believe.

The next morning the leaders and elders question Peter and John. Peter, being filled with the Holy Spirit, witnesses to them about the power of Jesus Christ of Nazareth. The officials threaten them and command them not to speak or teach in the name of Jesus. Peter and John report to the others what has happened. In one accord: they pray and ask God for more boldness to speak and work miracles, in the name of Jesus Christ. After they pray, the meeting place shakes and they are all filled with the Holy Spirit and speak the Word of God with boldness.

Those who believe are of one heart. No one claims his own possessions, but, shares everything with each other; so that no one lacks anything. Those who own land or houses sell them and bring the money to the apostles. A husband and wife, Ananias and Sapphira try to deceive the apostles and both fall dead. The apostles work many miracles among the people. The officials put the apostles in jail, but, that night an angel of the Lord led them out. They are brought before the council again. The apostles are beaten with a whip and warned not to speak in the name of Jesus. The apostles were happy to suffer for the sake of Jesus, and continued teaching and telling the good news that Jesus is the Messiah.

PRAYER
Dear God,
Thank You for the power that is in the name of Jesus Christ of Nazareth. Thank You for the Holy Spirit who imparts boldness and power to speak and to work miracles. I first partake of His miracles. Cause me to rise up in every area of my life where I have been disabled and beggarly. Please heal me and give me the boldness to be a witness. In the name of Jesus Christ, I pray. Amen.

TODAY'S CHALLENGE: To pray for more boldness when I feel intimidated because of my witness for the Lord Jesus Christ.

What else is God saying to me today?

What is my response?

DAY THREE HUNDRED AND SIXTEEN: READ Acts 6-9

As the number of disciples multiply, Stephen, who has great faith, and is filled with the Holy Spirit, along with six others, is appointed as Deacon. He does great wonders and signs among the people. A group called the Freedmen, begin disputing with Stephen and accuse him before the council. All of the council members stare at Stephen because his face looks like that of an angel. Stephen gives a history of the Jews beginning with Abraham and ending with Jesus. He tells them that they are stubborn and hardhearted and are fighting against the Holy Spirit. The council members become furious! They drag Stephen out and stone him to death. As they stone him, Stephen sees the heavens open and Jesus standing on the right side of the Father. He says, "Lord receive my spirit." He asks the Lord to forgive them.

Saul consents to Stephen's death. At this time, there is great persecution against the church in Jerusalem, especially by Saul, so the people are all scattered. Philip goes to the city of Samaria and tells the people about Christ. Peter and John join him. They lay hands on the people and pray for them to receive the Holy Spirit. An angel of the Lord directs Philip to go to Gaza. He tells an Ethiopian of great authority about Jesus. The Ethiopian believes and is baptized.

Saul continues harassing and threatening the disciples of the Lord. While journeying to Damascus, suddenly a bright light from heaven flashes around him. He falls to the ground and hears a voice saying, "Saul! Saul! Why are you persecuting me?" When Saul asks who he is, He says, "I am Jesus whom you are persecuting." He asks what he should do. The Lord tells him to arise and go to the city. Meanwhile the Lord speaks to one of His disciples in that city, Ananias, and tells him to lay hands on Saul so that his sight will be restored and he will be filled with the Holy Spirit. He later joins the apostles in Jerusalem.

PRAYER
Dear Heavenly Father,
If my faith causes me to be persecuted, please allow me to focus on You so that I won't feel the stones. Thank You for the price that some of Your followers have paid in order to get the gospel to the world. Please bless everyone, everywhere who is suffering or who has suffered for the sake of the gospel. I pray that Deacons in Your church will be full of faith and the power of the Holy Spirit as Stephen and Philip were. In the name of Jesus Christ, I pray. Amen.

TODAY'S CHALLENGE: To forgive those who have stoned me with their words.

What else is God saying to me today?

What is my response?

DAY THREE HUNDRED AND SEVENTEEN: READ Acts 10-12

There is a man in Caesarea who worships God and always prays. He also gives a lot of money to help the poor. One afternoon, in a vision, an angel tells him to send for a man named Simon Peter. After God shows him a vision three times, he sends him to meet the men from Caesarea. When Peter enters Cornelius' house, he tells them that God has shown him that He doesn't think that anyone is unclean or unfit. As Cornelius tells him what happened, Peter says, "In truth I perceive that God shows no partiality, but, in every nation whoever fears Him and works righteousness is accepted by Him." While Peter preaches to the group of people, the Holy Spirit falls upon all who hear the Word. Those Jews who are with Peter are astonished that the Holy Spirit is being poured out on the Gentiles also.

The apostles and followers in Judea hear that the Gentles have accepted God's message. Initially they chide Peter, but, after Peter relates to them what has happened, they begin to praise God that the Gentiles have turned to the Lord.

At this time, King Herod causes great suffering for some of the believers. He kills James with the sword. Seeing that this pleased the people, he seizes Peter and puts him in prison. He orders four squads of soldiers to guard him. The church prays without ceasing for him. That night, as Peter is asleep, bound with chains, and soldiers guarding him, an angel awakens him and leads him out of prison.

PRAYER
Dear God,
Thank You that You are no respecter of persons, nor do You show partiality. In every nation, You accept whoever accepts You. I praise God as the disciples did that Your followers include believers from all over the world. May Your word continue to be preached to every nation. Please use me to show love to those whom I may not usually associate with and may the Holy Spirit fall on them as they hear Your word. I also pray that physical, mental, emotional, and spiritual chains will fall off of me and the members of Your church as they pray. In the name of Jesus Christ, I pray. Amen.

TODAY'S CHALLENGE: To keep praying in the midst of crisis and persecution.

What else is God saying to me today?

What is my response?

DAY THREE HUNDRED AND EIGHTEEN: READ Acts 13, 14

There are several prophets and teachers at the church in Antioch. The Holy Spirit appoints Barnabus and Saul to go to the island of Cyprus. The governor of the Island wants to hear the gospel, but, a man named Bar-Jesus, who practices witchcraft, tries to prevent them and dissuade the governor. Paul rebukes him and pronounces blindness on him for a few days. The governor puts his faith in the Lord.

Paul and Barnabus preach in Antioch. Paul tells them the history of the Jews and the scriptures that testify that Jesus is the Messiah. Many Jews and Gentiles follow them. The Jewish people see the crowd and become jealous. The Gentiles rejoice, but, the Jewish leaders chase them from that part of the country. They shake the dust off their feet against them and go to Iconium.

There they speak in the synagogue and a great multitude of both Jews and Greeks believe. Eventually a violent attempt is made to stone them. They flee to Lystra and Derbe and preach the gospel. When they heal a crippled man, they have to restrain the crowd and forbid them to worship them. The Jews from Antioch come there and stone Paul and drag him out of the city supposing that he is dead. When the disciples gather around him, he rises up and goes into the city. He tells them, "We must through many tribulations enter the kingdom of God."

PRAYER
Dear Holy Father,
Thank You for the power of Your word and the power of prayer. I pray for boldness when I am persecuted, healing when I am wounded and the wisdom and fear of the Lord to restrain me if anyone tries to worship me because of the gift of God within me. In the name of Jesus Christ, I pray. Amen.

TODAY'S CHALLENGE: To give God the glory and point people to Him.

What else is God saying to me today?

What is my response?

DAY THREE HUNDRED AND NINETEEN: READ James 1, 2

James admonishes believers to count it all joy when we have various trials, because this will produce patience. When we allow patience to have its perfect work, we will be complete and lack nothing. God will give wisdom to anyone who asks and will not reproach them. James tells us that we should not doubt or be double-minded. He compares the rich and the poor. He calls the man blessed who endures temptation, for he will receive a crown of life. He warns us to be doers of the word and not hearers only, deceiving ourselves.

He condemns showing partiality, saying those who do such are sinning and are convicted by the law as transgressors. He makes the argument that "faith without works is dead." He cites Abraham who had faith, but, proved his faith by offering up Isaac. He concludes, "By works faith is made perfect."

PRAYER
Dear Lord,
Trials don't feel good. Please help me to learn how to 'count it all joy' and to be patient and allow You to work things out. Please give me the strength and power to endure every phase of testing without murmuring or complaining. I know that You will cause things to work out perfectly. Please take away all fear. I need Wisdom and I thank You that You will give it to me. Help me to exercise my faith by doing good works. Please help me to not show partiality as I live and work in a world that judges so readily on external factors. I submit to You, Lord, and ask You to perfect these things in me. In the name of Jesus Christ, I pray. Amen.

TODAY'S CHALLENGE: To allow patience to produce its perfect work in me.

What else is God saying to me today?

What is my response?

DAY THREE HUNDRED AND TWENTY: READ James 3-5

James cautions those who want to become teachers. He says they are judged with greater strictness. He talks about the power of the tongue saying that a person who can control their tongue is mature and able to control their entire body. He compares the tongue to a spark that sets a person's entire life on fire with flames that come from hell. He compares earthly wisdom with wisdom that comes from above.

He tells the believers that they fight because of selfish desires. He tells them that they will even kill to get what they want, but, (they won't get what they want by fighting and arguing), and that they should pray for what they want. He warns them not to expect to get what they pray for when they pray with selfish desires. He commands them. "Surrender to God. Resist the devil and he will flee from you." He admonishes them to stop saying cruel things about others and not to brag or be prideful.

He tells the rich people to cry and weep because of the terrible things that will happen to them. He says the Lord, All-Powerful, has heard the cries of the workers whom they have defrauded. He says they have murdered innocent people who cannot fight back. He tells the believers to be patient until the coming of the Lord, who will establish their hearts. He prescribes prayer for the sick; that they should call for the Elders of the church and the Elders should anoint the sick with oil and pray the prayer of faith for them to be healed.

PRAYER
Dear Heavenly Father,
What a strong word from the apostle James. I ask You to please forgive me for the many times I have allowed my tongue to spark a fire, rather than to light a path. Please rid me of selfishness and sinful desires. I humbly submit to You, I resist the devil and command him to flee from me, my family, and my situations. Help me to be humble enough to ask for prayer when I need it, and gracious enough to pray for others when they need it. In the name of Jesus Christ, I pray. Amen.

TODAY'S CHALLENGE: To examine myself under the microscope of these verses, and to repent as necessary.

What else is God saying to me today?

What is my response?

DAY THREE HUNDRED AND TWENTY-ONE:
READ Galatians 1-3

Paul identifies himself as an apostle chosen by God. He prays that the Lord will be kind to the believers and give them peace. He expresses shock that they have so quickly turned from God to believe another message. He says that he hopes that God will punish anyone who preaches a different message than theirs.

He gives them the account of his life; as a persecutor of the church and tells them that God chose him and he went to Peter and James in Jerusalem. Paul tells them not to return to the law. He tells them that he died through the law that he might live to God. Paul says, "I have been crucified with Christ."

Paul asks the Galatians who has bewitched them, causing them to not obey the truth. He reasons with them that if they did not receive the Spirit by works of the law, but by faith, they should continue the same pattern. He tells them that the law brings a curse, but, Christ has redeemed us from the curse of the law, that the blessing of Abraham might come on the Gentiles. He tells them that they are now sons of God through faith in Jesus Christ. "There is neither Jew nor Greek, slave nor free, male nor female, but we are all one in Christ Jesus."

PRAYER
Dear Lord,
I thank You for the life of faith that Jesus Christ has provided for me. I cannot perform appropriate works in order to gain His acceptance, nor does my ethnicity count with God. I, by faith, accept His finished work on the cross and the provisions that He made for me through His death, burial, resurrection and ascension. In the name of Jesus Christ, I pray. Amen.

TODAY'S CHALLENGE: To know that I am a child of God based on my relationship with Jesus Christ.

What else is God saying to me today?

What is my response?

DAY THREE HUNDRED AND TWENTY-TWO:
READ Galatians 4-6

A child who is under age does not differ from a slave though he is master of all. Because Jesus has redeemed us, we are no longer slaves, but, sons and heirs of God. Paul doubts the stability of those who he calls his little children. He differentiates between the sons of the bondwoman and the free woman and compares them to two covenants. He says there is a natural Jerusalem and a Jerusalem which is from above. He says that we are not sons of the bondwoman, but, of the free.

So he commands them. "Stand fast therefore in the liberty by which Christ has made us free, and do not be entangled again with a yoke of bondage." He laments that they were doing so well until someone made them turn from the truth. He convinces them that the work of the cross makes circumcision unnecessary. Paul teaches them: if you are guided by the Spirit, you won't obey your selfish desires. The flesh and the Spirit are at war with each other. He contrasts the works of the flesh with the fruit of the Spirit.

He instructs those who are spiritual to gently restore those who are trapped in sin and not to think himself to be something, deceiving himself. He reminds us that we will reap what we sow and not to grow weary in well-doing.

PRAYER
Dear Lord,
Thank You for the liberty that I have through Your Son, Jesus Christ, my Lord. I accept all of the benefits and responsibilities of being a child of God. Break off of me every form of bondage and entanglement, so that I may enjoy the freedom and blessings of being an heir of God. Please help me to not act in false pride, but, to gently help to restore others who may be trapped in sin and bondage. In the name of Jesus Christ. Amen.

TODAY'S CHALLENGE: To daily choose to walk in the Spirit and not fulfill the desires of the flesh.

What else is God saying to me today?

What is my response?

DAY THREE HUNDRED AND TWENTY-THREE:
READ Acts 15-18:11

Some Judeans begin teaching the Lord's disciples that they cannot be saved unless they are circumcised. After this matter is brought to the Apostles, and after much deliberation, James tells them that they should not place unbearable burdens on the Gentiles. They should only be commanded not to eat things offered to idols, things strangled, or any meat that still has blood in it. They also must not commit sexual immorality.

Paul and Silas go back to Derbe and Lystra where a disciple named Timothy joins them. Paul and the others go from city to city telling the disciples of the Lord to follow the apostle's instructions. One night in a vision, Paul sees a man from Macedonia begging him to come and help them. On the way there they stop in Philippi. There they meet Lydia, a businesswoman who is also a worshipper of God. She and her family are baptized.

One day while going to pray, they meet a slave girl who has a spirit of divination and makes a lot of money for her masters. She begins to vex Paul continuously. He orders the spirit to leave her alone. Her owners drag Paul and Silas to court. The officials beat them badly and put them in jail with chains on their feet. At midnight Paul and Silas pray and sing praises to God. Suddenly an earthquake shakes the jail to its foundation. As a result many people put their faith in God.

Paul and the others leave there and visit Thessalonica and Berea. Paul then goes to Athens. He is upset because of all the idols there. He tells them about the Lord Jesus Christ. Paul is brought to speak before the council. He then travels to Corinth. He stays there for a year and a half teaching God's people.

PRAYER
Dear God In Heaven,
Your love for people is so evident in the fervency and zeal of Your disciples and apostles. I pray that the freshness and excitement of my relationship with You will not be crowded out by the cares and demands of a busy life. Dear God, in the midst of my midnights may my prayers and praises break chains and destroy the foundations of any bondages in my life. Through every trial, please give me a testimony of victory that will cause others to come to the Lord. In the name of Jesus Christ I pray. Amen.

TODAY'S CHALLENGE: To sing and pray at midnight.

What else is God saying to me today?

What is my response?

DAY THREE HUNDRED AND TWENTY-FOUR:
READ I Thessalonians 1-5

This letter to the church of the Thessalonians is from Paul, Silvanus, and Timothy. The church members are appreciated for their work of faith, labor of love, and patience of hope in our Lord Jesus Christ. This church is cited as an example to others. Paul cites the good conduct and sound doctrine that he and his companions portrayed to them and encourages them to walk worthy of their calling.

He exhorts them to abound more and more and live to please God. He states that it is the will of God for followers of the Lord Jesus Christ to abstain from sexual sins, and possess their bodies in sanctification and honor, not in lust. He states that God will punish people who commit sexually immoral acts.

He comforts those who have loved ones who have died. He tells them that when Jesus returns from heaven with a shout, and the trumpet of God, the dead will rise first, and we who are alive will be caught up together with them in the clouds to meet the Lord in the air. He says that that day will come as a thief in the night to those who are in darkness.

He exhorts them to esteem their hard working leaders, to be patient with each other, to rejoice continually, to pray without ceasing, and to give thanks in everything. He blesses them by saying, "May the God of peace Himself sanctify you completely; and may your whole spirit, soul and body be preserved blameless at the coming of the Lord Jesus Christ."

PRAYER
Dear Lord,
Thank You for calling me to live a life that is holy and pleasing to You. I ask for and receive Your power to help me to abstain from all forms of sexual sins. I realize that You will punish me if I continually commit such. I thank You that there is hope for the reunion of all of my friends and loved ones who die with their faith in Christ. Please help me to express Your love in all of my interpersonal relationships. I commit and dedicate myself to You completely spirit, soul, and body. In the name of Jesus Christ, I pray. Amen.

TODAY'S CHALLENGE: To honor God with my body.

What else is God saying to me today?

What is my response?

DAY THREE HUNDRED AND TWENTY-FIVE:
READ II Thessalonians 1-3; Acts 18:12-19:10

Paul continues to teach and admonish the Thessalonians in a second letter. He says that he and his companions brag about them because of their ever-growing faith in God and love for each other, and because of their patience in enduring persecutions and tribulations. He assures them that God will punish those who trouble them, both presently and eternally at the coming of the Lord.

He corrects them concerning the coming of the Lord Jesus Christ, stating that, that day will not come until there is first a falling away and the son of perdition is revealed, who will exalt himself as God. Those who do not receive the love of the truth will be carried away with strong delusions, believing a lie.

Paul exhorts them to stand fast because God has chosen them for salvation and He offers them comfort and hope. Paul asks for them to pray for him that the word of God will spread swiftly and be glorified. He assures them that the Lord will establish them and guard them from the evil one. He tells them to withdraw from disorderly, lazy, and disobedient persons. He also tells them not to grow weary in well doing.

In Corinth, the Jews rise up against Paul, but the proconsul, Gallio, dismisses the case against him. After staying there for a while, he sails for Syria. Priscilla and Aquila are with him. He ministers for two years in Asia to both Jews and Greeks.

PRAYER
Dear Lord,
I thank You that through Your Son, Jesus Christ, I can have victory during persecutions and tribulations and You will defend me. I place the care of my future and eternity into Your hands, and ask for the strength to continue in well doing so that I my please You and be a testimony to other people. I thank You for guarding me from the evil one and for helping me to love the truth. I pray for Your comfort during times of suffering and pray to be a faithful witness wherever You send me. In the name of Jesus Christ, I pray. Amen.

TODAY'S CHALLENGE: To know that God will punish those who trouble me.

What else is God saying to me today?

What is my response?

DAY THREE HUNDRED AND TWENTY-SIX:
READ I Corinthians 1-4

Paul writes to the church at Corinth. He tells them that the testimony of Christ was confirmed in them and they do not lack any spiritual gift. He pleads with them to not be divided, to be perfectly joined in the same mind and to avoid contentions. He reasons with them that Christ is not divided. He points out that God confounds the wise and uses things that men count as foolish to astound them. Christ gives us wisdom and makes us holy and acceptable.

"Eye has not seen, nor ear heard, nor have entered into the heart of man the things that God has prepared for those who love Him," Paul says. He says, God has revealed these things by His spirit to us, but these things are foolish to the natural man.

Paul tells the Corinthians that he cannot speak to them as mature believers because of their carnality which is evident in envy, strife, and divisions. He tells them that no one can lay a foundation other than Jesus Christ. He also tells them that the day of judgment will reveal the quality of each person's work. Believers, he says, are temples of God and God's Spirit dwells in them. He tells them that if they defile the temple of God, He will destroy them.

PRAYER
Dear God,
What an awesome privilege to be chosen as a child of God. I praise You for accepting me into Your family and depositing Your Spirit within me, making me Your holy temple. I pray for the revelation of my worth to become a reality to my mind. I ask You to please cleanse and remove any defilement from my temple, so that You may have an undefiled dwelling place. I pray to be more spiritually mature and less carnal. Help me to keep the windows of my temple free from the smudges of envy, strife, bitterness, unforgiveness and anything that clouds my vision of who I am through You. In the name of Jesus Christ I pray. Amen.

TODAY'S CHALLENGE: To begin to respect myself as the temple of God.

What else is God saying to me today?

What is my response?

DAY THREE HUNDRED AND TWENTY-SEVEN:
READ I Corinthians 5-8

Paul expresses his abhorrence at the terrible things that he has heard about some of the Corinthians. A man in the congregation is sleeping with his stepmother. He chides them for being prideful instead of mourning over such an atrocity. He says that such a one should be expelled from the congregation. He chides them for not having enough wisdom to be able to judge each other's disputes. Paul warns them not to be deceived. "Neither fornicators, nor adulterers, nor homosexuals, nor sodomites, nor thieves, nor covetous, nor drunkards, nor revilers, nor extortionists will inherit the kingdom of God. He says, "The body is not for sexual immorality, but for the Lord."

The apostle responds to questions concerning marriage. He says that having a marriage partner should keep one from sexual immorality. He advises married people to be fair with each other and not to deprive each other of sex except to fast and pray. To widows and singles, he says, it is better to get married than to burn with desire. He also addresses the cases wherein one partner is unsaved. The most important thing is to obey God's commands. When the Lord comes it won't matter if you're married or not. For those who can, he recommends that they stay single. In response to inquiries about things offered to idols he answers. "Don't become a stumbling block to those who are weak."

PRAYER
Dear God,
I can hear in these scriptures Your demand for accountability to God for actions, behaviors and relationships. Please help me and others in Your church to assign more value to the things that You hold sacred and that will benefit our lives. I pray that a new respect for marriage as well as for the state of singleness will be established among Your people. Please let us not be distracted by either being married or single, but, focused on obeying Your commands. I pray for Your blessing and wisdom and power to be content in the state that I am in and to be a reflection of Your glory right where I am. In the name of Jesus Christ, I pray. Amen.

TODAY'S CHALLENGE: To be obedient to God in my relationships.

What else is God saying to me today?

What is my response?

DAY THREE HUNDRED AND TWENTY-EIGHT:
READ I Corinthians 9-12

Paul tells the church; that as apostles who sowed spiritual seeds among them, they have a right to receive material things from them, but, they have not exercised that right. He tells them that he deprives himself of certain rights and privileges in order to win people to Christ. The apostle tells the church about their ancestors who saw many miracles, but, did not please God. What happened to them is a warning to us to not do the shameful things that they did. He strictly warns them to stay away from idols, and always honor God. He outlines rules for worship and for taking the Lord's Supper.

Concerning spiritual gifts, he explains that there are different kinds of spiritual gifts, but they come from one Spirit. The church is one body with many parts. Together we are the body of Christ. Paul says that he wants them to desire the best gifts.

PRAYER
Dear Heavenly Father,
Thank You for the example of Your apostle, Paul. He illustrated and demonstrated what it means to be free, but to live in a state of humility and servant hood in order to glorify You. Please help me to walk in that humility, not insisting on exercising my rights if it will prevent someone from knowing You. Help us as members of Your body to understand that the purpose of spiritual gifts is to serve and benefit each other. Bless me and help me to be a blessing to others, and bring honor to You. In the name of Jesus Christ, I pray. Amen.

TODAY'S CHALLENGE: To know that I'm free but choose to be a servant.

What else is God saying to me today?

What is my response?

DAY THREE HUNDRED AND TWENTY-NINE:
READ I Corinthians 13-16

Paul regards love: above all of the spiritual gifts, such as tongues, prophecy, knowledge, faith and even self-sacrifice, saying that without love they are nothing. He describes the personality and behaviors of love and concludes that faith, hope and love are abiding, but the greatest of these is love.

He encourages them to pursue love and desire spiritual gifts, especially that they may prophesy. He points out the fact that tongues must be interpreted, and edifies the believer, but, prophecy edifies the church. He teaches them how to allow the gifts of the Spirit to operate in an orderly fashion during church meetings.

He tells them to remember the message of Christ's resurrection from the dead. Therefore, his followers will be raised from the dead also. He explains that just as we now have physical bodies that will die; we will have spiritual bodies that will be eternal. Our Lord Jesus Christ has given us victory over the sting of death. He gives them instructions concerning offerings and sends greetings from Priscilla and Aquila who hold church meetings in their home and from all of the churches in Asia.

PRAYER
Heavenly Father,
I thank You for the wonderful gifts of the Spirit, but, please help me to always remember that the greatest of these is love. Love is the motivation for employing spiritual gifts. I submit myself to all that love is and pray that I will daily grow in its grace. In the name of Jesus Christ, I pray. Amen.

TODAY'S CHALLENGE: To allow love to be my motive in serving and giving.

What else is God saying to me today?

What is my response?

DAY THREE HUNDRED AND THIRTY:
READ Acts 19:11-20:1; II Corinthians 1-3

God works unusual miracles through Paul. After the riot ceases, Paul embraces the disciples and departs for Macedonia.

Paul greets the church in Corinth and Achaia. He thanks God who is merciful and gives us comfort when we are in trouble; then we can comfort others with the same comfort. He tells them of the great trouble that they had in Asia, but God delivered them from death. He tells them that Christ says yes to all the promises of God to us. He also thanks God for always leading us to victory.

Paul notes that he and his companions are not self sufficient, but, their sufficiency is from God. He notes that the minds of the children of Israel are blind because only Christ can take the veil away. "Where the Spirit of the Lord is there is liberty."

PRAYER,
Heavenly Father,
You choose people as Your representative in the earth and You can use Your yielded servants in manner that You choose. Thank You. I praise You for being the God of all comfort. I ask for an abundance of Your strength and comfort in my times of suffering, and I pray for the strength to extend that comfort to others. I embrace the promises, the victory, and the liberty that I have through my Lord and Savior Jesus Christ. Amen.

TODAY'S CHALLENGE: To receive God's comfort and to pass it on to others.

What else is God saying to me today?

What is my response?

DAY THREE HUNDRED AND THIRTY-ONE:
READ II Corinthians 4-6

The Apostle endeavors to convince the church at Corinth that the gospel which he and his co-laborers preach is based in the truth and hidden only to those whose minds are blinded by the god of this world. He states that they do not preach about themselves; their message is that Jesus Christ is Lord. He describes believers as earthen vessels in which the treasure of the truth of Jesus Christ is stored. Therefore we are cast down, but not conquered. Though the outward man perishes the inward man is being renewed day by day.

We know that if our earthly house is destroyed, we have an eternal house in heaven which was made by God. When we are absent from the body we are present with the Lord. Our goal is to be well pleasing to God. Paul says that we no longer judge people after the flesh. "Anyone who belongs to Christ is a new person. The past is forgotten, and everything is new."

The apostle beseeches the church not to receive the grace of God in vain. "Today is the day of salvation," he says. He describes the trials and circumstances by which they have brought the gospel to them openly and with open hearts. He admonishes them to be likewise. He commands them to not be unequally yoked with unbelievers nor touch what is unclean.

PRAYER
Dear Heavenly Father,
May Jesus Christ be the central theme of my testimony, so that I do not speak about myself, but about Him who is worthy. I ask You to bless and protect me and my loved ones and Your people while we dwell in these earthly tents; but let us live cognizant of the fact that we do have another house, not made with hands which is eternal. Please give me circumstantial discernment to walk in wisdom and not be unequally yoked with unbelievers and help me to not touch that which is unclean through either thought or deed. In the name of Jesus Christ, I pray. Amen.

TODAY'S CHALLENGE: To believe that my past is forgotten, and I am a new person.

What else is God saying to me today?

What is my response?

DAY THREE HUNDRED AND THIRTY-TWO:
READ II Corinthians 7-9

Paul tells the church that God has made great promises to us. Therefore we should stay away from anything that defiles our bodies or spirits, and walk in holiness and the fear of the Lord. Paul says that he is comforted in his tribulations because of their love for him and their repentance.

He notes the willingness and liberality of the church in Macedonia. He notes that God loves a cheerful giver and is able to make all grace abound toward them, causing them to have abundance for every good work.

PRAYER
Dear God,
Thank You for all of Your precious promises to Your children. You make these promises because of Your great love for us. Please help me to not do anything that will defile my body or my spirit. I bow before You now and ask You to forgive me and cleanse me from anything that I have done in the past which would cause such. Let me right now feel the freedom that comes from having these defilements removed from me. I welcome Your purity, love, healing and deliverance in my spirit, soul and body. In the name of Jesus Christ, I pray. Amen.

TODAY'S CHALLENGE: To be a consistent and cheerful giver.

What else is God saying to me today?

What is my response?

DAY THREE HUNDRED AND THIRTY-THREE:
READ II Corinthians 10-13

The apostle Paul teaches the church on spiritual warfare. He states that although we live in fleshly bodies, our weapons for spiritual warfare are not carnal or natural, but, mighty through God for pulling down strongholds. Paul tells them that he chooses to walk humbly before them, but that he has authority that was given to him by God for their edification. He does not glory in this, but glories in the Lord.

Paul expresses concern for their faithfulness. He preached to them about Jesus Christ and they received the Holy Spirit, but, then they let someone tell them about another Jesus. He says these people only pretend to be apostles. "Even Satan tries to make himself look like an angel of light."

Paul tells them of his sufferings for Christ. He tells them that if he chooses to do so he could boast. He says that he was given revelations, but was given also a thorn in the flesh lest he be exalted above measure. God did not remove it, but, said to him. "My grace is sufficient for you, for My strength is made perfect in weakness."

He tells them that the signs of an apostle were accomplished among them through his ministry. He challenges those who question his authority and authenticity to examine themselves to see if they are in the faith.

PRAYER
Heavenly Father,
Sometimes we forget that there is an invisible, unseen realm which impacts our existence. I ask You to help me to sharpen my *spiritual weapons* of the word of God, prayer and praise so that I can effectively pull down appropriate strongholds and walk in freedom. Please give me discernment so that I will not follow any false teachings or teachers nor question those whom You have authenticated. In the name of Jesus Christ, I pray. Amen.

TODAY'S CHALLENGE: To discern and avoid those who pretend to be apostles of the Lord Jesus Christ.

What else is God saying to me today?

What is my response?

DAY THREE HUNDRED AND THIRTY-FOUR:
READ Acts 20:2; Romans 1-4

After going to Macedonia and encouraging them with many words, Paul goes to Greece. Paul writes this letter of introduction and intent to visit to the church in Rome. He identifies himself as a bondservant and apostle of the Lord Jesus Christ. He tells them that the prophets of God in the Holy Scriptures spoke of Jesus Christ, who was born of the seed of David. He commends them saying their faith is spoken of throughout the whole world, and that he does not cease praying for them. Paul says that he's ready to preach to them who are in Rome. "I am not ashamed of the gospel of Jesus Christ, for it is the power of God to salvation for everyone who believes."

God's wrath will be revealed from heaven against all ungodliness and unrighteousness of men. He is speaking about those who persist in uncleanness, lusts of the heart, idolatry and homosexuality and more. He asks, if those who practice such things think that they will escape the judgment of God. However, there is glory, honor and peace for everyone who works what is good. He says both the Jews and Gentiles are guilty before God. Paul says there is none righteous. "All have sinned and come short of the glory of God."

Paul elaborates on the futility of boasting and trusting in the law to establish righteousness. He cites Abraham of whom the scriptures say, "Abraham believed God and it was accounted unto him for righteousness." He shows that the promise came to Abraham by faith not through the law. Righteousness was imputed to Abraham because of his faith, and not only to him, but to everyone who believe in Him who raised Jesus our Lord from the dead.

PRAYER
O Dear God,
The scriptures immutably present You as the Christ. Help me to not see the truth and pretend that its not there. Help me to not reject God and embrace all forms of unrighteousness. I receive forgiveness for my sins by faith in Your Son Jesus Christ. I thank You that because of my faith in Jesus Christ, righteousness has been imputed to me by God. In the name of Jesus Christ. Amen.

TODAY'S CHALLENGE: To know that the only thing that makes me righteous is my faith in the Lord, Jesus Christ.

What else is God saying to me today?

What is my response?

DAY THREE HUNDRED AND THIRTY-FIVE:
READ Romans 5-8

The apostle Paul says that we who are believers have been justified by faith and have peace with God through Jesus Christ. We can even glory in tribulations which produce perseverance, character and hope which does not disappoint. He points to the fact that while we were still sinners, Christ died for us. How much more will He now save us from wrath. Just as sin entered the world through one man, Adam, and spread throughout the world, so grace entered through Jesus Christ and abounds to many.

We should not sin because grace abounds, we are dead to sin. We are no longer slaves to sin, but slaves of God. "For the wages of sin is death, but the gift of God is eternal life in Christ Jesus our Lord." Laws only have power over people who are alive. For example once a man dies, his wife is free to marry someone else. We are dead to the power of the law, but free to belong to Christ.

There is no condemnation for those who are in Christ and who walk after the Spirit. Life in Jesus Christ makes us free from the law of sin and death. We have not received the spirit of bondage, but of adoption which makes us heirs of God and joint heirs with Christ. So our present sufferings are not worthy to be compared to our future glory. The Holy Spirit helps us to pray as we ought to and He makes intercession for the saints according to the will of God. "And we know that all things work together for good to those who love God and are the called according to His purpose." Paul says through Christ we have been justified and glorified. With Christ He freely gives us all things and nothing can separate us from the love of God. In all things we are more than conquerors.

PRAYER
Heavenly Father,
Thank You for choosing me, adopting me into Your family, and giving me an inheritance with Jesus Christ. I desire to enjoy the freedom that I have in You. I thank You for freeing me from the bondage of sin. I thank You that the Holy Spirit prays through me and intercedes for me according to the will of God. Thank You for providing me the security of Your inseparable love and making me more than a conqueror. In the name of Jesus Christ, I pray. Amen.

TODAY'S CHALLENGE: To accept the gift of God which is eternal life.

What else is God saying to me today?

What is my response?

DAY THREE HUNDRED AND THIRTY-SIX: READ Romans 9-11

Paul grieves because Israel rejects Christ. He even wishes that he could be accursed if it would cause Israel, his countrymen to come to Christ. God showed them His glory, made a covenant with them, gave them the law and they have ancestors who are also ancestors of Jesus Christ. He notes that God has not broken His promise, but not all Israelites are the true people of God. God is just and has mercy on whom He wills. Paul asks if the clay has a right to question the potter. God has prepared vessels of mercy of both Jews and Gentiles.

Paul says his earnest and sincere desire for Israel is that they may be saved. He says they have zeal without knowledge and have ignorantly established their own righteousness. It is not a righteousness of faith but of the law. "But if you confess with your mouth the Lord Jesus Christ and believe in your heart that God has raised Him from the dead, you will be saved." The apostle quotes the prophet Isaiah who says that Israel is a disobedient and contrary people.

Paul explains that God has not cast away His people, noting that he himself is a Benjaminite. Paul notes that the failure of the Israelites made it possible for the Gentiles to be saved, but, God has not forgotten the promise that He made to His chosen people and they will be saved as it is written in the scriptures.

PRAYER

Dear God,
Thank You for Your great and wonderful plan for mankind. Thank You for making provisions for mankind, knowing that we would sin. I confess with my mouth and believe in my heart that You raised Jesus from the dead. I call upon You for complete and eternal salvation. I pray with the apostle Paul that Israel will be saved, and that those who You have assigned me to share the gospel with will also be saved. In the name of Jesus Christ I pray. Amen.

TODAY'S CHALLENGE: To pray regularly for the unsaved people in my life.

What else is God saying to me today?

What is my response?

DAY THREE HUNDRED AND THIRTY-SEVEN:
READ Romans 12-16

Paul's appeal to the Christians in Rome and to believers everywhere is for them to receive God's mercy which will enable them to offer their bodies to God as a living sacrifice, holy, pure and acceptable to Him. He states that this is our reasonable service. He cautions us to not be conformed to the way the people of the world thinks, but to be transformed by the renewing of our minds, then we will know the good, acceptable and perfect will of God.

He tells us not to think that we are better than we really are, but to use good sense and measure ourselves by the faith that He has given to us. We should each use our different gifts in a spirit of love to edify each other. He points out the manner in which those who follow Christ should behave toward each other, toward the government and to neighbors. He says that we should cast off darkness and put on the armor of light. He tells us to receive those who are weak in the faith, but don't dispute with them over matters of eating, holy days, and other practices, but to not put a stumbling block or cause a brother to fall. He says that if our faith is strong we should be patient with those who are weak. We are to honor God by accepting each other as Christ accepted us.

He commends the Roman saints to Phoebe, servant of the church in Cenchrea. He tells them to receive and assist her. He also sends greeting to Priscilla and Aquila and other saints. In his benediction he praises God who is able to establish us through the gospel and the preaching of Jesus Christ. To God alone wise, be glory through Jesus Christ forever. Amen.

PRAYER
Dear God,
I realize that I need Your help in changing the way that I think. Help me to attune my mind to Your word and to the Holy Spirit so that I will think and live according to Your perfect will instead of the way my society dictates. Help me to live by the faith that You have given me, and to be patient and loving to others. Please help me to know and assist those women and men who are servants of Yours and Your people. I ask these things in the name of Jesus Christ, amen.

TODAY'S CHALLENGE: To discover what it means to present my body to God as a living sacrifice.

What else is God saying to me today?

What is my response?

DAY THREE HUNDRED AND THIRTY-EIGHT:
READ Acts 20:3-22

Luke writes about the apostle's Paul ministry after he leaves Greece and returns through Macedonia. There are others with him. Luke meets them in Troas. There, on the first day of the week, when the disciples meet to break bread together, Paul speaks to them and continues until midnight. There are many lamps in the upper room where they are gathered. A young man named Eutychus goes to sleep while Paul is speaking. He falls from the third story and dies. Paul comes down and embraces him and says. "Don't worry! He's alive!" He goes back up and continues preaching until daybreak, he then departs. They all rejoice that the young man is alive. Paul intends to be in Jerusalem on the Day of Pentecost. He sails to Miletus. While there, Paul sends for the elders of the church at Ephesus. He reminds them of his ministry among them, and the trials he suffered because of the plots of the Jews. He tells them that he is headed to Jerusalem by the Holy Spirit's orders and does not know what awaits him there.

PRAYER
Heavenly Father,
Your power rested mightily on the apostle Paul after his conversion. He led many people into the kingdom through preaching Your word. Many are still being converted and strengthened through his writing. You also used him to work incredible miracles. However, before all of this, he terrorized the church until You revealed Yourself to him. Heavenly father I would like to ask You to use my life as You desire, for Your honor and glory.

I would also like to take this time to offer special prayer for those people in my life who seem to cause me the most trouble, and those who seem to be the most rebellious against You. I pray that You will reveal Yourself to them as You did to Paul; open their blind eyes, bring them to salvation, fill them with the Holy Spirit and employ them in Your service. I pray this in the name of Jesus Christ. Amen.

TODAY'S CHALLENGE: To pray for the rebellious people in my life, and trust God to reveal Himself to them.

What else is God saying to me today?

What is my response?

DAY THREE HUNDRED AND THIRTY-NINE: READ Acts 23-25

Paul is brought before the council so that he can answer the accusations that the Jews are making against him. He looks straight at the council members and tells them that he has served the Lord with a clear conscience until this day. Ananias, the high priest orders the men who are standing near by to strike Paul on his mouth. Paul says to him. "God will strike you, whitewashed wall!" Paul apologies when he is told that the man is the high priest. He quotes the scripture which says. "You shall not speak evil of a ruler of Your people." Paul causes dissention among them when he perceives that some of them are Sadducees and some are Pharisees. Fearing a riot, the commander has Paul taken into the barracks.

The following night the Lord tells him to take comfort. As he has testified of Him in Jerusalem, he will do also in Rome. Paul is made aware of a plot to kill him so the commander sends him under guard to Felix, the governor with a letter. After hearing Paul's case, Felix, who knows the way of the Lord, does not lock Paul up, but keeps him under guard and allows his friends to come and help him. Several days later Felix and his wife Drusilla go where Paul is kept under guard and listen to him speak about Jesus Christ. After this, Felix sends for Paul often hoping for a bribe. Two years later Porcius Festus becomes governor. When the Jews bring their charges before Festus, Paul asks to go before the emperor. Before he does, Festus asks King Agrippa and his wife Bernice to hear what Paul has to say before sending him to the governor.

PRAYER
Dear Heavenly Father,
The apostle Paul was submitted to You, in spite of being falsely accused and brought before high court officials. Because of his bold testimony, people of great influence heard the gospel. I pray that I will model his example and not be afraid or ashamed to confess the Lord Jesus Christ in such circumstances. The great salvation that the Lord offers is worthy to be proclaimed in all places to all people. In the name of Jesus Christ, Amen.

TODAY'S CHALLENGE: To be a bold witness in every circumstance.

What else is God saying to me today?

What is my response?

DAY THREE HUNDRED AND FORTY: READ Acts 26-28

Agrippa gives Paul permission to speak. He honors the King and asks him to listen patiently. Paul tells King Agrippa that the Jews have known him since he was a child and can testify that he was a Pharisee, and is now on trial because of the promise God made to his people. He tells the King about his persecution of the church and his conversion on the way to Damascus and the events that led to his arrest. Before he finishes speaking, Festus says with a loud voice. "Paul you are crazy, too much learning has driven you out of your mind." King Agrippa tells Paul that he almost persuades him to become a Christian. The king tells them that Paul is not guilty of anything, and that he does not deserve to die or be put in jail. He says that Paul could have been set free had he not asked to be tried by the Roman Emperor.

PRAYER
Dear God,
What an awesome testimony the apostle Paul had, and he never seemed to tire of sharing it. I pray that I will convey with perpetual freshness, the wonderful things that God has done and continues to do in my life. In the name of Jesus Christ I pray. Amen.

TODAY'S CHALLENGE: To tell my testimony often, and with perpetual excitement.

What else is God saying to me today?

What is my response?

DAY THREE HUNDRED AND FORTY-ONE:
READ Ephesians 1-3

Paul greets the church and praises God the Father of Our Lord Jesus Christ. He expounds the many benefits that we have received in Christ. We have received spiritual blessing, we've been chosen by God, esteemed holy and blameless, and adopted as children of God. Through Jesus Christ we have redemption, forgiveness of sins, grace, and an inheritance; we have been sealed with the Holy Spirit of promise.

The apostle prays that the church will be given the spirit of wisdom and revelation in the knowledge of God. He prays that they will be enlightened and know the hope of their calling, "and what is the exceeding greatness of His power toward us who believe, according to the working of His mighty power."

We have been made alive and no longer walk in the old things, but, God has loved us, raised us up, and seated us together with Jesus Christ in heavenly places. We have been saved by His grace through faith that God has given to us. Jesus Christ is our peace, the One who has torn down walls of separation and made us fellow citizens and members of the household of God.

Paul acknowledges that God chose him to minister to the Gentiles telling them of blessings that cannot be measured. Paul prays for the church to be strengthened, rooted and grounded in love, and able to comprehend the love of God which surpasses knowledge.

PRAYER
Dear Lord,
Thank You for the many benefits that I have in You. I pray for myself, my family and Your church to have revelation on the knowledge of God. Thank You that I am alive and seated with You in heavenly places. Thank You for these and others blessings that cannot be measured. In the name of Jesus Christ, I pray. Amen.

TODAY'S CHALLENGE: To know the love of Christ that passes knowledge.

What else is God saying to me today?

What is my response?

DAY THREE HUNDRED AND FORTY-TWO:
READ Ephesians 4-6

The apostle begs the believers to live in a way that is worthy of God's people; in humility, gently and patiently bearing with each other in love.

He orders followers of Christ to stop living like stupid, godless people whose minds are darkened. He admonishes them to put off the former conduct and be renewed in the spirit of their minds. He commands: put away lying, be angry and sin not, stop stealing, speak only good things out of your mouth that edifies other people. Do not grieve the Holy Spirit, let go of all bitterness and such and be kind, tenderhearted and forgiving toward each other, and walk in love and wisdom, "submitting to one another in the fear of God." Husbands and wives are taught to live in a manner that reflects Christ and His church. Wives submit to your own husbands as to the Lord. Husbands love your wives as Christ loves the church. Children are to obey their parents in the Lord and honor them. Fathers are to not provoke their children to wrath, but to train and admonish them in the Lord. He also speaks to bondservants and masters.

Finally, he teaches believers in Christ to be strong in the Lord and the power of His might. In preparation for spiritual warfare, the apostle tells us how to dress in God's armor, which enables us to stand against the wiles of the devil, being aware that we are not battling against flesh and blood, but, against powers, in the spiritual world.

PRAYER
Dear Loving Heavenly Father,
I submit to the admonitions, cautions and commands, as well as the blessings and benefits in these verses. With Your help, I will reflect Your love in all of my relationships, and endeavor to promote unity. I put on Your armor and defeat the tactics of the devil. Thank You for equipping me for spiritual warfare and assuring me of victory through the name of Jesus Christ. In His name, I make my confessions, supplications, and petitions. Amen.

TODAY'S CHALLENGE: To remember that my battle is not with humans, but with spiritual powers.

What else is God saying to me today?

What is my response?

DAY THREE HUNDRED AND FORTY-THREE:
READ Philippians 1-4

Paul writes to the Philippians who belong to Christ Jesus and thanks them for helping him to spread the gospel. He prays for their love to keep on growing and that that will be pure and innocent until Christ returns. He writes them from jail and expresses joy that the Roman guards and others know that his imprisonment is because of spreading the gospel of Jesus Christ. He states that whether he lives or dies he will be with Christ. He encourages them to be courageous when facing their enemies and to receive the love and comfort that God gives. He asks them to live in harmony and love each other with the same humility that Christ portrayed when He gave up everything to become a servant.

He tells them to be glad that they belong to the Lord, and watch out for those who are evil and pervert the truth. He says nothing is as wonderful as knowing Jesus. He desires to know Him in the power of his resurrection and the fellowship of his suffering. The apostle says that he does not consider himself as one who has already apprehended, but, "forgetting those things which are behind and reaching forward to those things which are ahead. He presses toward the goal for the prize of the upward call of God in Christ Jesus."

He urges them to help those women who have labored with him in the gospel whose names are in the Book of Life. He tells them to not be anxious for anything, but, to pray and thank God for everything, thereby assuring God's peace; and to meditate on the things that are true, noble, just, pure, lovely, virtuous, praiseworthy and of good report.

PRAYER
Dear Heavenly Father,
The apostle has given a perfect prescription of how to *attain* and *maintain* a peaceful state of mine. Don't be anxious for anything, pray about everything, and meditate on good things. At this moment, I pause to release my anxieties. I pray for Your will to be perfected in everything that I am concerned about, and I meditate on your love and grace to me. I thank You for Your love and concern for me. In the name of Jesus Christ. Amen.

TODAY'S CHALLENGE: To meditate on the right things.

What else is God saying to me today?

What is my response?

THREE HUNDRED AND FORTY-FOUR: READ *Colossians 1-4*

This letter is from the apostle Paul and from Timothy a follower of Christ to God's people who live in Colosse. He thanks God for them and for their hope which is stored in heaven for them. He tells them that the gospel is spreading successfully all over the world. He prays that they are grateful to God for giving them a part in His kingdom of light, having rescued them from the dark powers of Satan. He forgives our sins and sets us free.

The apostle Paul presents a clear and detailed exposition of who Jesus Christ is and his relationship with us. He explains that the reason for God sacrificing His Son was to bring us back to Himself so that we can now stand in His presence as holy, faultless, innocent people. He admonishes them to stay rooted in their faith. Since they have accepted Christ as Lord, they should continue following Him and not be swayed by foolish arguments. He elaborates what Jesus did for us on the cross. We have been raised to new life in Christ. We are chosen by God to be His own special people.

The apostle outlines some rules for Christian living. Wives are to put their husbands first, A husband must love his wife and not abuse her. Children must obey their parents, and parents must not be hard on their children. Both slaves and masters must honor God in their interactions with each other.

PRAYER
Heavenly Father,
How wonderful You are and how awesomely You have made us. The apostle was unable to visit the Christians in Colossi, but he could write to them. This gives me and millions of other people opportunity to read the truths and treasures in those letters also. Thank You for the gift of writing that can bring salvation, offer encouragement, and teach Your truths. I pray for myself and others who are called as writers of Your gospel in various styles. Whether through personal letters or formal books, magazines, television or movies, may Your word and Your testimony be broadcasted mightily throughout the world by those who write. In the name of Jesus Christ, I pray. Amen.

TODAY'S CHALLENGE: To use all of my gifts and talents for the glory of God.

What else is God saying to me today?

What is my response?

DAY THREE HUNDRED AND FORTY-FIVE: READ Hebrews 1-4

The author of the book of Hebrews establishes the truth that God spoke to his Jewish ancestors through the prophets, but in these last days has spoken through His Son. He points out the fact that Christ is higher than angels. "For to which of the angels did He ever say, you are My Son, today I have begotten you?" He reminds them that angels worship Jesus Christ, and that they are ministers, but the Son has been given a scepter and sits on the right hand of the Father.

He warns them to not neglect so great a salvation that necessitated Jesus lowering Himself so that He would bring many to glory. He tells them to be faithful and not harden their hearts as their fathers did in the wilderness. They did not enter into His rest because of unbelief. We should be diligent and not fall according to the same example. God's word is sharper than a two-edged sword and discerns the thoughts and desires of our hearts.

PRAYER
Dear God,
Please help to be diligent in studying Your word so that I will never be swayed from the truth. I renounce all doctrines and teachings that are contrary to absolute truth, and ask You to forgive me for entertaining any, knowingly or unknowingly. Help me to not in any way neglect God's gift of salvation to me, and help me to not fail through unbelief. In the name of Jesus Christ, I pray. Amen.

TODAY'S CHALLENGE: To be alert to erroneous teachings.

What else is God saying to me today?

What is my response?

DAY THREE HUNDRED AND FORTY-SIX: READ Hebrews 5-7

The apostle explains the qualifications for high priesthood and points out the fact that Christ did not glorify Himself to become high priest, but, God appointed Him. He chides them for their immaturity and discusses the perils of those who fall away who were once enlightened and have tasted of the heavenly gift and become partakers of the Holy Spirit and the powers of the age to come. The writer expresses his confidence for better things of them and tells them that God is not unjust to forget their work and labor of love.

He recalls that Melchizedek, King of Salem, priest of the Most High God, blessed Abraham and Abraham gave him a tenth part of all he had. Jesus Christ has become our high priest and the surety of a better covenant. He is a priest who continues forever, unlike the priests who serve and die. He is also able to save and to *always* make intercession. "For such a High Priest was fitting for us, who is holy, harmless, undefiled, separate from sinners, and has become higher than the heavens."

PRAYER
Dear God,
Sometimes because of our carnal desire for "more," we neglect what we already have. I thank You that Jesus Christ more than exceeds every requirement that is needed in order to be our great High Priest. Furthermore, He has been approved and appointed by God. That's good enough for me! I worship His majesty. Thank You, Jesus, for always making intercession for me and giving me a better covenant. In Your name I pray. Amen.

TODAY'S CHALLENGE: To honor Jesus Christ as my great High Priest.

What else is God saying to me today?

What is my response?

DAY THREE HUNDRED AND FORTY-SEVEN:
READ Hebrews 8-10

The author explains that his intention is to convey that we have a High Priest who is seated at the right hand of God in heaven. He is a minister of the true sanctuary and tabernacle which were erected by God. He has a more excellent ministry and is Mediator of a better covenant. The author describes the earthly sanctuary and its limitations, and the functions and duties of the earthly priests. However, Christ came as the High Priest of the good things to come and the more perfect tabernacle not made with hands. He offered Himself as the perfect sacrifice, pouring out His own blood once for the sins of many.

The law of Moses is a shadow of good things to come, but it cannot free people from sin. Christ came to free people from their sins. "When sins are forgiven, there is no more need to offer sacrifices." The blood of Jesus offers us courage by which we can now enter the most holy place by a new way. This way is Jesus Christ, who is the great High Priest in charge of God's house. We should keep our hearts pure, our consciences free from evil, and hold fast to the confession of our faith. We should encourage each other and not forsake the assembling of ourselves together.

"No sacrifices can be made for people who decide to sin after they discover the truth. They are God's enemies, and all that they can look forward to is a terrible judgment and a furious fire. "Jesus is coming soon! It won't be long very long. The people who accept Him, will live because of their faith."

PRAYER
Dear Heavenly Father,
Thank You for offering Yourself, the perfect and acceptable sacrifice for my sins and the sins of the whole world, once for all. I praise You that I can now enter the most holy place and present my praises and petitions before You. Please help me to keep my heart pure and my conscience free from evil, and hold fast to the confession of my faith. I pray to You, Heavenly Father, in the name of my great High Priest, Jesus Christ. Amen.

TODAY'S CHALLENGE: To hold fast to my faith in God and not turn back.

What else is God saying to me today?

What is my response?

DAY THREE HUNDRED AND FORTY-EIGHT:
READ *Hebrews 11-13*

"Faith makes us sure of what we hope for and gives us proof of what we cannot see." The author cites examples of faith in the elders, in our understanding of the creation, in Abel's offering, in Enoch being taken away, in Noah's obedience to build an ark, and in Abraham's obedience to go at God's command. "Without faith we can't possibly please God. We must believe that God is real and He rewards everyone who searches for Him." The writer continues to list those who died in faith without yet having received the promise, but embraced them afar off.

Such a great cloud of witnesses surround us. We must not be hindered, but, lay aside all weights and sin. We must keep our eyes on Jesus who leads us and makes our faith complete. He encourages us to receive correction from the Lord and to live at peace with everyone and live a clean life so that we won't miss out on God's wonderful kindness. He warns us to watch out for persons such as Esau who did not value his birthright. He tells us to continue being concerned about each other and remember God's people who are in jail. Don't fall in love with money or forget about your leaders who taught you God's message; emulate them. "Jesus Christ never changes! He is the same yesterday, today and forever."

PRAYER
Dear Heavenly Father,
I thank You for making faith available for everyone. I receive Your faith to accomplish Your will in every area of my life. Nothing is impossible for You. I ask for and accept Your strength, as a partner to my will, and I lay aside every hindrance and sin, so that I may endure to the end. I thank You for Your power to complete this in me. In the name of Jesus Christ, I pray. Amen.

TODAY'S CHALLENGE: To keep my eyes on Jesus.

What else is God saying to me today?

What is my response?

DAY THREE HUNDRED AND FORTY-NINE:
READ Philemon, I Peter 1, 2

This very personal letter is from the apostle Paul and Timothy to his friend and brother in the Lord, Philemon, who holds church meetings in his home. It is also addressed to the church and to their friends Apphia and Archippus. He lauds Philemon's faith in God and work on behalf of God's people. The occasion for this letter is to plead with him to help Onesimus, who has been like a son to him, because he led him to Christ while in jail. He asks Philemon to receive Onesimus back, not as a slave, but, as a friend and a follower of the Lord Jesus Christ. Paul pledges to pay anything that Onesimus might owe Philemon, but, tells Philemon not to forget that he owes him his life. He appeals to him as a dear friend and follower of Christ.

The apostle Peter writes to God's people who are scattered in various places. He tells them that they are holy because God chose them. Because they have obeyed Jesus Christ, they are sprinkled with His blood. He encourages them, telling them that there is hope within them through the new life. He tells them that though they may have to go through fiery trials for now, their faith will be found to praise, honor, and glory at the revelation of Jesus Christ. He tells them to gird up their lions and be sober and to rest in that hope. He commands them to be Holy in their conduct because God is holy, and has redeemed us not with corruptible things, but with the precious blood of Christ.

He tells them, "stop being hateful! Quit trying to fool people, and start being sincere. Don't be jealous or say cruel things about others." He says they should be like thirsty, newborn babes, desiring pure spiritual milk and they will find out how good the Lord is. He calls them to come to Jesus Christ, He is the living stone. Others rejected Him, "But you are a chosen generation, a royal priesthood, a holy nation, God's own special people." He begs them to therefore sojourn as pilgrims and abstain from fleshly lusts, and to live uprightly before others including those in government and those in authority.

PRAYER
Heavenly Father,
I ask You to forgive me and Your people for our conduct with each other, and especially among those who are unsaved. Please help me to be mindful that I am a chosen, royal priest no matter where I go. I ask You Holy Spirit to help me to always remember this. I can therefore cast away all insecurities, and unbecoming behavior. In the name of Jesus Christ I pray. Amen.

TODAY'S CHALLENGE: To realize my identity from God's perspective.

What else is God saying to me today?

What is my response?

DAY THREE HUNDRED AND FIFTY: READ I Peter 3-5

He admonishes wives to not depend upon outward things like style of hair to win their husbands, but to, by faith, submit to them, perhaps winning them to Christ. Husbands should be thoughtful and considerate to their wives and treat them honorable because they are more delicate. In this their prayers will not be hindered. He tells them all to be kind and humble and to treat everyone with kindness and compassion, not returning evil for evil. It is better to suffer for the will of God than for doing evil.

Christ suffered here on earth and we must be likewise armed. He tells them that they have walked long enough like the Gentiles and should live the rest of their time doing the will of God. Above all things, he tells them to have fervent love for each other.

He exhorts the elders among them telling them to shepherd the flock as overseers, not with compulsion or for dishonest gain, and when the good Shepherd comes they will receive a crown of glory. The younger people are told to submit to the elders. Those who humble themselves, God will exalt in due time. "Cast all of your care upon Him, for He cares for you." He tells them to resist the devil steadfastly in the faith.

PRAYER
Heavenly Father,
Your ways and plans are complete and perfect. If each of us would obey and please You, we would eliminate so much pain and suffering that we cause each other. Please help me to restrain myself and be compassionate and kind, and live to do the will of God. I humble myself before You and ask for Your strength, which enables me to do Your will. In the name of Jesus Christ, I pray. Amen.

TODAY'S CHALLENGE: To walk in honesty with God and other people.

What else is God saying to me today?

What is my response?

DAY THREE HUNDRED AND FIFTY-ONE: READ II Peter 1-3

The apostle Peter writes to all who share in the privilege that our God and Savior, Jesus Christ, will do what is just and fair. Peter says that we have everything we need to live a life that is pleasing to God. Through Him we have great and precious promises. He encourages us to grow in the faith by adding to our faith: virtue, knowledge, self-control, perseverance, godliness, kindness and love. Practicing these things will help us not to stumble. Peter alludes to his impending death and writes to remind us of these principles and promises.

He reminds his audience that he and his co-laborers did not devise fables, but, expounded to them the power and coming of our Lord Jesus Christ. This was not a private interpretation by the will of God, but, prophecy came by holy men of God spoken as they were moved by the Holy Spirit. He warns that false prophets and teachers are among them who bring destructive heresies. Those who follow them will be destroyed. He reminds us that God cast down the angels that sinned and did not spare them, nor did he spare the ancient world except for Noah. God punished the cities of Sodom and Gomorrah by burning them to ashes. This was a warning to all who sin.

Peter warns us that scoffers will come in the last days, casting doubt on the Lord's return. He reminds us that the Lord is long suffering and does not count years and days as we do. He is patient; because He wants everyone to turn from sin and not be lost. "The day of the Lord will surprise us like a thief." Everything will be destroyed. Peter tells us that while we are waiting we should make certain that the Lord finds us pure, spotless, and living at peace.

PRAYER
Dear Heavenly Father,
You have given Your followers the power to live successful, godly lives, without practicing sin, which will lead to destruction. Today, I fully embrace that provision and strength with renewed dedication and determination. Precious Holy Spirit, please remind me that I am strong in the Lord, even when I don't feel like I am. I pray, that I will be kept by God, and that I will safely enter into eternity with Him. In the name of Jesus Chris, I pray. Amen.

TODAY'S CHALLENGE: To not take God's grace for granted.

What else is God saying to me today?

What is my response?

DAY THREE HUNDRED AND FIFTY-TWO:
READ I Timothy 1-3

The apostle writes this letter to Timothy, his son in the faith. He tells Timothy that when he was leaving Macedonia, he asked him to stay in Ephesus and warn certain people to stop spreading false teachings and to ignore senseless fables and endless genealogies which only cause arguments, and do not edify anyone. He tells Timothy that the law was not given to control people whose lives are not pleasing to God, but for criminals, lawbreakers and sinners. He lists who these people are. The apostle Paul tells Timothy that the instructions that he is given him is based upon what some prophets said about him, and if he follows them he will fight like a good soldier.

He tells Timothy that he should pray for everyone, especially kings and those in power. Paul desires to see everyone everywhere praying with hands lifted, not arguing with each other or being angry. He expresses his desire to see women wearing modest apparel and conducting themselves properly. He says that church officials should have a good reputation, be faithful in marriage, self-controlled, sensible, well-behaved, gentle, and not love money. They must also be in control of their own families and children. He gives additional qualifications for church officials.

PRAYER
Dear God,
I admit that I do not consistently pray enough for those in power in the government or for church officials. Please forgive me. Your word teaches me that my prayers make a difference. I ask You to please help me with my prayer schedule. I commit to make prayer a priority. I pause now and pray for all of those in leadership in my world, my country, my state, my city, my church and especially in my home. May Your kingdom come, and Your will be done in their lives. In the name of Jesus Christ, I pray. Amen.

TODAY'S CHALLENGE: To develop a disciplined prayer life.

What else is God saying to me today?

What is my response?

DAY THREE HUNDRED AND FIFTY-THREE:
READ I Timothy 4-6

The apostle Paul tells Timothy that the Holy Spirit says: in the last days many people will turn from their faith and they will be fooled by evil spirits and teachings that come from demons. There will be heresies concerning the forbidding of marriage and abstaining from food that God has provided and for which we should be thankful. He tells Timothy to let no one make fun of him because he is young, but to be an example in word, conduct, love, faith and purity.

He tells Timothy the proper way to act toward others, how to treat older and younger widows, and how to treat church leaders. He also gives instructions to slaves and slave owners. He says to withdraw from people who are proud and full of fleshly works. He outlines the perils that come with greed and lust for wealth, stating that the love of money is the root of all kinds of evil. He charges Timothy to fight the good fight of faith and keep these commandments without spot, blameless until our Lord Jesus Christ appears.

PRAYER
Dear Heavenly Father,
I pray that my mind, body, soul and spirit will be united with Jesus Christ who is the Spirit of truth. I refuse and reject all heresies and teachings of demons. I submit to You, Holy Spirit, to lead me and direct me in my relationship with others. Bless me and help me to be an example in word, conduct, love, faith and purity. In the name of Jesus Christ. Amen.

TODAY'S CHALLENGE: To fight the good fight of faith and keep your commandments.

What else is God saying to me?

What is my response?

DAY THREE HUNDRED AND FIFTY-FOUR: READ Titus 1-3

The apostle Paul writes to Titus, his son in the faith. He recognizes that God, who cannot lie, manifested His word through preaching which was committed to him. He acknowledges that he left Titus in Crete to appoint leaders for the churches in each town. He points out that they must have a good reputation and be faithful in marriage. Their children should be followers of the Lord and not be wild and disobedient. They must teach and hold fast the faithful word that they have been taught. He rebukes false teachers and admonishes Titus to speak that which is proper for sound doctrine. He gives instructions for the older men and women and for servants and masters. Salvation has been brought to everyone by God's grace.

He tells Titus to remind the people to obey rulers and authorities and to be gentle and humble toward everyone. He reminds Titus that we who are now saved were once disobedient, but, the kindness and the love of God appeared and through His mercy He saved us through the washing and regeneration of the Holy Spirit. We then became justified by His grace and heirs according to the hope of eternal life. He says that those who have believed in God should be careful to maintain good works.

PRAYER
Dear Heavenly Father,
Thank You for the Word of God which leads to salvation. I pray that You will bless and protect and provide for the families of those who have been called to church leadership. Bless their marriages and their children. Please make financial provision for them and help them to keep their doctrine pure. Help everyone who believes in You to maintain good works. In the name of Jesus Christ, I pray. Amen.

TODAY'S CHALLENGE: To be gentle and humble toward everyone.

What else is God saying to me today?

What is my response?

DR. MINNIE CLAIBORNE

DAY THREE HUNDRED AND FIFTY-FIVE:
READ II Timothy 1-4

The apostle Paul writes to Timothy. He greets him as a dear child and prays for the kindness and mercy and blessings of God for him. He also greets Timothy's mother and grandmother. He encourages Timothy to make full use of the gifts that God has given him. "For God has not given us a spirit of fear, but of power, love and of a sound mind."

He tells Timothy to be strong in the grace that is in Jesus Christ, and endure hardship as a good soldier. He states that we are to be sanctified vessels fit for the Master's use, pursuing righteousness, faith, love, and peace with a pure heart. He says that servants of the Lord must not quarrel, but be gentle, able to teach and correct in humility those who oppose the faith.

He warns that in the last day, perilous times will come when people will love only themselves and money and commit many sins. They will have a form of godliness but deny the power. He reminds Timothy of his persecutions and states that those who desire to live godly, in Christ Jesus, will suffer persecution. He emphasizes the necessity of continuing in the scriptures, noting that they were all given by inspiration of God. He charges Timothy to be ready to preach the word at all times and to do the work of an Evangelist and fulfill his ministry. Paul states that the time of his death is at hand. He says, "I have fought the good fight, I have finished the race, I have kept the faith. Finally, there is laid up for me the crown of righteousness."

PRAYER

Dear Heavenly Father,

Thank You for the individual assignments that You have given to each of Your children. What a wonderful testimony Paul had. Although he started out as a persecutor of the church, God changed his life and he became great in the kingdom of God. He fulfilled his call and could peacefully look forward to meeting the Lord. He poured all that he was into the work of the ministry, obeying the call of God on his life. Heavenly Father, I too recognize that You have a task, a purpose, a call for my life. I ask for and receive the power, love and soundness of mind and an expulsion of the spirit of fear, so that I can fulfill my life's call and look forward to an eternal crown of righteousness. In the name of Jesus Christ, I pray. Amen.

TODAY'S CHALLENGE: To fulfill my ministry.

What else is God saying to me today?

What is my response?

DAY THREE HUNDRED AND FIFTY-SIX: READ I John 1, 2

John declares that God is light and there is no darkness in Him at all. If we walk in His light, we have fellowship with each other and the blood of Jesus Christ cleanses us from all sin. "If we confess our sins He is faithful and just to forgive our sins and cleanse us from all unrighteousness." John writes to us as to dear children and implores us to not sin, but, states that if we do sin, we have an advocate with the Father, Jesus Christ. We should always keep God's commandments and walk as He walked. He emphasizes the old commandment, to love each other. He addresses this commandment to children, fathers, little children, and young men. He tells us that if anyone loves the world, the love of the Father is not in him.

He tells us that in the last hour the Antichrist will come, even now antichrists have come. The antichrist denies the Father and the Son. He tells us that we have an anointing from the Holy One and the anointing that we received will teach us and abide in us.

PRAYER
Dear God,
I choose to walk in Your light and have fellowship with You and others. I confess all of my sins before You and ask You to forgive me and cleanse me from all unrighteousness. Thank You for the anointing that You provide that will teach me and keep me from being deceived in these last days. In the name of Jesus Christ, I pray. Amen.

TODAY'S CHALLENGE: To abide in God's anointing.

What else is God saying to me today?

What is my response?

DAY THREE HUNDRED AND FIFTY-SEVEN: READ I John 3-5

John writes of God's love for us, which is so great, that He calls us His own children, and promises that we will be like Him when He is revealed. Whoever abides in Him will not sin, he who sins is of the devil, but God's Son was manifested to destroy the works of the devil.

John warns us not to believe every spirit, but, test the spirits, whether they are of God because many false prophets have gone out into the world. "Every spirit that does not confess that Jesus Christ has come in the flesh is not of God." Those who believe that Jesus is the Christ are born of God, and overcome the world through faith. By these things we know that we have eternal life. We have confidence then, that if we ask anything according to His will, He hears us and we will have what we pray for.

PRAYER
Dear Heavenly Father,
You have given us Your word, Your prophets and Your Son, so that we all may have eternal life. I welcome Your life. I pray for Jesus to destroy all of the works of the devil in my life and the lives of my family and loved ones. May Your love be perfected in us and may we not commit sin. I pray for those who are lost and do not know You as their Lord and Savior. Please send me or other prepared laborers to bring the good news to them. May they not harden their hearts so that they too may know Your love. In the name of Jesus Christ. Amen.

TODAY'S CHALLENGE: To live and pray according to God's will.

What else is God saying to me today?

What is my response?

DAY THREE HUNDRED AND FIFTY-EIGHT:
READ II John III John, Jude

John writes this short epistle to the elect, or special lady and her children. He pleads with them to love each other and walk in God's commandments. He warns that many deceivers, who are antichrists, have gone out into the world, who deny that Jesus is coming in the flesh. He warns her to not receive such persons into her house or greet them. The third epistle is written to Gaius with a prayer that he prospers and be in health. John rejoices that he walks in truth and lauds him for the generosity shown to fellow laborers. He tells him of the misdeeds of Diotrephes and warns him not to imitate what is evil. "He who does good is of God, but he who does evil has not seen God."

Jude writes to all who are chosen and loved by God and kept safe by Jesus Christ. He states that he desired to write concerning their common salvation, but, finds it necessary to write to them, exhorting them to contend earnestly for the faith because certain ungodly men have crept in unnoticed who deny the Lord Jesus Christ. He reminds them that although the Lord rescued the people from Egypt, he later destroyed some of them who departed from the faith. Rebellious angels who left their domain are reserved in everlasting chains for judgment. Sodom and Gomorrah were punished with fire because of sexual immorality. But he tells the believers to build themselves up in their most holy faith by praying in the Holy Spirit, and keeping themselves in the love of God. He concludes. "Now unto Him who is able to keep you from stumbling, and to present you faultless before the presence of His glory with exceeding joy. To God our Savior, who alone is wise, be glory and majesty, dominion and power, both now and forever. Amen."

PRAYER
Most Holy God,
What You have done to redeem us back from destruction is enough. Thank You for the sacrifice of Jesus Christ. Thank You for the Holy Spirit of truth. I pray for people all over the world, of all races, languages and nations to receive this great love that You extend and be born again, avoiding eternal damnation. I pray for overcoming faith, endurance and persevering faith for myself and all followers of Christ during these last days. I pray that we will adhere to the truth and resist and refuse the antichrist and his doctrines. I pray that we will find added strength by praying in the Holy Spirit and keeping ourselves in the love of God. All praises, glory, dominion and honor to God our Father, to His Son the Lord Jesus Christ and to the blessed Holy Spirit. In the name of Jesus Christ. Amen

TODAY'S CHALLENGE: To remain steadfast in the faith.

What else is God saying to me today?

What is my response?

DAY THREE HUNDRED AND FIFTY-NINE:
READ Revelation 1-3

God gives Jesus Christ a revelation which He gives to an angel to convey to His servant John. John writes to the seven churches in Asia.

John's greeting elaborately identifies the source of these messages as God and Jesus Christ, who "was and is and is to come; the first to conquer death, the One who loved us and washed us from our sins in His blood and made us kings and priests to His God and Father, to Him be glory and dominion forever and ever."

John announces, "Behold He is coming with clouds!" All the people on the earth will see Him, including those who pierced Him. The Lord says, "I am Alpha and Omega, the One who is and was and is coming. I am God, All-Powerful!" John identifies himself as a sufferer with them and a follower of the Lord Jesus Christ, their king, who himself was sent to the Island of Patmos because he preached the word of God. On the Lord's day he hears a voice. He sees an incredible vision of the "Son of Man." Upon seeing this astonishing sight, John falls, as if dead. He lays His right hand upon John and tells him to write.

He writes and tells the church at Ephesus that God sees their hard work, and intolerance of evil, and all that they have gone through; however God has something against them; they have turned from their first love and must repent quickly. He comforts the church at Smyrna in their suffering and poverty, and tells them that they are rich. He tells them that God will reward them. He lauds the church at Pergamos for not denying His name, but, chides them for following false doctrines. He notes the love, faith and service of the church at Thyatira, but strongly chides them for tolerating Jezebel. He calls the church at Sardis, "dead" and commands them to wake up. The Philadelphian church is found faithful and He will open doors for them that no one can shut, and shut doors that no one can open. He threatens to spew the Laodicean church out of His mouth because they are neither hot nor cold, but luke-warm.

PRAYER
Dear Heavenly Father,
Thank You for visiting Your people during times of persecution, and warning them of things that they must do in preparation for Your return. Thank You for making me a priest and king unto God, and giving me Your peace. I welcome Your critique of my life. I pray for an ear to hear what You're saying to me and the wisdom and strength to make all necessary changes, so that I may be found faithful. In the name of Jesus Christ, I pray. Amen.

TODAY'S CHALLENGE: Don't be luke-warm!

What else is God saying to me today?

What is my response?

DAY THREE HUNDRED AND SIXTY: READ Revelation 4-6

John sees a door that opens into heaven. The Spirit takes hold of him and he sees a throne with some one sitting on it. He describes the splendor of the throne and the creatures which day and night cry, "Holy, holy, holy is the Lord." Twenty-four elders worship him and place their crowns in front of the throne. He sees a sealed scroll that only a Lamb from the tribe of Judah, that had once been killed, could open. The creatures and the elders then bow before the Lamb and sing a new song, praising the Lamb for being killed and redeeming God's people from every tribe, language, nation and race; and allowing them to serve God as priests and kings and allowing them to rule on the earth. Millions and millions of creatures and the elders begin praising the Lamb.

When the Lamb opens the first of seven seals a voice thunders, "Come and see!" A white horse with a rider carrying a bow is given a crown. He had already won victories and goes out to win more. A red horse comes out and is given power to take away peace from the earth. After that a black horse emerges; its rider carries a balanced scale. A pale green horse with a rider, whose name is Death, emerges, and his kingdom follows. They are given power over one fourth of the earth. Under the fifth seal, John sees the souls of many martyrs. The sixth seal reveals a great earthquake and God's great anger is revealed.

PRAYER
Dear Lord God,
Holy, holy, holy, is the Lamb. Words are inadequate to express the glorious splendor of our Mighty King. I join my language from earth with heaven's chorus and say, "Our Lord and God, You are worthy to receive glory, honor and power." Dear Lord, on that day when You judge the earth, You are my hiding place. In the name of Jesus Christ. Amen.

TODAY'S CHALLENGE: To offer appropriate praise to our Lord and King, Jesus Christ.

What else is God saying to me today?

What is my response?

DAY THREE HUNDRED AND SIXTY-ONE:
READ Revelation 7-9

John sees four angels holding back the four winds from blowing on the earth. They are instructed to do no harm until after God's mark has been put on the foreheads of His people. There are 124,000 from every tribe of Israel who receive the mark. After this John sees an innumerable multitude from every tribe, race, nation and language standing before the Lamb. They are wearing white robes and hold palm branches. They praise God. One of the elders tells John that these are the ones who have gone through great suffering and have washed their robes in the blood of the Lamb. God will wipe all tears from their eyes.

The Lamb then opens the seventh seal. There is silence in heaven for about half an hour. Seven angels who stand before God are given seven trumpets. As each angel blows the trumpet, a different type of destruction or plague or devastation is released upon the earth. Instructions are given to not harm those who have the mark of God on their foreheads. In spite of the woes that are released, the people who survive these atrocities do not turn away from their demon worship, murder, sorcery, theft or sexual immorality.

PRAYER
Dear God,
Thank You for protecting Your faithful people in the midst of great destruction. Thank You for loving people of all races, tribes, languages and nations. I pray that the mark of God is indelibly imprinted upon my forehead for eternity. I pray also for this to become a reality for my unsaved family members and loved ones. In the name of Jesus Christ. Amen.

TODAY'S CHALLENGE: To reach the unsaved.

What else is God saying to me today?

What is my response?

DAY THREE HUNDRED AND SIXTY-TWO:
READ Revelation 10-12

John sees an angel with a little scroll that he, John, is eventually given to eat. It tastes sweet, but, turns sour in his stomach. Some one tells him to keep telling what will happen to people from all races, tribes, nations, and languages on the earth.

He sees two witnesses who are killed by the beast who lives in the pit, because they preach God's message. Their dead bodies will lie in the street for three and one-half days. Then God will raise them from the dead. Everyone who sees them will be terrified.

Loud voices announce the opening of the seventh seal. They announce that it is time to reward God's servants and destroy everyone who has destroyed the earth. He sees a vision in the sky of a woman in travail. She has a male child whom a huge red dragon tries to devour. Her son will rule all nations with an iron rod. The boy is snatched up and taken to God. The woman runs to a place in the desert that God has prepared for her. Michael and his angels throw the dragon out of heaven down to earth. He is the same snake, Satan. God's people defeat Satan because of the blood of the Lamb and the word of God. The snake is angry at the woman and starts war against the rest of her children who are the people who obey God, and are faithful to what Jesus did and taught.

PRAYER
Dear God,
Thank You for showing us that in the end, You will save Your people who are faithful. Continue to give me victory over Satan, and help me continue to do what Jesus did and taught. In the name of Jesus Christ I pray. Amen.

TODAY'S CHALLENGE: To continue saying what God tells me.

What else is God saying to me today?

What is my response?

DAY THREE HUNDRED AND SIXTY-THREE:
READ Revelation 13-15

John sees a beast coming out of the sea. It has ten horns and seven heads, with a crown on each horn. One of its seven heads seems to have been fatally wounded, but, is now well. All the people on earth marvel at this beast and they worship the dragon from whom he receives his power. The beast is allowed to boast and claim to be God for a period of forty-two months. It curses God, and the name of God, and says many blasphemous things. It is given great authority over all nations of the earth. God's people are admonished to endure and be faithful. A second beast deceives many people and has power to work miracles. Anyone who does not wear his mark either in their forehead or right hand cannot buy or sell anything. This beast is a person. Everyone who worships the idol that the beast makes or accepts his mark will suffer God's eternal damnation. God's people are admonished to endure and have faith in Jesus.

John sees the harvest of the earth and a deep river of blood flowing. From the sky, seven angels bring the last terrible troubles. After this, God's anger is appeased. On a glassy-looking sea, John sees those who have defeated the beast and the idol. They are singing and playing their harps which God has given to them.

PRAYER
Oh Dear Lord,
Please help me to be faithful in whatever degree of tribulation I may have to suffer. Let my trust and faith in Jesus secure me. Help me to daily overcome Satan through the blood of the Lamb and the word of God. In the name of Jesus Christ, I pray. Amen.

TODAY'S CHALLENGE: To endure and remain faithful to Jesus.

What else is God saying to me today?

What is my response?

DAY THREE HUNDRED AND SIXTY-FOUR:
READ Revelation 16-18

The seven angels empty the seven bowls of God's anger on the earth; upon everyone who has the mark of the beast and worships idols. Other destructions are poured out on the sea, the sun, the throne of the beast, and the great Euphrates River. Demons go to the kings of the earth to gather them to do battle on the great day of the Lord, in a place known in the Hebrew language as Armageddon. The seventh bowl is released into the air. One of the angels shows John a shameless prostitute who sits on many oceans, has slept with every king, and is drunk on the blood of God's people. The woman, the angel explains, is the great city that rules over all kings on earth.

Another angel, having great power, shouts, "Fallen! Powerful Babylon has fallen and is now the home of demons." God's people must not take part in Babylon's sins or share her punishments. An angel picks up a great stone and throws it into the sea, demonstrating how Babylon will be thrown down, never to rise again.

PRAYER
Dear God,
Thank You for warning us that a day of wrath from God will come upon the earth to destroy all that is evil. Thank You for giving us an opportunity to chose to serve You before the great day of God's wrath. Thank You for giving me the grace and faith to chose Jesus Christ as my Lord and Savior. In the name of Jesus Christ. Amen.

TODAY'S CHALLENGE: To educate those who I can about the things to come.

What else is God saying to me today?

What is my response?

DAY THREE HUNDRED AND SIXTY-FIVE:
READ Revelation 19-22

John hears loud shouts in heaven: as multitudes rejoice over the overthrow of Babylon, who has corrupted many nations and murdered God's people. John is told to only worship God; everyone else who tells you about God, does so by the Spirit of God. A rider who is called "Word of God" rides on a white horse whose name is Faithful and True. On the part of His robe that covers His thigh is written, "KING OF KINGS AND LORD OF LORDS."

An angel from heaven chains the dragon for 1000 years. This is that old snake, known as the devil and Satan. He throws the dragon in a pit. After a thousand years, Satan will be set free. He will deceive the countries of Gog and Magog. A great multitude will follow him into battle against God's people. Fire from God will come down and destroy the entire army. After this, the devil will be thrown into the burning lake of fire, with the beast and the false prophet. They will be in pain day and night forever and ever. The great white throne judgment takes place and after that John sees a new heaven and a new earth.

The angel shows John walls of jasper, and a city made of pure gold, clear as crystal. He sees all manner of precious stones. The gates are made of pearls and the streets of gold. "The Lord, God, All-Powerful and the Lamb are its temple and light. Only those whose names are written in the Lamb's book of life will be in the city. Jesus says: that Jesus is coming soon and God will bless everyone who pays attention to the message of this book.

PRAYER
Dear Lord,
Thank You that You have a day set aside for the final and ultimate destruction of Satan and all that is evil. I look forward to the day when You will reign in the fullness of Your glory as KINGS OF KINGS AND LORDS OF LORDS! Thank You for the magnificent place that You have prepared for Your people. Thank You, Lord, in the name of Jesus Christ. Amen.

TODAY'S CHALLENGE: To know that God and His people will reign triumphantly forever.

What else is God saying to me today?

What is my response?

READ
AND *PRAY*

THROUGH THE BIBLE

Our nation and world is in serious need of prayer. Dr. Minnie Claiborne's book is an incredible and powerful tool to help us pray biblically and effectively. It makes the Bible come alive! It is one of the most helpful resources in my entire Christian walk.

Florence La Rue—
Entertainer, Speaker, Lead Vocalist of the 5th Dimension.

This book is unquestionably a classic! Every person in the family should have their own personal copy. Dr. Minnie, your book will bless people all around the world.

April Perry—President, CEO—Infinity Inc,

I might be talking myself out of a job, but if everybody would read Dr. Claiborne's book, they might not need me. The book is easy to read, profound in its impact.

Troy Maxwell, Pastor Frazier Park, Vineyard Church.

Dr. Minnie, your book should be in every language of the world!

Evy E.E.

About the Author

Minnie Claiborne, Ph.D. LHD, is an ordained Minister, Christian Counselor/Therapist, Professor, Author and Speaker. She is Founder and President of the Prayer Therapy Training Institute. She has 5 earned degrees and delights in teaching people to have a more intimate, personal relationship with the Lord and Savior, Jesus Christ. She has been in ministry for 27 years; with an extensive background in Radio and Television. She resides in Southern California with her family. Dr. Claiborne has been a member of The Church on The Way for 18 years. She ministers to people of all denominations. www.drminniecounseling.com

CPSIA information can be obtained
at www.ICGtesting.com
Printed in the USA
FSOW02n1816240117
29988FS

9 781453 545829